KIM JONG UN AND THE BOMB

ANKIT PANDA

Kim Jong Un and the Bomb

Survival and Deterrence in North Korea

OXFORD
UNIVERSITY PRESS

OXFORD
UNIVERSITY PRESS

Oxford University Press is a department of the University of Oxford. It furthers the University's objective of excellence in research, scholarship, and education by publishing worldwide. Oxford is a registered trade mark of Oxford University Press in the UK and certain other countries.

First published in the UK by Hurst Publishers, 2020

Published in the United States of America by Oxford University Press
198 Madison Avenue, New York, NY 10016, United States of America.

© Ankit Panda 2020

CIP data is on file at the Library of Congress
ISBN 978–0–19–006036–7

9 8 7 6 5 4 3 2 1
Printed by LSC Communications, United States of America

CONTENTS

CONTENTS

O gentlemen, the time of life is short;
To spend that shortness basely were too long
If life did ride upon a dial's point,
Still ending at the arrival of an hour.
An if we live, we live to tread on kings;
If die, brave death, when princes die with us.
Now, for our consciences, the arms are fair
When the intent of bearing them is just.

Hotspur, in *Henry IV, Part 1*, Act V, Scene II

ACKNOWLEDGEMENTS

This book was written over the course of one year, representing the culmination of more than a half-decade of my work on North Korea, nuclear weapons, and international security. Over the course of 2017, I, alongside many other analysts working on North Korea's military capabilities, found that my prior years' work on the country had suddenly garnered a great deal of public interest amid the twin developments of Donald Trump's election to the American presidency in November 2016 and Kim Jong Un's historic missile testing campaign that year.

By the time of the Singapore Summit between Trump and Kim in June 2018, I had authored scores of analytical articles and commentaries on the U.S.–North Korea relationship and Pyongyang's fast-advancing military capabilities. At public events during this period, I frequently made the case against the folly of considering military action against North Korea—despite the distasteful and apparent reality of its increasingly sophisticated capabilities. During travel to Seoul and Tokyo at the time, I focused on listening to the perspectives of officials and experts—all with the aim of making sense of what North Korea's new-found capabilities and subsequent turn toward diplomacy would mean for the region and for the world.

ACKNOWLEDGEMENTS

Around the time I started writing the manuscript that became this book, Kim Jong Un had embarked on a charm offensive to transform his international image from that of an irascible "rocket man" (as Trump had memorably dubbed him, with no due credit to Elton John) to that of an international statesman who could rub shoulders comfortably with the likes of China's Xi Jinping, South Korea's President Moon Jae-in, and, of course, Trump. The diplomacy in 2018 was unparalleled in its form and briefly raised hopes that North Korea might disarm and reorient decades of its national defense, foreign, and security policies to herald a new age in Northeast Asia.

By the time this manuscript was finished in the second half of 2019, those hopes had largely been dashed. The underlying thesis of this book—that a nuclear-armed North Korea is a de facto reality that the international community will have to live with—was one that underpinned much of my ongoing commentary and analysis at the time. In this book, I look back on the evidence supporting it while interrogating possible alternatives and the policy approaches that might best support a turn toward a more peaceful, stable Northeast Asia within the ever-tightening constraints that emerge from North Korea's maturation as a possessor of nuclear weapons.

This book would ultimately not have been possible without the support of countless individuals: friends, mentors, teachers, colleagues, sources, and family.

Over the course of my study of North Korea, I have benefited tremendously from the insights and work of countless analysts and scholars that preceded me. Many of them I have spoken to personally for hours and hours, and others I have corresponded with remotely or read and referenced. While by no means an exhaustive list, I'd like to especially thank James Acton, Nobu Akiyama, Jieun Baek, Andrea Berger, Joe Bermudez, Laura Bicker, Bob Carlin, Victor Cha, Chun In Bum, Shea Cotton,

ACKNOWLEDGEMENTS

Ferenc Dalnoki-Veress, John Delury, Abraham Denmark, Catherine Dill, Michael Duitsman, Michael Elleman, Mark Fitzpatrick, Aidan Foster-Carter, Go Myong-hyun, Sheena Greitens, Melissa Hanham, Nathan Hunt, Kentaro Ide, Van Jackson, Robert Kelly, Duyeon Kim, Bruce Klingner, Scott LaFoy, Marco Langbroek, Lee Byeonggu, Minyoung Lee, Seongmin Lee, Jeffrey Lewis, Grace Liu, Jonathan McDowell, Curtis Melvin, Adam Mount, Vipin Narang, Junya Nishino, Stephen Noerper, Ramon Pacheco-Pardo, Jung Pak, Kee Park, Sokeel Park, Anne Pellegrino, Marty Pfeiffer, Dan Pinkston, Tom Plant, Joshua Pollack, Mira Rapp-Hooper, Cheryl Rofer, David Santoro, Markus Schiller, Dave Schmerler, Sugio Takahashi, John K. Warden, and Xu Tianran. I'm especially grateful to Kelsae Adame for her exceptional research assistance. Chris Biggers and Rob Simmon at Planet made looking at North Korea from afar a much easier task for me.

A few others not in the preceding list above requested they not be named specifically given security concerns. I am nevertheless grateful for their contributions. Moreover, this book could not have been what it is without the willingness of those with special insight in intelligence analysis and military operations who were willing to speak with me, sharing their unparalleled insight. Because they were not authorized to share what they did with me and did so at personal and professional risk, their contributions to my understanding of the matters discussed in this book are uncredited except where anonymously footnoted. Nevertheless, I am endlessly indebted to these sources and their willingness to share what they could to expand our public understanding of North Korea.

Without the support I've received as a writer and thinker at *The Diplomat*, I could not have arrived at a point personally and professionally where I would be capable of writing this book. My colleagues there over the years, including Shannon Tiezzi, Katie

ACKNOWLEDGEMENTS

Putz, Prashanth Parameswaran, Franz Stefan-Gady, and Zachary Keck, have been a constant source of inspiration. James Pach, *The Diplomat*'s publisher, deserves exceptional thanks for taking a chance on me when I was starting out as a young, aspiring writer on international affairs. With James' encouragement and support, I found space to grow and mature at *The Diplomat*.

I also extend particular thanks to my supportive colleagues at the Federation of American Scientists, including my friend Adam Mount, who has been highly supportive of my research efforts on North Korea and other matters. I am also deeply grateful for the support of FAS President Ali Nouri, Hans Kristensen, Matt Korda, Abigail Stowe-Thurston, Mercedes Trent, and Pia Ulrich. I'm additionally deeply grateful to Chad O'Carroll, Oliver Hotham, and the entire Korea Risk Group (KRG) team, including staff at NK News, for their exceptionally deep ongoing coverage of North Korea and the region. The site's KCNAWatch tool, in particular, was an invaluable research resource for referencing years of archived North Korean state media. Some of the analysis that appears in this book was initially presented in written work for KRG's NK Pro portal, where I have been a contributing analyst since 2018.

The very opportunity for this book to come into existence would very likely not have been possible without a fortuitous encounter over a dinner in Brooklyn, New York, with Mike Dwyer, publisher at Hurst. I'm grateful to Mike for his active support and friendship. As an editor myself, I've learned that the role may be one of the most thankless in the publishing world; accordingly, it must be said that this book benefited tremendously from the edits made by Lara Weisweiller-Wu at Hurst. I'm grateful also to Tom Feltham and Daisy Leitch for stewarding months of copy edits and fact checks and Alison Alexanian for help promoting the book. Whatever errors remain are mine and mine alone. I also appreciate support from

ACKNOWLEDGEMENTS

Dave McBride and Macey Fairchild at Oxford University Press in New York City.

Getting this book to where it needed to go would not have been possible without the support of family and friends. My parents, Minati and Sanjay, ensured that I'd have the sort of upbringing that'd leave me forever endlessly curious about world affairs. I am grateful for their love and support as I pursued a career as a writer. My brother, Aman, meanwhile, continues to serve as a reminder of what hard work looks like. For always keeping me good spirits, I owe quite a bit to my friends at the Lampshade and Crowbar Society and other dear friends in New York City (if you've been to one of my holiday parties recently, this means you).

A boundless thank you above all to my partner, Lindsay, who endured months of my absence as I traveled, wrote late into the night, and obsessively pored over images, spreadsheets, and documents to write this book. Without your support and love, none of what I do could be possible—quite literally. Without you at my side, it would have been impossible to find the time or space to conclude a project of this length. It's because of you that I'm a better writer, thinker, and person now than I was when we first got to know each other at sixteen. Thank you.

Ankit Panda
New York City
May 2020

AUTHOR'S NOTE

This book generally uses preferred North Korean romanization for North Korean names (i.e., Kim Jong Un, not Kim Jeong-un) and preferred South Korean romanization for South Korean names (i.e., Moon Jae-in). Exceptions include North Korean place names, which are represented using the Anglicized Variant name types used by the U.S. National Geospatial Intelligence Agency, which in many, but not all, cases correspond to preferred North Korean romanization.

All measurements appear in SI units.

KIM JONG UN AND THE BOMB

INTRODUCTION

The atomic mushroom cloud—that ominous and ubiquitously known symbol of nuclear destruction—has not made an appearance on our planet's surface in nearly four decades. Following the last known atmospheric test of a nuclear weapon, conducted by China on October 16, 1980, no man, woman, or child has had the terrible opportunity to see one with their own eyes. Nevertheless, the threat posed by nuclear weapons remains very much real. Even past the end of the Cold War, the threat of nuclear destruction has remained ever present. As the Cold War deterrence theorist Thomas Schelling put it in 2005, "The most spectacular event of the past half century is one that did not occur. We have enjoyed sixty years without nuclear weapons exploded in anger. What a stunning achievement—or, if not achievement, what stunning good fortune."[1]

Nearly two decades into the twenty-first century, global trepidation about nuclear war has quickly zeroed in on the Korean Peninsula. There, in November 2017, a young leader in his early thirties triumphantly declared that he had "finally realized the great historic cause of completing the state nuclear force." Kim Jong Un, North Korea's third supreme leader, had seen through a vision initiated in the mid-twentieth century by his grandfather, Kim Il Sung, and carried forward into the twenty-first by his father, Kim Jong Il. His announcement in 2017 came after months of serious crisis with the United States—a crisis that brought the world to the brink of nuclear war. Shocked by the rapid progression of North Korean capabilities, the United States, led by President Donald J. Trump, was making regular threats to attack Kim. At the United Nations, before gathered world leaders and senior officials, Trump had even threatened North Korea with "total destruction."[2]

Fortunately, no such war occurred, but even so, the world changed. Now, North Korea is a nuclear power and it will likely remain a nuclear power for decades to come. The exact moment it reached this status is debatable and depends on one's perspective. Some might point to the day it first exploded a nuclear weapon—October 9, 2006—while others might point to 2013, when North Korea chose to adopt an internal law describing itself as a "full-fledged nuclear weapons state." Others—certainly Kim Jong Un himself—waited longer, until a very specific capability had been credibly demonstrated: the ability to strike anywhere on the continental United States of America with a thermonuclear warhead. For this North Korean leader, only with that achievement in 2017 has his country been able to declare its deterrent complete.

The distinction might now be mostly philosophical—like the question of when precisely an oyster prepared for human consumption dies. For the paranoid and perennially insecure regime in Pyongyang, nuclear weapons had long been seen as the ultimate guarantee of survival. For all three Kims, the objective behind pursuing these weapons was not to explode them "in anger"—or to strike out of the blue at Washington, D.C. and leave the American imperialists in ruin—but to hold at risk crucial military and civilian targets in the United States and across Northeast Asia, with the aim of deterring those adversaries from contemplating any attempt at forcible regime change. Some are still not satisfied with North Korea's capabilities, continuing to view the country as a paper tiger, but Kim's demonstrations of nuclear capability in 2017 rightly transformed the threat perceptions of many others. In January 2018, for instance, operator error resulted in the dissemination of an emergency alert to the residents of the U.S. state of Hawaii, warning of an incoming ballistic missile: "SEEK IMMEDIATE SHELTER. THIS IS NOT A DRILL."[3] The alert caused very real panic, even if there was no launch, and in this sense Kim's deterrent is indeed operational: the reality of a nuclear North Korea has begun to hang over the heads of Americans. And not only Americans: in the final days of December, 2019, Japan's national broadcaster, NHK, sent out an accidental alert—later proven false—that a North Korean ballistic missile had overflown Japan and landed in the Pacific Ocean.

The story of how North Korea "nuclearized" itself is unique in the world. Once derided in the 1970s as a "fourth-rate pip-squeak" of a country by U.S. President Richard M. Nixon, by 2017 the Democratic People's Republic of Korea, as North Korea formally calls itself, came to dominate U.S. airwaves as the pre-eminent nuclear threat to the United States. Years of economic isolation and internal hardship and famine after the fall of the Soviet Union, partly due to what has become an extensive UN-backed sanctions regime, has done little to deter North Korea's quest for the bomb. Even before its first nuclear test in 2006, going back to the early-to-mid-1990s, Pyongyang has entertained multiple attempts at diplomacy with the United States and regional state over the years, designed on their part to disarm the country and denuclearize the Korean Peninsula. But each such initiative, including the latest efforts of the Trump administration in 2018–19, has failed—due variously to misunderstandings, Pyongyang's active deception, or Washington's lack of interest in serious diplomacy.

At the end of it all, North Korea has become the tenth country to successfully develop and weaponize nuclear arms, making it the world's ninth existing nuclear power (given South Africa's unilateral disarmament in 1989), and the eighth declared nuclear power. It now joins India, Pakistan, and Israel as a nuclear weapons-possessor outside of the Treaty on the Non-Proliferation of Nuclear Weapons (NPT), which recognizes just five countries—the United States, China, Russia, France, and the United Kingdom—as legitimate nuclear weapons states. However, North Korea represents a unique challenge to the future of that treaty: unlike the other three non-NPT nuclear powers, Pyongyang first joined the NPT and then left it to pursue its nuclear program, ultimately successfully. The NPT is otherwise one of the world's most remarkably successful treaties, having headed off fears that there would perhaps be tens of nuclear states by the turn of the millennium; North Korea's nuclearization represents one of the greatest challenges for its future.

The world has not yet given up on North Korea. Multiple UN Security Council resolutions still set out the objective of disarming North Korea in a "complete, verifiable, and irreversible" manner—dismantling all of its weapons of mass destruction. The policy of the United States, South Korea, Japan, Russia, and China remains the "denuclearization of the Korean Peninsula." "Denuclearization" is a word that we will be very familiar with by the end of this book—it's a peculiar framing, unique to the Korean Peninsula. It is a persistent source of misunderstanding that Kim Jong Un himself remains committed to the concept; in 2018, he signed his name to three documents—joint texts with the United States and South Korea—pledging himself to that outcome. This is because, in the context of the Korean Peninsula, denuclearization does not and never did mean unilateral North Korean nuclear disarmament. By the time the two Koreas coined the term in a 1992 agreement, North Korea had already begun covertly pursuing nuclear weapons. More than twenty-five years later, when Kim and Trump came to the table and again agreed to work toward the "complete denuclearization" of the Korean Peninsula, talks ultimately fell apart over Kim's unwillingness to surrender those weapons.

Rather, to Kim—and his father and grandfather—denuclearization would include concessions by the United States, too. North Korea has bristled for decades about the American "nuclear threat" to its territory and complained of a U.S. "hostile policy" toward it. While no authoritative, public document from the regime has described the precise steps that the United States could take to realize its "denuclearization" obligations, there is good reason to believe that, for all intents and purposes, the Korean Peninsula will only be "denuclearized" when nuclear weapons are abolished worldwide. In 2005, North Korean diplomats told American counterparts that a denuclearized Korean Peninsula was Kim Il Sung's dying wish. In March 2018, Kim Jong Un himself told South Korean officials that this was also the dying wish of his own father, Kim Jong Il. The Korean Peninsula may one day be denuclearized, but Kim Jong Un does not expect it to happen in his lifetime. In the meantime, his nuclear weapons are here to stay. The reason for this is simple: Kim faces a hostile superpower adversary—the United States— and his survival can only be guaranteed by these weapons, which must be credibly useable.

* * *

The longevity of the adversarial relationship between the United States and North Korea is often underappreciated. From North Korea's founding in 1948 to Kim Jong Un's declaration of a complete nuclear deterrent in January 2018, sixty-nine years transpired without a normal diplomatic relationship between the two sides. Just two years after its birth, North Korea found itself facing down a U.S.-led United Nations coalition in the Korean War, which would come to be known in the country as the Great Fatherland Liberation War. The war, initiated at Kim Il Sung's behest, is at the center of the national founding mythos. While South Koreans are portrayed in North Korea as misled countrymen at best and hapless "puppets" of Washington at worst, internal North Korean propaganda has cultivated a deep national skepticism and hatred of Americans. By the time North Korea had developed and demonstrated its nuclear threat to the United States in 2017, it had been an adversary of Washington for longer than both the Soviet Union and China.

With its first successful test-flight of an intercontinental ballistic missile on July 4, 2017, North Korea introduced a new nuclear challenge to the United States for the first time in forty-six years. Since China's own flight-test of its first successful true ICBM in September 1971, American nuclear strategists and defense planners had been used to a world with just two nuclear-armed adversaries that could wreak havoc on U.S. mainland targets. This fundamentally changed with North Korea's triumph in 2017, and American policymakers and military planners must now begin accounting for this new reality.

But the story of a nuclear North Korea neither begins nor ends with that 2017 test. Rather, it is a story that extends back to the earliest days of the Cold War and the aftermath of the Korean War. One year after the Cuban Missile Crisis brought the United States and the Soviet Union to the brink of nuclear Armageddon in 1962, North Korea, with assistance from the Soviet Union, initiated construction on its first research reactor.[4] In the 1970s the country turned toward more ambitious plans for additional nuclear reactors, culminating in construction from 1979 of a reactor at the sprawling complex which would come to be known as the Yongbyon Nuclear Scientific Research Center. North Korea also acquired its first ballistic missiles in the late

1970s, of Soviet manufacture and design. Over the ensuing decades, North Korea would master these liquid-fueled short-range ballistic missiles, reverse engineer them, and extensively modify and iterate on their fundamental design, creating a largely indigenous North Korean arsenal.

In 1985, Kim Il Sung assented under Soviet pressure to joining the NPT, but a year later, the Yongbyon reactor started operating, quickly becoming a concern to U.S. intelligence and an item on the diplomatic agenda right up to the 2018–19 summits between Kim Jong Un and Donald J. Trump. Momentum continued in the 1990s, with the collapse of the Soviet Union offering North Korea the services of out-of-work Soviet scientists with knowledge of ballistic missiles. In the 2000s, cooperation developed on ballistic missile technology with Iran, a customer of North Korean technology and a long-range missile aspirant itself. Under Kim Jong Il, whose rule began in 1994, North Korea started to amass materials for a highly enriched uranium program, tapping into the nuclear proliferation network set up by the infamous Pakistani metallurgist AQ Khan. Thus the DPRK gained access to both fissile material paths to the bomb: plutonium and uranium. By this time, around the turn of the millennium, much relevant knowledge had also become available in the open source, further accelerating North Korea's progress in its nuclear development.

In 1998, North Korea stunned the world by launching the Taepodong-1, a satellite launch vehicle revealing various pieces of kit that could find themselves in future long-range ballistic missiles. This launch was a watershed event in the relationship between North Korea and the United States, straining the 1994 Agreed Framework between the two countries that had agreed a testing moratorium until 2006. It sparked the United States into taking North Korea's long-range nuclear ambitions seriously; Japan, over whose territory the Taepodong-1 had flown, began a serious and sustained effort to collaborate with the U.S. on various ballistic missile defense platforms. The start of the Kim Jong Un era at the end of 2011 saw an intensified focus on development, with flight-testing in 2016 of North Korea's first attempt at an intermediate-range ballistic missile. After a dizzying raft of further tests in 2017, including the successful development of intercontinental ballistic missiles that could reach the U.S. homeland, Kim Jong Un used his New Year's Day address on January 1, 2018 to declare North Korea's nuclear deterrent "complete".

Many in the west have long underestimated North Korea's overall knowhow and capacity to progress. Repeated refrains by many analysts in the United States and elsewhere that North Korea was an inherently backward country have turned out to be mistaken, at least with regard to its nuclear capability. Any U.S. or U.S.-allied interruptions to North Korea's nuclear resolve, in the end, have been temporary. By the end of 2019, Kim Jong Un had overseen more than one hundred ballistic and cruise missile tests across his first eight years in power.[6] With more than fifty years of slow nuclear development under its belt, North Korea has developed and used largely self-sufficient means to produce its own nuclear weapons and means of delivery of remarkable breadth and complexity.

While Pyongyang may still have fewer manufactured nuclear warheads than any other nuclear weapon-possessing country, its qualitative capabilities in terms of range and payload now outclass those of countries like India, Pakistan, and even Israel in many ways. The country's unique position as a highly insecure and small state, with a need to deter adversaries both near (South Korea, Japan) and far (the United States), has led it to develop the constellation of conventional and nuclear capabilities it possesses today.

For nearly three decades, policymakers in the United States and elsewhere sought to prevent today's reality, seeking to freeze and eventually eliminate North Korea's burgeoning capabilities. The end of the Cold War and the intensification of American concerns over nuclear proliferation in North Korea and elsewhere marked the end of bilateral nuclear competition between the United States and Soviet Union, and the start of what Yale scholar Paul Bracken argued was a "Second Nuclear Age." Today, North Korea's self-proclaimed "complete" nuclear deterrent, combined with a historic but unsuccessful bout of U.S.–North Korea diplomacy in 2018 and 2019, has all but closed that ignominious chapter. We are now living in a new nuclear age, where—despite all international efforts to the contrary—North Korea has emerged as a *de facto* nuclear power. This book is about how and why that happened, and what it means for peace and stability in Northeast Asia.

PART ONE

SURVIVAL

1

A NEW EMPEROR

Kim Jong Un didn't grow up expecting to inherit North Korea. His father, Kim Jong Il, had known for more than a decade that he was walking an unambiguous path to leadership, paved by his own father, the country's founder Kim Il Sung. The rest of the Workers' Party, North Korea's ruling party, had had plenty of exposure to the "great leader" in waiting before he came to power. At the 6th Workers' Party Congress in 1980, Kim Jong Il was anointed as Kim Il Sung's heir, a full fourteen years before he inherited power. But Kim Jong Un didn't enjoy this long period as heir apparent. He was one of Kim Jong Il's five children: the oldest, Kim Jong Nam, was the son of Song Hye Rim, an actress and once Kim's favored mistress. The second, Kim Sol Song, was the daughter of Kim Yong Suk, the wife his father had chosen for him. Kim's three younger children by Ko Yong Hui were two boys—Kim Jong Chol (b. 1980) and Kim Jong Un (b. 1984)— and one girl, Kim Yo Jong (b. 1988). In other words, Kim Jong Un's succession was hardly written in the stars at his birth.

By 2003, Kim Jong Il's paranoia about being forcibly removed from power had reached new heights—particularly as American military power laid waste to Saddam Hussein's Iraq from March. Kim vanished from public view for months. A short time thereafter, preparations began for a succession that pointed toward one of Ko Yong Hui's children becoming the next *suryong*, or supreme leader.[1] By the mid-2000s, South Korean intelligence had ruled out Kim Jong Nam, Kim Jong Il's oldest son. Jong Nam was deemed unfit—particularly after he was caught attempting to enter Tokyo in 2001 under an assumed identity with the intention of visiting Disneyland, embarrassing the regime.[2] Given North Korean state propaganda's celebration of Ko Yong Hui, who died of cancer in 2004, it was becoming clearer that one of her two sons would become the next leader. Kim Jong Il's sense of mortality grew more acute by 2008, when he suffered a major stroke. State planning for a succession accelerated as a result and, on January 8, 2009—Kim Jong Un's presumed twenty-fifth birthday—his father made clear that he was the chosen one.[3]

Jong Un's personality made him the ideal successor: he was brash, confident, ruthless, and headstrong. His youth, however, would be a problem—particularly given the existence of powerful greybeards around Kim Jong Il who might sense an opportunity to influence the young leader. To facilitate the succession, official accounts of Jong Un's credentials burnished his inherent strategic and tactical wisdom in military matters. The basis of a minor personality cult was put in place for the leader-in-waiting. Soon enough, this youngest son of Kim Jong Il was showered with Party and military credentials, and elevated to the highly powerful National Defense Commission. Soon to be known as "General Kim," Jong Un was thought to have been central in the dual 2010 attacks on South Korea: the March sinking of ROKS *Cheonan*, and the November 2010 shelling of Yeonpyeong-do Island.[4]

At the October 10, 2010, celebration of the Workers' Party of Korea's sixty-fifth anniversary, Kim Jong Un appeared alongside his father in the flesh, confirming his status as heir. He watched and clapped alongside his ailing father as military hardware rolled down Kim Il Sung Square, including mock-ups of ballistic missiles. A little more than a year later, Kim would be back on the balcony of the Grand People's Study House without his father at his side. Kim Jong Il died at approximately 8:30 a.m. on December 17, 2011. With his passing, the Kim Jong Un era had begun.

Those who had expected the regime's imminent collapse in 1994 after Kim Il Sung's death had been wrong, and once again in the 2010s Kim Jong Un would defy all predictions of crisis and collapse. Kim's cruelty and ruthlessness were apparent early on in his attempts to consolidate power. While optimists suggested that his childhood years in the docile Alpine setting of Switzerland might have given him a predisposition toward liberalization and reform, the young leader had no such plans.[5] Kim Jong Un was no North Korean Gorbachev and no *perestroika* or *glasnost* was on the cards for the 25 million people who found themselves under the rule of yet another hereditary tyrant. Shortly after the two-year anniversary of his father's death, Kim made global headlines for executing his uncle-by-marriage, Jang Song Thaek, one of his father's most trusted and powerful deputies. On February 13, 2017, just one day after Kim oversaw his first ballistic missile launch of the Trump era, his overseas agents used a powerful chemical nerve agent to stage an attack on his own half-brother, Kim Jong Nam, at Kuala Lumpur International Airport—one of the thirty busiest airports in the world. After painful convulsions, Jong Nam succumbed to the nerve agent, and was found to have on his person antidotes for a range of poisons and nerve agents, including the VX that killed him.[6]

By killing his brother in this way, Kim Jong Un not only ensured a brutal and agonizing last few moments for Kim Jong Nam, but also announced to the world, without saying a word, that North Korea possessed advanced chemical weapons and was able to smuggle them overseas for use in targeted assassinations. To date, North Korea has not officially acknowledged its possession of chemical and biological weapons, but independent experts and overseas intelligence agencies have long believed these capabilities were within the country's reach. Kim Jong Nam was coming to represent an alternate locus of legitimacy that could threaten the new leader, even as he lived overseas in China. In 2012, Jong Nam had even chided his younger brother, saying that he was "just a nominal figure and the members of the power elite will be the ones in actual power ... The dynastic succession is a joke to the outside world."[7]

What was clear from these two interfamilial assassinations was that Kim Jong Un would do whatever it took to keep his hold on power, at any cost. He quickly appeared at ease inheriting what one scholar had called North Korea's "mafia state."[8] North Korea's record on human rights and state-sponsored crime remained unchanged. Adapting to the times, North Korea's use of cybercrime skyrocketed, and older, reliable methods of raising funds for the leadership's vanities continued. In other words, the Kim regime's *nature* did not change. What did change, however, was policy guidance. Remaining in power—sustaining the Kim regime—would require an accelerated effort to perfect a nuclear deterrent.

On March 31, 2013, Kim Jong Un, barely two years into his reign, declared a "new strategic line" under the aegis of *byungjin*, or 'parallel development'. This *byungjin* line borrowed an old idea from his grandfather, first articulated in a 1962 speech to the Workers' Party Central Committee. That year, months after the conclusion of the Cuban Missile Crisis, Kim Il Sung had made the case that North Korea would have to pursue "parallelism" in its national objectives: pursuing national armament and economic prosperity side by side. The slogan employed, according to one telling, was "A gun in one hand, and a sickle and hammer in the other!"[9] Now, in March 2013, Kim Jong Un chose to recast his grandfather's call for *byungjin* in a contemporary light, explicitly referring to those days of high tension: "The line was put forward ...when the U.S. was running amuck to invade the DPRK and other Asian countries, elevated after the Caribbean Crisis."[10]

A year after the swift rise and fall of the February 2012 'Leap Day Deal' with the Obama administration, Kim declared his *byungjin* policy of simultaneously pursuing economic prosperity and a powerful nuclear deterrent. These objectives would be mutually reinforcing. Economic wellbeing would free up resources to build the ultimate tool of national defense, while that very tool would offer North Korea the unbreakable shield necessary to sustain its way of life and its regime, protecting it from what it saw as the constant threat of annihilation at the hands of the United States. For the five years from March 2013 to April 2018, this *byungjin* line drove a remarkable period in North Korea's history. Every major, publicized space launch, ballistic missile test, and nuclear test under Kim Jong Un was tied back to the *byungjin* objectives. Together, this unprecedented intensification of missile and weapon testing might be called the *byungjin* campaign.

During this time, Kim Jong Un oversaw four nuclear weapon tests and scores of ballistic missile launches. In April 2018, days before his first summit meeting with South Korean President Moon Jae-in, he "declared with pride that the historic tasks under the [*byungjin*] strategic line ... [have been] successfully carried out."[11] In January that year, he had declared North Korea's nuclear deterrent "complete." How, in just five years, had Kim Jong Un fulfilled the dream of his father and grandfather's combined sixty-three-year rule?

Scientists to the Front

Kim Jong Un's *byungjin* was the successor to his father's *songun* policy, which had put the Korean People's Army at the forefront of affairs of state, expending tremendous resources on improving the quality of the KPA's conventional armaments. Kim Jong Il's *songun* obsession had combined with unfavorable factors in the mid-to-late 1990s—including a lack of Soviet support, floods, droughts, and poor public food distribution—to produce a period of mass starvation, known in North Korea as the Arduous March. Casualty figures vary greatly, but most estimate that somewhere between 250,000 to 600,000 people perished; higher-end estimates cite as many deaths as 3.5 million—more than 10 per cent of the country's total population at the time. Under Kim Jong Un, however, the relationship between the supreme leadership and the KPA has undergone a transformation, both elevating the country's burgeoning nuclear force and ensuring that it is answerable only to Kim himself.

In April 2012, the erstwhile Missile Guidance Bureau of the KPA was transformed into a Strategic Rocket Force, granting it the status of first-among-equals with the KPA's three branches (Army, Navy, and Air Force).[12] This reorganization mirrored the Chinese People's Liberation Army's structure, where what is now known as the PLA Rocket Force has stewarded the country's strategic nuclear forces. Four years later, in 2016, a constitutional amendment saw the abolition of the powerful National Defense Commission—once an organ at the apex of state guidance under Kim Jong Il—and its replacement with the more civilianized State Affairs Commission, unless and until a time of war. Kim Jong Un was quietly implementing a restructuring: one where he would reign supreme over a consolidated nuclear force—a "treasured sword"—with a prized position in the country's national defense strategy.

Kim had been careful, however, not to present these reforms to national defense as a break from his father or grandfather's traditions. In the Kim Jong Un era, North Korean propaganda has repeatedly emphasized the contribution of all three generations to the realization of the nuclear deterrent. Days after the first successful flight-test of North Korea's largest intercontinental-range ballistic missile, the 8th Conference of the Munitions Industry credited Kim Il Sung with creating "the precious tradition of building the Juche-based national defense industry in the flames of the anti-Japanese revolution in his early years," and Kim Jong Il with "bolstering up the arms as the most important matter of the Party and revolution and lifeline of building a socialist power." Arriving at Kim Jong Un, the state media account celebrated the young leader's heralding of a "fresh heyday" for North Korean national defense, hailing his *byungjin* line as a "historic turning point." Though Kim's father and grandfather have stronger personality cults and command greater respect, descriptions of Kim Jong Un's contributions to the country's nuclear forces were detailed and effusive.

> Under his strategic decision, the DPRK carried out two successful H-bomb tests, "March 18 revolution" and "July 4 revolution" and won the miraculous July 28 victory and the great November 29 victory. These are extra-large auspicious events in the history of the nation as they opened up the era of radical changes and fully realized the long-cherished desire of our people for powerful national defense capability.[13]

In the story told today in North Korea about the country's nuclear arrival, none of it would have been possible with Kim Jong Un and especially his *byungjin* campaign. Without these, North Korea's nuclear weapons capabilities would not have made the final jump necessary from the mostly symbolic, ramshackle deterrent they represented during his father's tenure to the serious threat they had become by New Year's Day, 2018, sowing terror in the minds of Americans. By the same token, had Kim agreed to abandon nuclear weapons, he would, in effect, have been repudiating the legacy left by his father and grandfather in an act akin to a national betrayal.[14]

It is true that Kim Jong Un himself has personally left his mark on the nuclear program. He appears to have taken a particular liking to a fundamental, human component of the program. If his father's tenure was defined by a military-first ethic, then Kim Jong Un's tenure might be defined by a scientists-first approach. Repeatedly, North Korean propaganda in the Kim Jong Un era has emphasized the critical role played by the country's scientists, engineers, and technicians in bringing the national "treasured sword" to reality. As early as 2013, Kim underscored that technological progress would be the way to thrive under the sanctions imposed by the outside world. In 2017, he feted the hundreds of personnel who had been involved in the development of the country's ICBM and thermonuclear technology, holding major rallies in Pyongyang and even a celebratory concert with the well-loved Moranbong Band—an all-girl group sometimes called North Korea's 'Spice Girls.'[15] As the band performed, a slideshow played behind them, showcasing decades of North Korean advancements in strategic weaponry, including ballistic missiles and nuclear weapons. Kim himself has been enthusiastically photographed with his munitions industry workers and scientists after important tests. In March 2017, Kim baffled the world upon the test of a new rocket engine—one that now powers some of North Korea's most fearsome weapons—by releasing a photograph of him self giving a uniformed military officer a piggyback ride. For an apparently ruthless tyrant, capable of killing his own family in cold blood, Kim was showing remarkable intimacy with these men who had sharpened the blade of his "treasured sword."

Under Kim Jong Un, North Korean scientists—even those with a marginal association with the national nuclear and ballistic missile programs—have found themselves receiving preferential access to housing in Pyongyang, including a glitzy new residential district on Ryomyong Street. Kim has also demonstrated a particular care for the younger generation of up-and-coming missile engineers. In August 2019, after overseeing the first successful test-firing of a "super-large" multiple launch rocket system, Kim reportedly expressed his delight that "our young national defense scientists are so clever as to conceive out of their own heads." The national newspaper, *Rodong Sinmun*, reported that Kim was very happy to have such "promising talents who will shoulder ... the rapid development of ...defense."[16] For Kim, scientists and engineers have become a core constituency in the economic flourishing of the country, too, having demonstrated their value by developing and testing the military technologies pivotal to his regime's survival.

Byungjin's Success and the Aftermath

By April 2018, when Kim declared the success of the *byungjin* line, a rapprochement was already underway. Taking note of the inauguration of a pro-engagement president in South Korea, Moon Jae-in, and of course using the leverage of his now-complete nuclear deterrent, Kim embarked on a long year of remarkable diplomacy, culminating in a visit to Chinese leader Xi Jinping, the first inter-Korean summit of the 2010s, and the first-ever U.S.–North Korea summit meeting in June 2018 in Singapore. These events (see Part Three) underscored a reputational payoff for Kim after the *byungjin* testing campaign. Instead of continuing to face "maximum pressure"—what the Trump administration had called its hardline strategy toward North Korea—and total global isolation, Kim was given an audience with a U.S. president less than one year after testing three missiles capable of ranging U.S. territory.

In Kim's view, his June 2018 summit with Trump was the beginning of a process by which the United States and North Korea would come to deliberate the terms on which these two longstanding adversaries could coexist as nuclear-armed equals. In the mid-2000s, North Korean officials had often told American interlocutors that what they really sought was something akin to what India enjoys: normal diplomatic relations with the United States, unfettered global economic access, including to civil nuclear technologies, and toleration of its nuclear weapons, for national defense purposes. In 2018, one expert even brought up an Israel-style arrangement of *amimut*, or opacity: Israel is vague about its capabilities, not recognized as a nuclear power under the Treaty on the Nonproliferation of Nuclear Weapons (NPT), and the United States humors it by refusing to bring up the open fact of its nuclear possession.[17]

The bet did not pay off for North Korea, however. It was not long before the United States dawdled on the issue of sanctions relief, which had long been a hope of the regime in Pyongyang, even though it had long mastered sanctions evasion and illicit finance. The talks process ended in February 2019 in Hanoi with a North Korean walk-out and no deal. After all, Kim Jong Un had not flown to Beijing, Singapore, and Hanoi to turn over the keys to his nuclear kingdom; with his regime's survival at stake, and his deterrent complete, he had no reason and no intention to disarm. But why is this nuclear force so precious to him? What purposes does it serve?

What Does Kim Jong Un Want?

In January 2016, shortly after North Korea's fourth nuclear test, the *New Yorker*, a venerable and generally well-regarded American magazine, chose to reference the event on its cover. *New Yorker* covers attract the interest and appreciation of a certain type of well-educated, well-read, mostly American reader. The covers are evocative and often reflect the zeitgeist around their subject matter. In this instance, the January 18, 2016, cover, by artist Anita Kunz, pictured a caricature of Kim Jong Un as a chubby toddler, playing with a missile bearing the North Korean flag and an airplane bearing the American flag. The piece was titled "New Toys."[18] Days prior, North Korea had claimed that it had tested its first-ever hydrogen bomb. Yet the popular American reaction was largely still one of bewildered amusement.

This was an old tendency in the popular perception of North Korea in the United States. Perhaps one of the best-known manifestations of this in the 2010s was the film *The Interview* (2014), starring popular actors Seth Rogen and James Franco. Featuring Korean-American actor Randall Park as a gormless Kim Jong Un, the film catalogued a clandestine American attempt to assassinate Kim, with Franco and Rogen portraying tabloid-journalists-cum-assassins. The film's cultural relevance ballooned after a major cyberattack against Sony Pictures Entertainment in November 2014. While the United States government would officially attribute the attack to North Korea much later, private investigators strongly suggested early on that the intrusion was state-sponsored; this view made support for the film surge as an act of protest against what was seen as an attempt by a thin-skinned regime to suppress satire overseas.

The Interview was not the first piece of popular culture in this vein, however. One older entry was a 2004 comedy film, courtesy of *South Park* creators Trey Parker and Matt Stone, called *Team America: World Police*. This satire of 1980s and 1990s action films, featuring marionettes, follows the deeds and misdeeds of an American paramilitary group seeking to protect the world from a very-early-2000s panoply of bad guys, corresponding somewhat to the Bush administration's "Axis of Evil." Chief among the antagonists in the film was a caricature of North

Korea's then supreme leader Kim Jong Il, who bemoans his national and personal isolation in a racist musical number "I'm So Ronery." Kim Jong Il's cachet as a subject of mockery in American pop culture persisted into the 2010s and even beyond his 2011 death. A popular Tumblr blog titled "Kim Jong-Il Looking At Things" continued updating through December 2012, featuring North Korean state media-released images of Kim's many so-called on-the-spot guidance visits. The final image, shared on December 17, 2012, shows a somewhat disappointed Kim, surrounded by suited Party cadres, examining a roasted pig.

This portrayal of North Korean leaders, state objectives, and even military capabilities as befuddling, infantile, or silly even spills over to the ostensibly more serious American political commentariat and policymaking community. In 2017, the year Kim Jong Un demonstrated an astounding seven new missile types, U.S. President Donald J. Trump mused that "Kim's missiles keep crashing" in a leaked private phone call with the president of the Philippines, Rodrigo Duterte. In a tweet the day after Kim Jong Un's 2018 New Year's Address—the speech in which he celebrated the completion of his proverbial "nuclear button"—Trump guffawed and suggested that the button might not actually work. Trump's unwillingness to take Kim's capabilities seriously was far from unique, but it was not consistent with the findings of the U.S. intelligence community. In reality, at the time Trump made these comments, Kim had a missile testing success record of roughly 75 per cent.[19]

Beyond misreading Kim's growing capabilities, U.S. officials have also routinely offered assessments that the North Korean leader is erratic and irrational. In 2014, Adm. Samuel Locklear, the commander of U.S. Pacific Command, called Kim "unpredictable," saying: "His behavior, at least in the way it is reported and the way we see it in sense, would make me wonder whether or not he is always in the rational decision-making mode or not. And this is a problem."[20] Trump's second national security advisor and a scholar of history, Lt. Gen. H.R. McMaster, once mused that "classical deterrence theory" likely would not apply to Kim Jong Un, who was dangerous and untrustworthy.[21] To this day, even with the nuclear deterrent complete, numerous commentators—including some with a high degree of technical expertise and training in international security issues—underestimate North Korea, viewing its capabilities as a calibrated mirage, designed to cause Americans to quake in their boots without reason.

The reasons for these perceptions are multiple. Human beings tend to fear and mock what they do not understand and North Korea is both geographically distant and politically idiosyncratic in the eyes of most Americans. Contrary to the American perception of North Korea as a confusing and seemingly impossible place, South Korean and Japanese citizens—now long in the line of fire—take a different view. The regime's well-deserved reputation for almost unparalleled cruelty also contributes to a fallacious perception of irrationality on the part of its leader. Similar concerns existed in the United States in the mid- and late-1960s after China, then led by Mao Zedong, tested a nuclear weapon. Following the deaths of millions in the famine that followed the catastrophic Great Leap Forward and amid the madness of the Cultural Revolution, egged on by a zealous Mao, American leaders wondered out loud if such a cruel, incompetent, and capricious regime as Beijing might be trusted with nuclear weapons. In 2014, Michael Kirby, the chief UN human rights investigator in the country, described a "Holocaust-type phenomenon" in North Korea.[22]

Cruel regimes might not approach foreign policy-making with strategic precision and acuity, but it does not follow that they are irrational. The overbearing authoritarianism that manifests itself today in North Korea stems in great part from concerns about the regime's own security—and ultimately its own survival. These same concerns drive much of the country's investments in defense materiel and, ultimately, nuclear weapons, at the expense of food, shelter, and other necessities for the country's poorest and most vulnerable citizens. Under the Kim family, North Korea has behaved as what economists might call a means-ends rational actor, adapting its rather limited means to best realize a well-defined and remarkably constant set of end objectives.

In many ways, the country is the archetype of the self-interested state that international relations theorist Kenneth N. Waltz described in his seminal 1979 *Theory of International Politics.* For Waltz, the international system is the first-order principle that drives state decision-making. This system is fundamentally anarchic—that is to say, no sovereign reigns supreme above the system's constituent states and no authority can enforce any sort of global rule-set on behaviors. While other international relations theorists have disputed this view, we might surmise that North Korean leaders, at least, have largely agreed with Waltz. States in this anarchic system ultimately seek to maximize their security as a means to ensure their survival. For Waltz, the actions and strategic decision making of a state like North Korea can be explained by the fact that states are fundamentally unable to cooperate with one another over the long term, due to an inherent situation of insecurity and unbalanced coalitions. Kim Jong Un, for example, is insecure not only because of his inferior material capabilities, but also because of his inability to ascertain with certainty the intentions of other countries.

So if we accept that North Korea is a state with a rational leader and strategy, what might that strategy be? For pessimists, a commonly cited objective of North Korean state policy is the "final victory"—a longstanding and constant theme in national propaganda. This relates to the unfinished business of the Korean

War and the prospect of Korean unification under North Korean rule. On April 15, 2012, Kim Jong Un, then just four months into his rule, commemorated his grandfather's birth centenary with a speech titled "Let Us March Forward Dynamically Towards Final Victory, Holding Higher the Banner of *Songun* [Military First]." This speech marked an important moment in the young, enigmatic ruler's establishment as *suryong*, or supreme leader. He not only demonstrated that he was far more outgoing than his introverted father, who famously avoided speaking in public, but he also showed the world a commitment to ideological continuity, citing both the life's dream of his grandfather and the policy line of his father.[23] A few months later, North Korean state media began airing a propaganda hymnal titled "Onwards Toward the Final Victory."

There is no sugarcoating it: the objective of reunification is fundamentally coercive, threatening, and an existential threat to South Korea. However, under Kim Jong Un, the rigidity of this objective and its place in the hierarchy of North Korean strategy is questionable. Nevertheless, Kim's nuclear weapons would have limited use for achieving this objective. Some analysts are determined to cite evidence that Kim's "treasured sword" will not be left sheathed until called on to repel a U.S. invasion, but rather might be willfully drawn and held to the throat of the South Korean public, demanding their subjugation. However, the pessimists are likely wrong: the realization of a nuclear deterrent has made North Korea's use of conventional provocations *less*—not *more*—frequent. Under Kim Jong Un, no crisis has come close to matching the harm wrought on South Korea in 2010, with his father's twin attacks on the ROKS *Cheonan* and Yeonpyeong-do Island. Those crises occurred at a time when Pyongyang's nuclear development was ongoing and very much incomplete.

For a better answer to the question of what Kim Jong Un is looking to achieve with his nuclear force, we can go back to Waltz. In his neorealist telling, states would never "willingly place themselves in situations of increased dependence."[24] Instead, they would practice "self-help," where "considerations of security subordinate economic gain to political interest."[25] This radical tendency to favor "self-help" on the world stage manifests itself in the North Korean strategic lexicon in *Juche*, or "self-reliance" in the usual English translation. North Korea elevated *Juche* to the guiding principle of the state in the 1950s. Yet the country's history reveals a different story, and this story has clearly informed Kim Jong Un's vision for his nuclear forces. For the better part of its existence, Pyongyang has had a great reliance on, at best, the generosity, and, at worst, the noninterference, of proximal great powers, mostly China—the country's massive neighbor, Marxist-Leninist fellow traveler of sorts, and economic bulwark. Kim Il Sung spent much of the Cold War benefiting from Soviet military support as well.

Thus Kim Jong Un has sought to achieve self-reliance to avoid the pangs of great power abandonment that his country has always suffered. The collapse of the Soviet Union, for instance, plunged North Korea into a period of economic destitution from which it was never recovered—just years after Kim Il Sung found himself pressured by Moscow to enter the NPT. Similarly, the relationship with Beijing is permeated with a deep-seated mistrust about Chinese intentions in Pyongyang. Commentators have attributed this particular suspicion to pre-twentieth-century Korean history and the often difficult relationship between various imperial rulers in China and Korean leaders. Kim Il Sung's unease about the role of foreign powers grew more acute with the so-called August Incident of 1956, when factions with backing in Beijing and Moscow sought to remove him from power.[26] Kim survived and his resolve for strategic autonomy hardened, even as he would continue for decades to benefit from Soviet and Chinese commerce and generosity.

Even as North Korea sought to augment its security through cooperation with China and the Soviet Union—eventually

Russia—it also continued to see value in radical self-reliance. As the political scientist Van Jackson has observed, "the precise extent of *Juche*'s relevance is less important than the fact that reference to *Juche* is pervasive in North Korean propaganda aimed at foreign audiences."[27] The message to the outside world is clear: North Korea's destiny—and the destiny of the Korean Peninsula—will be determined by the North Korean leadership alone. Pyongyang regularly calls Seoul a "puppet" of the United States. Embedded in that epithet are years of simmering North Korean unease and insecurity about its own subservience—real and imagined—to the neighboring giants China and Russia; these same anxieties have driven and still drive Kim to develop, hold on to and expand his nuclear force.

Beyond self-reliance, what does Kim Jong Un want? Much depends on this question in a monolithic and authoritarian system of government like North Korea's, where Kim might, without any sense of irony or exaggeration, repeat Louis XIV's *l'État, c'est moi* (I am the state). Above all, like most anyone else, Kim Jong Un wants to die comfortably in his own bed of natural causes—preferably with a lifespan well in excess of North Korea's male life expectancy of sixty-eight: not exactly an irrational impulse. If Kim were to ever launch an invasion of South Korea or employ nuclear weapons in wartime or peacetime, he would likely meet a swift end at the hands of a combined U.S.—South Korean or U.S.—Japanese assault. But it is not just foreign forces that might threaten Kim's fate: his survival is predicated on him successfully consolidating and maintaining power, insulating himself from any would-be coup plotters or detractors. Kim Jong Un's overarching goal, and the regime's core objective, is survival. Part of this objective will be for Kim Jong Un to successfully raise his suspected three children, bequeathing the North Korean throne to one of them as his father did to him, and continuing the so-called *paektusan* bloodline that has made North Korea the world's sole *de facto* communist monarchy.

Underpinning these objectives of survival and self-reliance are a set of policy goals that drive North Korean state planning and foreign policy. First, Kim seeks to improve North Korea's economic lot. The purpose of this drive is not any sense of altruism or obligation to the North Korean people. Rather, Kim appreciates that a baseline level of economic prosperity is critical to sustaining his grip on power. Despite his power atop the North Korean state, Kim is no island: his ability to survive as ruler depends on convincing a core group of high-ranking Workers' Party elite that their lives are better served by supporting, rather than upending, the current party-state system. As a result, during Kim's rule the capital city of Pyongyang and the coastal city of Wonsan have received a seriously disproportionate amount of civil economic development spending. Even in monolithic *Juche* Korea, there are politics, and Kim's patterns of economic prioritization and modernization are well-supported by selectorate theory, which claims that rational leaders like Kim need to satisfy certain important internal constituencies to retain power.[28]

For Kim, unfortunately, the drive to improve North Korea's economic destiny has suffered as a result of the country's decision to pursue nuclear weapons, due to the international sanctions regime against Pyongyang—the widest-ranging imposed on any country. Beginning effectively in July 2006, after a series of missile launches by Kim Jong Il, and running through to December 2017, one month after Kim Jong Un's test launch of the country's largest-ever, intercontinental ballistic missile, North Korea has come under eleven successive UN Security Council sanctions resolutions. These have been augmented by unilateral sanctions by the United States, the European Union, and others. But, now that Kim's nuclear deterrent is "complete," economic motivations are back on the agenda. When Kim acknowledged in early 2018 that his *byungjin* line (parallel nuclear and economic development) had succeeded, he proceeded to announce a "new strategic line," focused exclusively on economic development. As of 2020, North Korea has experienced no relief from UN Security Council sanctions, but it continues to survive, adapting and evading sanctions with a greater degree of ingenuity than before. Using its nuclear weapons as leverage in negotiating sanctions relief seems an obvious strategy—and another reason not to give them up.

In short, Kim's project is to ensure his self-reliant survival, and central to this strategic vision is the perfection of a robust, diverse, and sufficiently large nuclear force, as well as the augmentation of North Korea's status on the international stage. These two objectives are related, in theory and reality. A state's possession of nuclear weapons—weapons of awesome, mass destruction with a taboo unique in the history of ordnance for precisely those reasons—confers a certain status and prestige. In April 2016, long before Kim's testing of his ICBM or thermonuclear weapon, the Korean Central News Agency (KCNA) offered a glimpse of Pyongyang's interest in foreign analyses and statements about North Korea's nuclear activities. "Experts and media around the world assert that the DPRK's nuclear weapons will increase and get more powerful as time passes and in turn it will set the country up for nuclear negotiations," an article in the *Pyongyang Times* noted, citing statements from the United Kingdom, India, the United States, and Russia on its activities.[29]

Of course, any nation-state wishes to be a strong presence on the international stage, but few regimes have had to think as carefully and seriously as the Kim dynasty about survival in a hostile world. Without understanding this North Korean peculiarity, it's simply not possible to appreciate where Kim Jong Un is coming from as he seeks to wield a nuclear force. Before we explore Kim's plans for his nukes, therefore, the next chapter will explore this history of precarity and peril on the Korean Peninsula.

2

HISTORY'S TRIALS

In his 1984 State of the Union address, U.S. President Ronald Reagan declared that "a nuclear war cannot be won and must never be fought." He identified the "value" of possessing nuclear weapons: "to make sure they will never be used." Put in scholarly terms, international relations expert Robert Jervis has described the "nuclear revolution" as a seminal sea-change in military strategy, rendering war between two nuclear states too costly to contemplate, dissuading unilateral aggression.[1] As Bernard Brodie, one of the original American nuclear strategists, put it: "Thus far the chief purpose of our military establishment has been to win wars. From now on its chief purpose must be to avert them. It can have almost no other useful purpose."[2]

Here, we really get to the heart of why Kim Jong Un has risked and spent so much to develop a nuclear force. Nuclear bombs and their means of delivery are neither cheap nor unsophisticated, but the states that develop them have spent untold sums keeping these weapons of apocalyptic destruction usable, precisely so they might never be used. At the center of this paradoxical idea is the concept of nuclear deterrence. Stated in its power, and that it had been provoked to this path largely by U.S. behavior.

In June 2003, after Bush declared that combat operations in Iraq had transitioned toward occupation, a senior North Korean Foreign Ministry official warned that if the United States encroached on Pyongyang's sovereignty, North Korea would respond "with an immediate, physical retaliatory measure."[33] There was that word again: *physical*. Nuclear weapons were not explicitly mentioned, but in hindsight this was clearly an early articulation of North Korea's aggressive nuclear strategy, designed around first use to ensure the survival of the country's leadership. Any attempt at invasion and regime change would be met with use of nuclear weapons.

The Foreign Ministry statement added: "As far as the issue of nuclear deterrent force is concerned, the DPRK has the same status as the United States and other states possessing nuclear deterrent force."[34] This equivalence was purely rhetorical: much work lay ahead before North Korea could actually demonstrate the capabilities to realize that status. As was the case in the early 1990s, and as we will see again in Part Three for 2017–19, two simultaneous sets of events arose out of this standoff: renewed diplomacy, alongside continued efforts toward achieving a nuclear force.

* * *

In 2005, North Korea came to the table once again. After the accession of Hu Jintao to the Chinese presidency in 2003, Beijing became a major driver of efforts to revive diplomacy, lest a U.S.—North Korea crisis spiral out of control to the detriment of political and economic stability in Northeast Asia. This diplomatic effort was known as the Six-Party Talks, after the involvement of the six states with a direct stake in the region: the United States, China, Russia, Japan, South Korea, and North crudest and simplest form, the massive destructive capability that North Korea can wield through nuclear weapons should prevent its adversaries from doing anything to harm its interests by threatening such use. Survival is what Kim's nukes mean to him—but deterrence is the reason why the two are tied together. As for the reason why survival through deterrence is of such unparalleled importance to Kim, we need to look to the broader story of his fragile country's birth, and its pursuit of the bomb almost ever since.

The history of North Korea's journey towards nuclear power status has been painstakingly litigated and relitigated by diplomatic historians, scholars, nonproliferation analysts, Koreanists, and journalists. In the United States, the appetite for diplomacy with Pyongyang has waxed and waned. Critics cite the low baseline trust in the seventy-year-old U.S.—North Korea relationship and Pyongyang's historic tendency to defect on its commitments—be it against the spirit or the letter of its agreements—as reasons to remain wary of diplomatic efforts. North Korea did not come into existence as a nuclear weapons possessor out of a void, after all. This chapter will chart in more detail the global history of nuclear weapons development, in North Korea and beyond, up to the end of the Obama era in 2016. (For obvious reasons relating to American politics as well as North Korean nuclear development, the period 2017–19 marked a crucial new direction in our story, and will be explored in Part Three.) The precise twists and turns of North Korea's nuclear program, including Kim Jong Un's final sprint toward completion of the deterrent by 2018, will be charted in Part Two—but first they need to be placed in context. So here we will begin at the beginning.

* * *

At 5:29 a.m. on July 14, 1945, the nuclear age began.

In truth, it had begun much earlier, with years of research and development under the aegis of the Manhattan Project. Now, on this fateful morning in the New Mexico desert, the United States became the first country to harness the power of the atom for mass destruction, of a scale unimaginable using conventional explosives alone.

Within two months, two nuclear weapons—affectionately dubbed 'Fat Man' and 'Little Boy'—had been dropped on the Japanese cities of Hiroshima and Nagasaki, respectively, killing tens of thousands. To this day, these bombings are credited with having altered the course of the most devastating total war that mankind had ever known. Other strategic factors—including the Soviet Union's decision on August 8 to join the allied campaign in the Pacific—may have played a more significant role in Japan's decision to capitulate and end the Second World War, but at the very least Imperial Japanese leaders balked at the atom bomb's colossal destructive power, resulting in Japanese surrender.

Four years later, another nuclear power emerged on the world stage. On the morning of August 29, 1949, the Soviet Union successfully conducted what U.S. intelligence would call 'Joe-1,' after the Soviet leader Joseph Stalin: the first test of a nuclear weapon outside of the United States. The weapon was modeled on the 'Fat Man' implosion bomb used on Hiroshima. Following that demonstration of the atomic bomb's awesome power, Soviet leader Joseph Stalin had directed Moscow's nascent nuclear weapons program into overdrive. The effort was abetted by years of Soviet espionage within the top-secret Manhattan Project. For the young Kim Il Sung, however, this first Soviet bomb likely served as a sign that his longtime benefactors in Moscow had acquired a significant capability that might allow him to push on with his ultimate objective: to unite both halves of the divided Korean Peninsula under the Workers' Party of Korea.

1945–50: Division, The Original Sin

The Soviet Union would not test another nuclear device until September 1951, but in the meantime, the Korean Peninsula had emerged as one of the Cold War's first major flashpoints. The events that would lead up to the start of the Korean War (1950–53)—most importantly the preliminary division of the North and the South—had taken root in the early 1940s, at the height of the Second World War. Korea's fate, like so much of the world, was decided by the Allied great powers. It was U.S. President Franklin D. Roosevelt, British Prime Minister Winston Churchill, and Soviet leader Joseph Stalin who recognized Korea's subjugation under Japanese imperial control in the Cairo Declaration of 1943. The three leaders resolved to address the matter of a sovereign and free Korea in "due course."[3]

Following the end of the war, attention in the west quickly turned to the spread of communism, particularly as the Chinese Civil War entered its final years, culminating in the founding of the People's Republic of China in 1949. The U.S.—Soviet alliance that had defeated Nazi Germany and Imperial Japan gave way to ideological struggle and contest as the Cold War was slowly but surely emerging. Witnessing the Soviet incursion into northern China and the Korean Peninsula in the weeks leading up to Japan's defeat, U.S. anxieties had begun to grow about an inexorable communist bulwark taking hold across from Japan, which had come under American occupation.

In Washington, D.C. on the night of August 10, 1945, one day after the bombing of Nagasaki, two American military officers were given the task of figuring out how exactly post-war American interests in Korea would be protected. One of them was Dean Rusk, who would later go on to serve as secretary of state under the Kennedy and Johnson administrations. Chris Bonesteel, or "Tic," was the other. Rusk recounted their deliberations in his memoirs, underscoring that "neither Tic nor I was a Korea expert."[4] All Rusk and Tic had by way of cartographic assistance that night was a 1942 National Geographic map of *Asia and Adjacent Areas*, which lacked any substantial detail about Korea's internal administrative structure. Nevertheless, the two men had enough to go on: the northern part of the Peninsula was vulnerable to Soviet control and Seoul, the largest city and the capital, held strategic value.[5] Rusk and Tic came up with a proposal for the Soviets: a demarcation line would be drawn at the 38th parallel north. This "made no sense economically or geographically," Rusk would later note, but if the Soviets accepted it, Seoul would remain in the American sector, just under 50 kilometers from the demarcation line. The Soviet Union assented, and the original sin of division on the Korean Peninsula was thus committed: a communist zone of responsibility in the north and an American-aligned zone in the south. On August 24, the Soviet Red Army entered Pyongyang.

A little less than a month later, Kim Il Sung, a young Korean major in the Soviet Red Army, landed at the northern Korean port city of Wonsan, ending twenty-six years of effective exile. He had been hand-picked by none other than the infamous head of Stalin's secret police, Lavrentiy Beria, as a suitable ward for the Soviet-backed half of Korea.[6] Beria had overruled the selection of Major General Nikolai G. Lebedev, a Soviet officer who was part of the occupation force and charged with the delicate task "to find and prepare several Koreans as candidates for the country's leaders, including the post of General Secretary."[7] In 1984 Lebedev recounted the circumstances of Kim Il Sung's elevation as the anointed leader of communist Korea: Beria, then the minister of internal affairs, had convinced Stalin in favor of Kim Il Sung, whom he had repeatedly interviewed. Lebedev also described his own experience meeting Kim Il Sung, the man who would become North Korea's *suryong*, or great leader:

Kim Il Sung was soon delivered to us. I thought it odd that he was dressed in a Soviet captain's uniform and had an Order of the Red Banner on his chest, while the man who brought him was dressed as a civilian. The thickset, round-faced Korean spoke good Russian, but in terms of political qualifications he was utterly ignorant. He failed the Marxism-Leninism exam completely. But we had no choice; we could not just go to Stalin and report that his candidate wasn't qualified. We had to create a General Secretary from what we were given. Whilst we were teaching him theory, we ... acquainted Kim with important Koreans in influential governmental and non-governmental organizations. Kim had to understand the importance of his mission and in this he succeeded very quickly and was bursting with pride.[8]

By the end of the year, Kim had been declared the chairman of the Korean Communist Party. In 1948, Kim founded the Korean People's Army and, after winning a Soviet-managed election for the premiership of a communist-dominated government, proclaimed the founding of the Democratic People's Republic of Korea (DPRK), its southern administrative border matching the declared demarcation line between the Soviet and American zones: the 38th parallel.

Meanwhile, south of the new border, another leader took up his own place in Seoul: Syngman Rhee, an avowed capitalist with an education spanning George Washington, Harvard, and Princeton Universities. While Japan's dominion over the Korean Peninsula had ended, both Kim and Rhee sought to realize Korean self-determination—as had been acknowledged by Stalin and Roosevelt in Cairo. They both wanted to unify Korea.

1950–90: The Korean War and the Cold War

On June 25, 1950, the Korean People's Army poured south across the 38th parallel. The Korean War had begun. By the July 1953 armistice that ended the conflict, nearly 2.5 million combatants and support personnel from more than thirty countries had been drawn in. Korean civilians on both sides suffered. While death toll estimates vary, at the higher end, 5 million people were estimated to have been killed over the course of the hostilities. Years after the war, in 1984, General Curtis E. Lemay told U.S. Air Force interviewers that "Over a period of three years or so, we killed off—what—20 per cent of the population of Korea as direct casualties of war, or from starvation and exposure."[9] Both Koreas lost a significant proportion of their population, for the North some 10 per cent of its pre-war population of around 10 million. In the end, the war ended in a stalemate, with an armistice but no peace treaty, and did little to resolve the political and territorial questions concerning the Korean Peninsula. Histories of the war differ within the two Koreas. In North Korea, tales of American atrocities—real and imagined—are central to sustaining what amounts to a founding myth for the country. The Korean People's Army's greatest feats during the conflict—all under Kim Il Sung's stewardship—are recounted as examples of the country's unique hardiness, self-reliant spirit, and bravery.

For more than two decades after the 1953 armistice, the Korean Peninsula simmered with unease and near-conflict. Under Kim Il Sung, North Korea remained risk-acceptant and eager to bloody the nose of the Americans and the South Koreans—all in the name of working toward a Korea reunified under the North Korean flag. Kim ordered infiltrations across the inter-Korean demarcation zone and attempted to punish the United States for its continued involvement on the Peninsula. In 1965, a Korean People's Air Force fighter shot at and damaged an RB-47 reconnaissance aircraft. In 1968, the Korean People's Navy seized the USS *Pueblo*, taking the vessel back to North Korea where the American crew were milked for propaganda value. Around this time, North Korean special forces staged a daring assassination attempt on South Korean President Park Chung-hee at the Blue House itself—the presidential residence in Seoul. In 1969, some 50 nautical miles away from the North Korean coast, a KPAF fighter successfully shot down a U.S. EC-121 reconnaissance aircraft.

None of these incidents caused a return to all-out war on the Korean Peninsula, but they kept the United States and South Korea committed to their alliance, which was sealed in a 1953 Mutual Defense Treaty, and vigilant. By the 1970s, Kim Il Sung's approach had softened—partly in response to U.S. President Nixon's opening to China. But risks remained on the Korean Peninsula: after the murder of two U.S. soldiers in the Joint Security Area along the DMZ in 1976, the two sides once again faced the prospect of an all-out conflict. By the 1980s, low-level infiltrations and cross-border firefights were still taking place. But things were about to change for the two Koreas, even if they couldn't foresee it. By the twilight years of the Cold War, Kim Il Sung had presided over the indigenous building of North Korea's first major operative nuclear reactor, but had also succumbed to Soviet pressure and acquiesced to the Non-Proliferation Treaty. Little did he know, however, that his world was on the cusp of change.

1990–92: The End of the Cold War and the Birth of 'Denuclearization'

The failure to prevent North Korea's breakout as a nuclear power was not for a lack of trying. Beginning in the early 1990s, both South Korea and the United States took an interest in what was quickly becoming apparent: North Korea's aspiration to produce nuclear weapons. As the Cold War was drawing to a close, this was a period of significant diplomatic progress between the two Koreas. Seoul, following a 1987 democratic uprising, had transitioned from an authoritarian state to a nascent democracy. Pyongyang, meanwhile, lost one of its most important allies, the

Soviet Union, heightening its sense of insecurity and isolation. Alongside this geopolitical transformation, the two countries' economic fortunes were also shifting: South Korea had rapidly industrialized as one of the "Asian tiger" economies, and by the 1988 Seoul Summer Olympic Games—widely seen as South Korea's "coming out" to the world—its economy had launched a period of unstoppable exponential growth that would make it one of the world's wealthiest nations.[10] North Korea, meanwhile, was doomed to a stagnation that would intensify with the collapse of the Soviet Union and culminate in famine by the late 1990s. With the loss of Soviet patronage, North Korea entered an economic slump from which it would never really recover.

Moreover, both Koreas were watching the experience of German unification, which showcased the absorption of East Germany by the West. What would be viewed in Seoul as a model for Korean unification was seen in Pyongyang as a stark warning of the uncertainty that lay ahead. Separately, in 1990 and 1991 North Korea watched in awe as the United States prosecuted large-scale conventional warfare against Iraqi dictator Saddam Hussein. Pyongyang's perception of a threat from the United States was acute and, while Saddam was not removed from power in 1991, Washington's ability to have done so did not go unappreciated by North Korea. The regime's growing insecurity in the post-Cold War world was bound to have consequences: a sometimes uneasy mix of diplomacy and nuclear development.

* * *

It was shortly after the collapse of the Soviet Union that the world first became familiar with the term 'denuclearization'—a word now used casually in everyday international discourse around North Korea. On January 20, 1992, the North and the South signed a joint declaration on the "Denuclearization of the Korean Peninsula," building on several developments between the two countries in 1991. Both had been admitted to the United Nations as member states after years as observers (South Korea since 1948 and North Korea since 1971, after the People's Republic of China was given a seat). This recognition symbolized the beginning of a new era in which two Koreas might coexist peacefully, even though both Seoul and Pyongyang maintained unification as a core national long-term objective. On December 13, 1991, high-level representatives of the two countries had signed a "Basic Agreement," which outlined a set of principles for inter-Korean exchange and relations. It underscored that each Korea would "recognize and respect each other's system."[11] The agreement was an important trust-building exercise between the two countries, after nearly four decades of hostile relations under the 1953 armistice regime.

It was in this context that the 1992 inter-Korean agreement on denuclearization was forged. North and South Korea pledged not to "test, manufacture, produce, receive, possess, store, deploy or use nuclear weapons" or to "possess nuclear [fuel production] facilities." Both sides agreed to reciprocal inspections for verification. This came seven years after Kim Il Sung's reluctant accession to the Treaty on the Nonproliferation of Nuclear Weapons (NPT) in 1985, under considerable pressure from the Soviet Union. Moscow had strongly supported the NPT and opposed development of nuclear weapons even by Communist bloc countries: for years, Soviet satellite states in Eastern Europe receiving civil nuclear technology to operate reactors had had "all aspects of the nuclear fuel cycle" controlled by Soviet technical specialists.

South Korea was also a member of the NPT, having been induced to set aside its own nuclear ambitions after Washington forestalled its attempts to procure equipment and facilities from France. Seoul's contemplation of an indigenous nuclear program had been prompted by Nixon's withdrawal of some 20,000 troops from the Korean Peninsula. According to a 1974 secret U.S.

cable, South Korean President Park Chung-hee had "told Korean journalists that he had directed scientists to build atomic bombs by 1977; he had also informed an industrial conference that he wanted long-range missiles for retaliation against North Korean provocations."[12] By entering the NPT in 1975, Seoul had foresworn the possession of nuclear weapons indefinitely in exchange for access to civil nuclear technology.

American tactical nuclear weapons had remained in South Korea, but in 1991 the United States withdrew these, under the reciprocal Presidential Nuclear Initiatives agreed between Mikhail Gorbachev, the last Soviet leader, and U.S. President George H.W. Bush. The two superpowers engaged in substantial nuclear reductions and a worldwide pulling back of overseas nuclear forces, including, on Bush's end, a pledge to withhold their redeployment under "normal circumstances" (i.e., peacetime).[13] Those weapons had been on the Peninsula since 1958 and had initially offset the North's quantitative military superiority: the Korean People's Army outnumbered South Korea's armed forces at the time, and still do. Their removal from the Peninsula created the conditions for the 1992 inter-Korean declaration.

At the time of the declaration, North Korea did not have in place any infrastructure for uranium enrichment, but a reactor at Yongbyon had been in operation since 1986; this could be used for production of plutonium for use in nuclear weapons. "Denuclearization of the Korean Peninsula" came to mean something very particular: no nuclear weapons anywhere from the southern tip of South Korea all the way up to the Yalu and Tumen rivers that separate North Korea from China. Even as the two Koreas arrived at this agreement, the North carefully avoided acknowledging that the South had, in fact, already denuclearized with the loss of the U.S. nuclear weapons. As of 2020, North Korea still has yet to make any public acknowledgement of this reality. Just ten days after the declaration, on January 30, 1992,

North Korea acceded to a safeguards agreement with the International Atomic Energy Agency (IAEA), following through on one of its obligations as an NPT member state—but the confusing language of 'denuclearization' would persist for years to come.

1992–94: The First Inspection Crisis and the Agreed Framework

The demise of the 1992 comprehensive safeguards agreement between North Korea and the IAEA hinted at the verification debates that would obstruct diplomacy regarding North Korea's nuclear program for years. After joining the NPT in 1985, North Korea should have concluded such a safeguard agreement by mid-1987, but Washington and Seoul saw this as better late than never—that is, until the agreement began to mean something for Pyongyang. In February 1993—almost exactly one year on from the inter-Korean denuclearization declaration—the director-general of the IAEA invoked the "special inspection procedure" at two sites that it believed were involved in the storage of nuclear waste. The North Korean reaction was swift indignation.

In May 1992, one month after the safeguards agreement was ratified, North Korea had voluntarily declared its nuclear materials and sites, and the IAEA was working to verify the information. Hans Blix, a Swede, then the agency's head, became the first citizen of a Western country to visit the Yongbyon complex, where he met senior North Korean nuclear energy officials.[14] The facilities Blix viewed included the reactor as well as underground tunnels and facilities, which one *New York Times* report at the time cited as "the firmest evidence yet that North Korea may have tried to build a nuclear bomb, or perhaps is still trying."[15] Blix chose his words carefully in describing to the press what he had seen in North Korea, eager not to anger Pyongyang and make the IAEA's task in the country more challenging. He remarked that at least one building in the Yongbyon complex—what the North Koreans euphemistically called the "radio chemical laboratory"—met the IAEA's standards to be classified as a "reprocessing plant."

The North Koreans had undertaken some measures to deceive Blix—efforts that were only uncovered decades later.[16] The IAEA also found evidence at the time that North Korea had previously carried out undisclosed shut-downs of the reactor at Yongbyon after the start of its operations in 1986—which would have been necessary for Pyongyang to produce more plutonium than it had declared.[17] Concerns over the sincerity of North Korea's engagement with the NPT obligations began to grow under the IAEA's scrutiny. The United States, in a move that apparently left North Korea "flat-footed," provided the IAEA with access to satellite images showing two buildings that North Korea had not declared to the agency.[18] A 1997 IAEA account noted that, in hindsight, it "was clear that the DPRK authorities had attempted to disguise the function of the two facilities by planting trees and using other camouflage."[19] One policy expert has suggested that Pyongyang "did not fully appreciate the technical competence of IAEA personnel" and their ability to see through such deceptions.[20]

By September 1992, the Agency had serious questions about the completeness of North Korea's declaration. It was this suspicion that had led to the invocation of the agency's special inspection power in February 1993. Perhaps Pyongyang had expected the safeguards agreement to have no practical consequences, but it was now abundantly clear that this was not the case. As the IAEA pressed for inspections at sites of interest where North Korea was unwilling to grant access, Pyongyang took the dramatic step of announcing its decision to withdraw from the NPT altogether. The safeguards agreement had hardly been in force for eleven months. The North Korean justification cited Article X of the NPT, which carved out withdrawal rights if "extraordinary events, related to the subject matter of this Treaty, have jeopardized the supreme interests of its country." For North Korea, the IAEA's demands were precisely such a threat; this was the simplest way of averting it.

Even as North Korea made known its intention to leave the NPT in 1993, it would be another decade before it would actually make good on its threat. On June 11, the United States and North Korea signed their first-ever written denuclearization agreement in New York, which paused North Korea's withdrawal from the NPT for "as long as it consider[ed] necessary." The crisis, however, was just beginning. In April, the IAEA had found North Korea in violation of its safeguards agreement obligations. In May, U.S. Secretary of Defense Les Aspin had classified the North Korean decision to leave the NPT as a major concern of the new Clinton administration, describing the U.S. effort to forestall Pyongyang's withdrawal as a "full court press."[21] He expressed uncertainty about whether North Korea had manufactured a nuclear weapon, stating that he had "conflicting" reports from U.S. intelligence. For Clinton, North Korea was not a back-burner national security issue; it had become a priority and a crisis.

By late 1993, a CIA assessment concluded that, contrary to its declarations to the IAEA, North Korea had likely reprocessed enough spent fuel for 12 kilograms of weapons-grade pluto-nium—enough for "one, possibly two" nuclear bombs. This was not a unanimous view within the U.S. intelligence community,[22] yet on Boxing Day, 1993, a stark headline appeared in the *New York Times*, stating boldly that "INTELLIGENCE STUDY SAYS NORTH KOREA HAS NUCLEAR BOMB."[23] Clinton and top U.S. national security officials all agreed that North Korea had to be stopped, lest it harm U.S. national security and undo years of successful efforts to develop a global nonprolifera-tion regime. The Clinton administration was aware of what unchecked progress in Pyongyang could represent for India and Pakistan's ongoing efforts to acquire the bomb.

The June 1993 bilateral agreement had opened a door for diplomacy, and Washington was inclined to go through it. But the path forward in these early months of the Clinton administration was perilous. The two countries came close to a conflict, with de-escalation and diplomacy only becoming possible largely as a result of a trip by former U.S. President Jimmy Carter to North Korea. Carter met with Kim Il Sung, helping the two sides cool off, but Pyongyang and Washington remained at odds over how to proceed on the nuclear issue.[24] Amid North Korean threats to turn Seoul into a "sea of fire," and following the presentation to Clinton of U.S. war plans, the two countries somehow managed to arrive at an agreement, signed in Geneva on October 21, 1994. It is known as the Agreed Framework, to date the most successful effort to cap North Korea's development of a nuclear capability, and the longest verified freeze on North Korea's nuclear fuel production.

The 1993–94 forging of the Agreed Framework amid crisis is among the best covered episodes in the history of U.S.—North Korean relations, including by U.S. officials involved in the negotiations. This is no surprise, since the Agreed Framework is key to understanding the state of play today. Kim Il Sung, speaking to Carter, had emphasized the long history of mistrust between their two countries, but offered a way out. A basic exchange had to be made: the United States would furnish North Korea with reactors for civil nuclear energy production and sufficiently robust security guarantees, while North Korea would "freeze" nuclear activities of concern at Yongbyon and allow the IAEA back into the country. Carter's trip kicked off a difficult four months of detailed, technical negotiations, not helped by Kim Il Sung's death by heart attack and the uncertainty of North Korea's first ever leadership transition. Nevertheless, under Kim's son and long-trained successor, Kim Jong Il, the Agreed Framework was signed.

In addition to the supply of civil nuclear energy facilities, the second and shortest part of the agreement pertained to the "full normalization of political and economic relations" between the two countries, outlining provisions to open commercial linkages and, ultimately, upgrade to normal diplomatic relations. The third section set out an agenda for "denuclearization of the Korean Peninsula," with Washington providing "formal assurances" that it would not attack or use nuclear weapons against North Korea, and Pyongyang pledging to continue dialogue with the South. The final component pledged both sides to "work together to strengthen the international nuclear non-proliferation regime"—a core U.S. concern. With its signature in October 1994, this short document cemented North Korea's place within the NPT, and punctuated the crisis of the early 1990s with a moment of hope that North Korea's nuclear development could be halted.

In hindsight, the Agreed Framework is equally notable for what it did not deal with: the alternative path to the bomb (highly enriched uranium), and ballistic missiles. American officials were aware of the agreement's relatively narrow technical scope, but North Korea's capabilities at the time were apparently nonexistent in the first instance, and rudimentary in the second. From a 2020 point of view, the Agreed Framework draws a sharp contrast with the 150-plus page Joint Comprehensive Plan of Action on Iran's nuclear program, for instance—a considerably more technical document, with multilateral buy-in and endorsement by the UN Security Council. But the Agreed Framework was the first serious bilateral attempt to codify an approach toward dealing with the North Korea issue, so naturally it was not lengthy or detailed; and, though critics swipe at its ultimate failure to prevent the emergence of a nuclear North Korea, it did succeed in delaying the accumulation of weapons-grade nuclear material for some seven years. Its signature was a remarkable turn of fortune from what had appeared to be a lurch toward conflict in the first half of 1994.

1995–2002: The Life and Death of the Agreed Framework

The Agreed Framework would survive until late 2002. In its lifetime it encountered several difficulties, including partisan obstruction to the Clinton administration's implementation of the agreement, the North's continuing proliferation activity, and, in 1998, a major North Korean satellite launch. In 1995 a consortium was set up to oversee development of the light water reactors that North Korea had been promised under the agreement, following IAEA ratifications. But, through 1996–98, the United States and North Korea largely found themselves in conversations over the missile proliferation issue: Washington had serious concerns about Kim Jong Il's plans to raise revenue for his regime by selling abroad both North Korean knowhow and fully assembled ballistic missiles. The Clinton administration imposed multiple rounds of unilateral sanctions on North Korea for this proliferation activity—most notably to Iran and Pakistan. Amid sustained American pressure, North Korean negotiators told their U.S. counterparts that the missile exports could only be ended if there were direct financial compensation to the regime for foregone revenue.

On August 31, 1998, tensions worsened as North Korea launched the Taepodong-1, a prototype satellite launch vehicle, overflying Japan. U.S. intelligence found that Pyongyang's claims of success were exaggerated, but North Korea's demonstration of a long-range rocket was cause for concern, particularly given the recent findings of an independent U.S. congressional commission led by former Secretary of Defense Donald Rumsfeld: a little more than two weeks before the launch, the commission had concluded that North Korea might one day bring the United

States under a ballistic missile threat. The Taepodong-1 launch invigorated the U.S.—Japanese alliance to begin serious consultations on missile defense cooperation.

Meanwhile, in Washington, the satellite launch sparked something of a "crisis stage", as Clinton's then secretary of defense William J. Perry recounted in his memoirs. Under congressional pressure that now reached a fever pitch, the White House convened a North Korean Policy Review. Republicans had vocally opposed the entire premise of the Agreed Framework itself; many now sensed an opportunity to allow its collapse. One thing led to another and Perry, determined to both salvage the Agreed Framework and prevent a lurch toward confrontation, found himself in Pyongyang in 1999.[25] "The North Koreans obviously valued their missiles, and saw them as providing deterrence, prestige, and cash from foreign sales," Perry has observed. "But they understood that giving up long-range missiles as well as nuclear weapons was the path to normalization of relations."

In September 1999, U.S. and North Korean officials met in Berlin for talks and arrived at a historic compromise. In a fillip to the Agreed Framework, negotiators arrived at a simple but compelling agreement for both sides. North Korea committed to a moratorium on long-range missile development, which would include a test freeze, for the duration of talks with the United States. In exchange, the United States would lift most economic sanctions against Pyongyang.[26] After U.S. inspections of a suspected clandestine nuclear facility at Kumchang-ri, Clinton authorized the lifting of sanctions in June 2000—and North Korea would not test another ballistic missile for six years. This settlement was known as the Berlin Agreement.

This was Clinton's final year in office, and the second half continued to see prominent, high-level U.S.–North Korean interactions. Vice Marshall Jo Myong Rok, Kim Jong Il's *de facto* number two, visited Washington as the leader's special envoy in October 2000, paving the path for a reciprocal visit to North

Korea by U.S. Secretary of State Madeleine Albright. Albright's talks with Kim Jong Il were productive and wide-ranging, and resulted in discussion of a possible trip to Pyongyang by Clinton himself. The trip never materialized—on December 28, 2000, with less than a month before George W. Bush's inauguration, Clinton said that there was simply "insufficient time to complete the work at hand." This was perhaps an augur of things to come. Before he departed office, Clinton imposed one final round of sanctions on a North Korean company, for further proliferation to Iran.

* * *

North Korea's first nuclear test had its harbingers. The political and diplomatic context in Northeast Asia declined precipitously following the U.S.–North Korea crisis in October 2002, when the Bush administration confronted the North Koreans about what it claimed was the covert pursuit of a uranium path to the bomb in contravention of the spirit of the Agreed Framework. During the fateful October 2002 visit of then-U.S. Assistant Secretary of State James Kelly to confront Pyongyang about the uranium enrichment issue, the American diplomat was apparently told by his senior North Korean counterparts that Pyongyang "was entitled to possess" nuclear weapons to defend its sovereignty from the "ever-growing nuclear threat of the U.S."[27] In early 2003, after the suspension of U.S. heavy fuel oil deliveries to North Korea under the Agreed Framework, Pyongyang declared the end of that agreement. North Korea now committed to reviving the nuclear operations at Yongbyon that had been suspended since 1994.

2003–05: The Rise and Fall of the Six-Party Talks

On January 10, 2003, North Korea became the first country to have both signed and quit the NPT—the cornerstone of the international nuclear nonproliferation regime. It described its withdrawal as "automatic and immediate" and underscored that it was no longer bound by IAEA safeguards. All this—the departure from the NPT, the signaled intention to resume plutonium production at Yongbyon, and the suspected covert uranium enrichment—came against an important international backdrop. The Bush administration was laying the groundwork for the invasion of Saddam Hussein's Iraq on the pretext of Hussein's pursuit of weapons of mass destruction.

The scenes on March 19 and 20, as American conventional weapons rained down on Baghdad, were no doubt taken to heart in North Korea as a reminder of just what the United States was capable of. In April, the Associated Press reported that, as the invasion began on March 19, U.S. stealth fighters had been dispatched to Dora Farms outside Baghdad, based on the belief that Saddam and his sons were present there—in other words, that the war could be swiftly concluded with a so-called "decapitation" strike on Iraqi leadership.[28] The strike was carried out, but the intelligence was bad—Saddam had not visited Dora Farms since the mid-1990s. Nevertheless, Kim Jong Il had seen all he would need to. During the first phases of the invasion of Iraq, the North Korean leader was absent from public view—"his longest disappearance since 1994."[29] A foreign observer in the country during these months described North Korea's posture as "a virtual war footing."[30] Bush himself had done little to assuage Kim's paranoia, having already given a 2002 State of the Union address publicly including North Korea in the "axis of evil"—alongside its proliferation customer Iran, and the now invaded Iraq.

Circumstantially, the months between late 2002 and early 2003 appear to have been critical in Kim Jong Il's decision to depart the Agreed Framework and double down on a physical nuclear deterrent—what would become known as North Korea's "treasured sword"—as the sole means of averting the fate that would eventually befall Saddam Hussein. On April 7, 2003, days after the start of major U.S. combat operations in Iraq, a spokesman for the North Korean Ministry of Foreign Affairs released a landmark statement through the Korean Central News Agency (KCNA), outlining the country's intentions:

> The UN [Security Council]'s discussion of the Iraq issue was misused by the U.S. as an excuse for war. The U.S. intends to force the DPRK to disarm itself. The Iraqi war shows that to allow disarming through inspection does not help avert a war but rather sparks it.
>
> This suggests that even the signing of a non-aggression treaty with the U.S. would not help avert a war. Only the physical deterrent force, tremendous military deterrent force powerful enough to beat back an attack supported by any ultra-modern weapons, can avert a war and protect the security of the country and the nation.

That same month, *The Washington Post* reported that, during negotiations held in Beijing, "The top North Korean official at the talks, Li Gun, pulled aside the highest-ranking American present, Assistant Secretary of State James A. Kelly, and told him that North Korea has nuclear weapons," that North Korea could not "dismantle them" and the choice would be in Washington's hands "whether we do a physical demonstration or transfer them."[31]

Although Li's claims about nuclear fuel production went beyond U.S. intelligence assessments at the time, there had indeed been signs of renewed activity at the Yongbyon facilities, as U.S. satellites concluded from truck activity near the site in early 2003. This was backed months later by South Korean intelligence on suspected activity at the 'radiochemical lab.'[32] With the end of the Agreed Framework, U.S.—North Korean relations were quickly spiraling back into crisis. Pyongyang continued to make statements underscoring that it could not be dissuaded from its commitment to breaking out as a nuclear

Korea. The first round had started as far back as August 2003, in Beijing, but the first three rounds of talks (concluding in June 2004) were overshadowed by signs of North Korea's persistent pursuit of the "physical" demonstration that had obsessed Kim Jong Il since the collapse of the Agreed Framework.

In early 2004, a U.S. delegation visited the Yongbyon reactor complex. One of the delegation's nongovernmental technical experts, Siegfried Hecker, testified to the Senate Foreign Relations Committee with a series of worrying conclusions: the reactor at Yongbyon had been restarted, and the 8,000 fuel rods that had been frozen under the Agreed Framework had now been moved. These rods would be needed for plutonium production. Hecker offered his interpretation of North Korean motivations:

> They have publicly stated that they have reprocessed the fuel rods to extract plutonium and strengthen their "deterrent." It appears they were concerned that the United States (and perhaps others) did not believe them. So, they may have invited us to provide independent confirmation of their claims.[35]

There was scant progress over the two rounds of talks in 2004, with Washington continuing to seek acknowledgement from North Korea that it had a covert uranium enrichment program. Tensions remained high and all parties were skittish about the prospect of escalation. In September 2004—coinciding with North Korea's founding anniversary day of September 9—South Korea's Yonhap news agency reported what appeared to be a giant cloud near North Korea's border with China, stemming from an explosion in Ryanggang province. Reporting in subsequent days described the cloud specifically as a "mushroom cloud," stoking speculation that the worst had happened: that North Korea had conducted the world's first nuclear test inside the earth's atmosphere since October 1980.[36]

The explosion was entirely conventional, even if its origins remained mysterious. U.S. and South Korean officials immediately pushed back on speculation that the incident was a nuclear test, and the North Korean foreign minister told a British counterpart that it was "part of a planned demolition of a mountain for the construction of a hydroelectric plant."[37] Days later, South Korea's then deputy unification minister, Rhee Bong-jo, added to the confusion by suggesting that "the cloud ... was a natural phenomenon."[38] In any case, both the explosion and the global reaction to it highlighted the level of international concern that North Korea might test a nuclear bomb. By late September 2004, Bush administration officials were openly addressing the prospect of North Korea testing a nuclear weapon in an attempt to influence the upcoming U.S. presidential election. On cable TV, National Security Advisor Condoleeza Rice warned, "The North Koreans would only succeed in isolating themselves further if they're somehow trying to gain negotiating leverage or their own October surprise."[39]

At this time, experts working on North Korea were skeptical that Pyongyang would conduct a test. However, following the start of Bush's second term, matters quickly escalated. On February 10, 2005, the North Korean Ministry of Foreign Affairs announced that the country had "produced nuclear weapons." This was an explicit claim about the physical deterrent—that Pyongyang had produced and, ostensibly, weaponized a nuclear device, for self-defense to cope with the Bush administration's "undisguised policy to isolate and stifle [North Korea]."[40] Pyongyang announced its suspended participation in the Six-Party Talks, but promised to return when the "conditions and atmosphere" would suit it. The Ministry of Foreign Affairs followed up on this provocative and ominous declaration just weeks later, with a March 2 memorandum to state media announcing that Pyongyang no longer considered itself bound by the 1999 Berlin Agreement's moratorium on long-range missile testing, because this had been agreed only for as long as talks were underway, and "the DPRK—U.S. dialogue was totally suspended when the Bush administration took office in 2001."

Around this time, North Korea's decision to conduct a nuclear test had likely been made. In April 2005, North Korea ceased operations at its Yongbyon reactor and removed spent fuel for reprocessing. This would have produced sufficient plutonium for one, if not two, weapons—in addition to whatever plutonium North Korea already had in its possession from the reprocessing campaign after the 2002 crisis. In May, the Ministry of Foreign Affairs confirmed these plans. Amid this, U.S. Assistant Secretary of State Christopher R. Hill traveled to Seoul, Tokyo, and Beijing to discuss apparent U.S. concerns that a North Korean nuclear test might now be likely.[41] Even if there was no strong, high-confidence consensus among U.S. intelligence about this, political concerns were acute enough for Hill to be dispatched with urgency. He met in early July with North Korean Vice Foreign Minister Kim Kye Gwan, who agreed that North Korea would return to the Six-Party Talks on the basis of U.S. assurances to recognize Pyongyang's sovereignty, and further "not to invade it."[42] Later that same month, Kim Jong Il met Chinese President Hu Jintao, and was reported by Chinese state media to have remarked that "denuclearization [was] a dying wish of North Korean founder Kim Il-sung."[43]

This was not a poignant recollection of his dying father's wish so much as a restatement that denuclearization would be a tango for two, requiring nuclear concessions from Washington as well as Pyongyang. But a fourth round of the Six-Party Talks did convene on the basis of this progress, and had some success. On September 19, 2005, the six participants concluded what remains to this day the most recent, wide-ranging expression of a North Korean commitment on denuclearization and disarmament. Pyongyang pledged to abandon "all nuclear weapons and existing nuclear programs," never to "receive or deploy nuclear weapons," and to soon return to the NPT and the IAEA safeguard regime; the United States "affirmed that it has no weapons on the Korean Peninsula and has no intention to attack or invade the D.P.R.K. with nuclear or conventional weapons."

There was language about mutual respect of sovereignty, observation of the UN charter and principles, and the aspiration for a peace treaty to formally end the Korean War. North Korea's right to "peaceful uses of nuclear energy" was confirmed, with assistance and provision from the five other countries. All six parties "undertook to promote economic cooperation" and "security cooperation" in Northeast Asia, and Japan and North Korea agreed to take steps towards normalizing relations. Finally, a fifth round of Six-Party Talks was set for early November.

2006–09: The Road to Nuclear Testing

Before long, however, matters soured once again. The fifth round was scuppered by a U.S.—North Korean standoff dating back to September over a major U.S. Treasury action: a then little-known Macau financial institution, Banco Delta Asia, had been dubbed a "primary money laundering concern" pursuant to Section 311 of the PATRIOT Act. It just so happened that BDA was host to around $25 million of the Kim regime's funds. In October, Pyongyang's anger was compounded by a follow-up Treasury action, which designated eight North Korea-based entities, including the Korea Mining Development Corporation, over proliferation concerns.[44] North Korea's apoplexy about these financial hostilities colored its approach to diplomacy throughout the fall of 2005.

In December, North Korea made its frustration clear by announcing that it would build more reactors like the one already in operation at Yongbyon, "because the U.S. has completely given up on the construction of the [light water reactors for energy generation]" that had been promised under the Agreed Framework.[45] Pyongyang would announce the formal termination of the two light-water reactor projects in June 2006.[46] Meanwhile, Pyongyang and Washington continued to bicker over BDA, with Pyongyang demanding the release of the funds, and the slide away from cordial diplomacy continued.

On July 4, 2006, North Korea launched six ballistic missiles and a Taepodong-2 satellite launch vehicle, shattering the 1999 Berlin Agreement's moratorium on long-range missile launches. UN Security Council resolution 1695 condemned the testing bonanza, called on Pyongyang to restore its observation of the moratorium, and required all UN member states to avoid commerce that could enable North Korea to acquire "items, materials, goods and technology" related to ballistic missile development.[47] By September, both Japan and Australia were taking action against a range of entities under the resolution, enraging the North Koreans. One month later, in October 2006, North Korea conducted its first nuclear test, crossing an important rubicon.

2007–8 marked a crucial period, one that could have inaugurated a wind-down of the nuclear facilities at Yongbyon. This was the last chance for the Six-Party Talks. The September 2005 joint statement was the gold standard and, despite Kim's nuclear bomb test in 2006, the impulse within the outgoing Bush administration was to push ahead. The Six-Party Talks continued, seeking to implement the joint statement. The United States worked to resolve the BDA impasse, seeing this gesture as a worthwhile measure to move forward with North Korea. For the first time since the 1990s, the IAEA found itself robustly involved in verification and so-called disablement activities in North Korea. By July 2007, the IAEA had verified that eleven nuclear fuel-cycle facilities of concern, including the existing operational reactor at Yongbyon, had been shut down. In October that year, South Korea's progressive president, Roh

Moo-hyun, made time during his last few months in office to meet Kim Jong Il for a second inter-Korean summit meeting—the first since 2000. The mood on the Peninsula briefly shifted toward optimism.

The signs looked better for U.S.—North Korea relations, too, as progress continued through the first half of 2008. In May, the North Koreans turned over nearly 19,000 pages constituting what they called a full disclosure of plutonium activities and holdings within their borders.[48] In June, this was followed by a grand gesture: with international media watching, Kim Jong Il oversaw the demolition of the prominent 60-foot cooling tower at Yongbyon. Sung Kim, a U.S. State Department official, described the measure as a "very significant disablement step."[49] The public relations value was undeniable insofar as the *idea* of disarmament was concerned, but independent experts were more circumspect, pointing out the reversibility of the gesture.

By late 2008, realities had set in: the North Koreans were allergic to discussions of a verification protocol with their negotiating partners. Pyongyang's position had been further soured by the Bush administration's willingness to hang North Korea's exclusion from the "state-sponsor of terrorism" list on its acceptance of such a protocol.[50] To make matters worse, the progressive Roh had stepped aside in Seoul—South Korean presidential terms being nonrenewable—and had been succeeded in February by a hard-nosed conservative, Lee Myung-bak. By the end of the year, the Six-Party Talks were "dead," according to the North Koreans.

As Barack Obama settled into the White House in spring 2009, diplomatic relations were in free fall. The IAEA was ejected from North Korea on April 16 after removing safeguarding equipment from the facilities that had been disabled at Yongbyon. One month later, to hammer the nail in the coffin of the Six-Party Talks, the North Koreans conducted their second nuclear test, which was considerably more powerful than the first. In June, in light of Kim Jong Il's stroke the previous year and his increasingly frail health, Kim Jong Un was announced as his father's successor and heir. At the time of writing—more than ten years on from these events—Kim Jong Un rules in North Korea, and the IAEA has yet to return to the country. The Six-Party Talks have become a distant memory.

2010–12: Kim Jong Il's Demise and the Great Leap to Nowhere

The Obama administration's first year in office ended with a stark reminder of the stakes on the Korean Peninsula. In November 2009, the navies of the two Koreas became engaged in a major skirmish along the Northern Limit Line, the maritime extension of the de facto border along the 38th parallel.[51] The South Koreans prevailed, sinking a North Korean gunboat, killing an unknown number of North Korean sailors on board. The North Koreans acknowledged the incident, blaming the South Koreans for instigating the conflict. The South Koreans, meanwhile, said they had fired warning shots to warn the North Korean vessel, which had transgressed across the NLL. The incident would presage a tumultuous year for the Korean Peninsula.

As Kim Jong Il and the North Korean party elite prepared the succession for Kim Jong Un, the Korean Peninsula came to the brink of all-out war. In January 2010, with tensions still high, the governing South Korean conservatives got into a verbal spat with the North, with the defense minister warning that Seoul would strike Pyongyang's nuclear missile operating bases with precision weaponry if the North's threats escalated. The North Koreans pushed back in a statement attributed to a spokesperson for the General Staff of the Korean People's Army, announcing that they perceived this as a declaration of war.[52] Between February and December 2010, North Korea staged two major provocations—some of its most serious in the post-Korean War period. In March, a North Korean midget submarine fired a torpedo at the South Korean ROKS *Cheonan*, killing 46 sailors. Pyongyang did not claim responsibility, but a South Korean investigation attributed the attack to the North. In November, Korean People's Army artillery units fired on the island of Yeonpyeong, where South Korean marines were stationed. That attack killed four South Korean civilians and was nearly interpreted as the start of a war.

This period of brazen escalation put the U.S. alliance with South Korea to the test, and the Obama administration found itself largely hewing to South Korean President Lee's preferences. The United States unveiled a new set of punitive sanctions against North Korea, and the two allies stepped up the intensity of their military exercises, drawing nuclear threats from Pyongyang, despite its still rudimentary nuclear capabilities at the time. By the end of 2010, the South Korean government was faced with an indignant public and a hawkish commentariat calling for everything from a limited attack on North Korea to the development of a South Korean nuclear deterrent. Seoul began its own form of verbal and physical brinksmanship with the North.[53] This was a deeply uncertain period on the Korean Peninsula and for the U.S.—South Korea alliance, which had to navigate what appeared at the time to be a lurch toward greater risk-acceptance from the North. Making matters worse, days before the strikes on Yeonpyeong Island, the North Koreans had invited a visiting team of U.S. experts to tour Yongbyon, revealing the existence of new facilities for nuclear fuel production. At the time, U.S. intelligence also knew of the existence of another, covert site called Kangson, which had not been disclosed by the North Koreans. By 2011, U.S.—North Korea diplomacy was largely moribund—as was an increasingly infirm Kim Jong Il. With the exception of another visit to Pyongyang by former

U.S. President Jimmy Carter that April, little materialized bilaterally. On December 17, 2011, Kim Jong Il died. Twelve days later, Kim Jong Un was anointed leader. North Korea's new era had begun, and the prospects for denuclearization were bleak.

* * *

Beginning in late 2010 and into early 2011, North Korea was experiencing a food crisis. In March 2011, the World Food Program, the UN's nutritional assistance and food security agency, advised that as many as 6.1 million North Koreans would face nutritional stress and that 434,000 metric tons of food would be necessary.[54] Pyongyang began to get proactive on the issue, seeking out food aid through appeals to humanitarian organizations and possible donor countries. In the United States, this task had fallen to the country's New York-based permanent mission to the United Nations, the *de facto* North Korean liaison office for diplomatic talks with the United States.

American food aid to North Korea would not have been novel; the Bush administration had initiated such a delivery in 2008, using nongovernmental organizations. A needs assessment was carried out to determine the extent of nutritional stress in North Korea, with the State Department confirming in February 2011 that, if need was ascertained and Washington could be confident aid would reach civilians and not be diverted by the regime, then assistance might move forward. Later that year, a U.S. government team visited North Korea and spent "seven days or so" touring the country, according to one official. "[The team] did not find a famine, but they found evidence of very deep chronic malnutrition, malnutrition that has been almost countrywide." The U.S.—North Korean engagement on food aid quickly broadened into conversations around security issues, even though the Obama administration sought to make clear that humanitarian assistance was not being positioned as a bargaining chip for security or nuclear concessions from North Korea.

For a while, therefore, it looked as though it might be possible to reach a new, effective settlement, using the Six-Party Talks as the building blocks. By the summer of 2011, Kim Kye Gwan, a senior North Korean Foreign Ministry official with considerable experience dealing with the United States, found himself in New York. The U.S. sought North Korea's re-endorsement of the September 2005 joint statement and acquiescence to conditional "pre-steps" toward a new deal, in the form of a missile-testing and nuclear fuel production moratorium. The two delegations held a second meeting in Geneva in October 2011 and, finally, a third in December, in Beijing.

Both sides left the Beijing meeting with the basic contours of a deal firmly in place, and the U.S. view was that Pyongyang must have well understood the "pre-step" requirement from the get go, given that it had been widely discussed with counterparts in Seoul and Beijing. But, unfortunately, history has a tendency to repeat itself when it comes to U.S.—North Korean negotiations. Just as the Agreed Framework had been infused with an early sense of unease following Kim Il Sung's death, so too were these talks, as a result of Kim Jong Il's sudden death on December 17, 2011. The transition to Kim Jong Un began just as the Obama administration was, for the first time, starting to see the possible contours of its own deal with North Korea. The succession did not result in an imminent crisis and, finally, on February 29, 2012, both countries released "readouts" on the outcome of their talks, known as the Leap Day Deal. However, it quickly became apparent that this was neither a conventional 'deal' nor a real breakthrough.

The limited optimism of Obama's so-called Leap Day Deal was indicated in both sides' reluctance to refer to the 2011 encounters as negotiations, instead preferring the more cautious designation of "high-level talks." Yet the U.S. State Department press release claimed that North Korea had agreed to allow IAEA inspectors back to "verify and monitor" a new moratorium on uranium enrichment, and to pick up where they had left off when they were evicted from North Korea in 2009: verifying the "disablement of the [Yongbyon] reactor and associated facilities." That would have been a major accomplishment. In exchange, "nutritional assistance teams" from both sides would meet to work out the monitored delivery of "240,000 metric tons of nutritional assistance." At its core, the Leap Day Deal was a food-for-freeze arrangement.

However, things unravel at another point in the State Department readout: the announcement of "a moratorium on long-range missile launches, nuclear tests and nuclear activities at Yongbyon."[55] The U.S. side seemed to have left the talks with the impression that "long-range missile launches" was understood to include space launches, given that the underlying technologies of concern were similar. According to the Americans, this had been given the nod in private, but not said publicly. This misunderstanding, or at least the failure to put a common understanding to paper, would be the downfall of the entire deal. What may have been agreed in the room during talks did not necessarily translate to what was publicly committed to in the releases. The State Department's readout was not the final say on the food-for-freeze arrangement, and certainly did not come bearing the signature of any North Korean. Each side had left the final round of talks in Beijing and issued its own text, without submitting it to the other side for review.

When the North Korean readout emerged, this quickly became apparent. The Korean Central News Agency described it as a somewhat unofficial-sounding "answer to questions raised by KCNA concerning the result of the latest DPRK—U.S. high-level talks."[56] The issuing authority for the "answer" was a nameless "spokesman of the Ministry of Foreign Affairs." Above all, the content of the readout revealed the interpretation gap between the two countries, with North Korea omitting the plutonium program from its moratorium—the very activities the IAEA had been trying to monitor in 2007–09. Astute journalists and analysts were quick to raise questions about this in the aftermath of the 2012 'deal.' Its failure was further solidified three days before Kim Il Sung's centennial birthday, when the North Koreans went ahead with testing a satellite launch vehicle that they had announced some weeks earlier, ignoring all warnings from the United States.

Perhaps Kim Jong Un, who had only been in power for a few months, felt he could not be seen to cave in to demands from the Americans, even if the launch might have been a plan set in place by his father. In the end, the Leap Day Deal marked the last serious and substantive round of U.S.—North Korea interaction during the Obama years, yielding to a near-four-year period of maintaining and gradually increasing sanctions pressure on North Korea, in the hopes that the young new *suryong* would see the benefits of coming back to the table to negotiate in good faith. That was a bad bet.

2012–17: "Strategic Patience"

With the exception of a short-lived, aborted attempt at engagement with North Korea in late 2015, during Obama's second term Washington largely sought to contain Pyongyang. Observers pejoratively dubbed this approach "strategic patience." While applying sanctions pressure and diplomatic signaling, the Obama administration waited for an indication that Pyongyang was ready for further talks. With North Korea's third (2013), fourth (2016), and fifth (2016) nuclear tests, its February 2016 satellite launch, scores of ballistic missile tests, and significant cyber intrusions, the United States had its hands full. As testing picked up in tempo under Kim Jong Un, Washington ramped up its use of sanctions. For the first time, Kim Jong Un himself came under U.S. unilateral sanctions, on the basis not only of his continued pursuit of weapons of mass destruction, but also of his place atop one of the world's cruelest regimes. The U.S. government cited North Korea's use of torture and forced labor to justify the sanctions against Kim, which, though largely symbolic, outraged Pyongyang, which described such sanctions as tantamount to declarations of war.

North Korea also bristled at the U.S.—South Korean joint military exercises, which maintained a high intensity as the Obama administration sought to reassure two successive conservative governments in South Korea. In Obama's final years in office, significant North Korean testing events were often followed by the dispatch of a U.S. strategic bomber from Guam as a display of protection for South Korea and Japan. Once again, the North Koreans saw these gestures as a form of nuclear coercion. From Kim Jong Un's vantage point in Pyongyang, the United States was scoffing in the face of his nuclear advancements, showing off the continued primacy of its forces.

Meanwhile, North Korea's tactics were shifting, as would become more clear after the presidential inauguration of property magnate Donald J. Trump in 2017. In 2014, Pyongyang-backed hackers calling themselves the 'Guardians of Peace' infiltrated the networks of Sony Pictures Entertainment, apparently provoked by the studio's release of a satirical comedy depicting a mission to kill Kim Jong Un. The episode marked what was then one of the most serious cybersecurity breaches ever experienced by a private U.S. firm; North Korea was evasive in confirming responsibility, but issued a statement hinting that it may indeed have been behind the cyber-attack.[57] The Obama administration responded by imposing yet more sanctions.[58]

The Obama administration's North Korea policy in the second half of 2015 and throughout 2016 was influenced by two important realities. First, in contrast with the failure of the 'Leap Day' overture, Obama had seen far greater success in non-proliferation with Iran; in his second term he had doubled and tripled down on securing a deal to verifiably cap Iran's civil nuclear program, ensuring that it would not be able to resume the work toward nuclear weapons that it had abandoned in the early 2000s. That effort had culminated in the July 2015 signing of the Joint Comprehensive Plan of Action—an impressive technical pact, but one with great political costs for Obama. The White House had expended considerable domestic political capital defending its Iran overtures against the sharp criticisms of the opposition Republicans. In this environment, the appetite for any bold risk taking—or a late-term policy review—toward North Korea was low.

The second reality informing Obama's late North Korea policy regarded who would succeed him in the Oval Office. The administration—like much of the U.S. political media establishment—was working on the assumption that Hillary Rodham Clinton, Obama's former secretary of state, would be elected. It would be Clinton inheriting a North Korea more dangerous than ever, and it would be Clinton needing and willing to expend the political capital on whatever had to be done. Many officials who staffed the Obama executive branch and worked on Northeast Asian security and nonproliferation had expected a seamless continuation of their work in a Clinton White House. They "would be handing ... foreign policy problems, with North Korea foremost among them, to a Clinton team staffed with likeminded, familiar faces."[59] Where was the rush for Obama to pack in a last-minute breakthrough with Kim Jong Un when Clinton would soon be coming in to continue his work?

In any event, as we know, the election of Donald Trump in November 2016 shocked the world. During the transition, Obama attempted to impress on the newly elected U.S. president—a real estate mogul and reality television star with no aptitude for foreign affairs—that North Korea would be the most serious national security challenge he would inherit.[60] Obama implored his successor to treat Pyongyang as the priority it should be. Within a year, Trump would learn firsthand that Obama had not been exaggerating, as Kim Jong Un pressed ahead with and claimed to have completed his nuclear deterrent. This has been the life's work of the North Korean state since Kim Il Sung's day, at the very heart of Kim Jong Un's global and domestic strategy—as we will see in the next chapter.

3

DETERRENCE

They serve the purpose of deterring and repelling the aggression and attack of the enemy against the DPRK and dealing deadly retaliatory blows at the strongholds of aggression until the world is denuclearized.

Article 2 of North Korea's 2013 Law on Consolidating the Position
of Nuclear Weapons State

Given North Korea's origins, and the first two Kims' history of fraught encounters with South Korea and the United States, it is hardly surprising that the regime's top priority has remained unchanged in the Kim Jong Un era: survival. In this chapter, it's time to look more closely at Kim's chosen means for survival—a nuclear deterrent, long pursued by his father and grandfather—and his strategy for using it.

As long as humans have sought to prevent outcomes adverse to their interests, they have practiced deterrence of some form—in a range of fields, from law enforcement and criminal justice to developmental psychology and parenting. At its core deterrence is this idea: for me to deter you from a specific action, I must credibly communicate that I am capable of imposing a cost greater than the action's perceived benefit.

71

Take threatening to send children to their rooms without dinner for poor behavior as an example. The child knows the parent's threat would represent a significant cost, because, presumably, they enjoy food; the child also knows the parent's threat is credible, because the parent can cook whereas the child cannot. By the same token, states can deter crime by communicating the likelihood that the long arm of the law will apprehend, prosecute and punish criminals.

While the above definition of deterrence might appear neat and formalized, its implementation is much more an art than a science, based as it is on perceptions and calculations by fallible human beings. Deterrence can fail—and fails regularly. In societies with worse-functioning institutions and features like corrupt police forces, the credibility of the state's threat is reduced, generally leading to more observed crime. Children clearly are not always perfectly behaved, despite the possibilities of punishment. Fortunately, the consequences of the failure of deterrence by a police force or a strict parent are manageable. With weapons and warfare, especially nuclear weapons, the consequences are more severe—even existential.

The history of conventional warfare is littered with examples of deterrence failures. For instance, the causes and courses of the First World War can realistically be characterized this way. In the lead-up to the war, the Triple Entente comprising the United Kingdom, France, and Russia was not intended as an offensive military alliance; on the contrary, it was designed to serve as a countervailing and deterrent coalition against Germany—an enterprise that failed. Tsarist Russian support for Serbia was also meant to deter greater powers from aggressing the small Balkan kingdom. Following the assassination of Archduke Franz Ferdinand of Austria-Hungary on June 28, 1914, the Austro-Hungarians perceived Serbian capabilities to be low, and Russia's willingness to enter a war on Serbia's behalf improbable. Similarly, had Germany better understood Franco—British capabilities—rather than underestimating the effectiveness of the British Expeditionary Force—it might not have embarked upon the disastrous Schlieffen Plan that precipitated the country's eventual defeat in the First World War.

In other words, deterrence failure has to do with all-too-human factors—especially the tendency of different agents to perceive differently the same material facts about a shared reality. Two sides may perceive the benefits to outweigh the costs, or one side may not find the other a credible threat. Here perceptions begin to mingle with emotions and even inter-personal communication between world leaders. There are many plausible explanations for why we have peace, and many have nothing to do with the mechanics of practicing deterrence. That leaves the other side of the ledger: we know—and know with certainty—when deterrence has failed. We do not necessarily know whether—or why—deterrence is working if at all.

Nuclear Deterrence: A Revolution or a Chimera?

Where conventional military balances in previous conflicts like the First World War were prone to misperception and misreading based on faulty intelligence, with the arrival of nuclear weapons, there is now a credible threat of unacceptably massive, virtually infinite and existential costs to war. The U.S. military's largest conventional chemical explosive today weighs 8,500 kilograms and can yield an explosive force equivalent to 11 tons of TNT; the smallest U.S. nuclear weapon weighs just 320 kilograms and can produce an equivalent of 300 tons of TNT. These weapons were game-changers in the Cold War, and they are just as revolutionary for North Korea in the twenty-first century.

Until the Soviet Union's first nuclear test in August 1949, the United States enjoyed a nuclear monopoly, and so nuclear deterrence remained in its infancy, with U.S. Air Force war-planners effectively seeing these bombs as simply a more powerful conventional weapon. But then U.S. President Harry S. Truman, the only national leader ever to have ordered use of nuclear weapons, quickly recognized their value. At the height of the Berlin crisis in the late 1940s, Truman brandished American nuclear power by dispatching B-29 bombers to Europe, reminding the Soviets of the potential costs of escalation. Under Eisenhower, the United States adopted a "massive retaliation" nuclear posture, identifying a low threshold of enemy action for an American nuclear response. This posturing—for instance during the First Taiwan Strait Crisis in the mid-1950s—was one of the principal factors prompting Mao Zedong to move ahead with China's nuclear weapons program.

By the 1960s, the two global superpowers' nuclear capabilities and stockpiles had grown, and we saw history's most famous nuclear "close call": the Cuban Missile Crisis of October 1962. To help communist Cuba deter future U.S.-backed invasion attempts, the Soviet premier Nikita Khrushchev agreed to base nuclear-capable missiles in Fidel Castro's Cuba. Kennedy publicly warned that detonation of these missiles anywhere in the western hemisphere would be treated as an attack "requiring a full retaliatory response on the Soviet Union."[1] That bold declaration of brinksmanship ramped up the crisis, and was a result of simple human psychology as much as anything else: at the Vienna Summit a year prior, Kennedy had felt utterly humiliated by Khrushchev, telling the *New York Times* that the encounter was the "worst thing in my life" and that Khrushchev "savaged" him.[2] Khrushchev in turn made a serious miscalculation, deciding to push back on Kennedy's threat and taking the world to the edge of nuclear crisis.

The crisis ultimately ended with a mutual deal to pull back nuclear weapons: the Soviet missiles from Cuba, American missiles from Turkey. It was in the aftermath that Stanley Kubrick released his black comedy *Dr. Strangelove*, which poked fun at the absurd ideas underlying nuclear deterrence: from Mutually Assured Destruction (MAD), to nuclear fail-safes, and, fundamentally, the so-called "balance of terror" that drove a nuclear arms race while also ostensibly preventing a nuclear war.[3] The close call with the apocalypse in 1962 allowed a more nuanced understanding of the rules of the game in both Moscow and Washington, with discussions of "strategic stability" and arms control ultimately resulting in a reduction of nuclear deployments. These attempts to manage the costs of unbridled nuclear competition led to significant arms control measures, and the Intermediate-Range Nuclear Forces Treaty in 1987, which resulted in the destruction of an entire class of US—USSR weaponry and prohibition of their use anywhere on earth. The Cold War ended without a catastrophic nuclear war, but no one can say for certain that this was because nuclear deterrence worked as it should have.

Kim Jong Un's pursuit of nuclear weapons is also driven by the pursuit of stable deterrence with the United States; establishing this would force the United States to deal with North Korea as a nuclear power. North Korea's nuclear breakout, and its status as the only state to have left the NPT to build nuclear weapons, may represent one of the nonproliferation regime's greatest failures, but the treaty otherwise remains successful. Outside of the five UN Security Council permanent members—the United States, Russia, the United Kingdom, France, and China, only three other states today have nuclear weapons—India, Pakistan, and Israel—and they never signed the treaty to begin with. Even so, the end of the Cold War marked the start of what is popularly known as the "second nuclear age,"[4] one of nuclear multipolarity.

Starting in 1991, the U.S. arsenal and that of the new Russian Federation—the successor state that has inherited the Soviet nukes—began to shrink in size. But, by the early 1990s, there were serious concerns about the possibility of nuclear breakout in both India and Pakistan[5]—a reality that came to pass with eleven weaponized tests by the two states over mere weeks in May 1998. At the same time, the earliest concerns about North Korea's interest in nuclear weapons had emerged by the early 1990s. This "second nuclear age" is seen by many as having brought about the end of global disarmament; instead, with nuclear weapons finding their ways into the national defense strategies of multiple states—and even concerns, post-9/11, of non-state actors staging radiological attacks—the policy prescription is now nuclear risk reduction and management. The thesis is a gloomy one, but all new nuclear powers emerge under the timeless logics of deterrence. Indeed, deterrence is the entire purpose of Kim Jong Un's "treasured sword."

North Korea's Strategy: Go First, Go Big

North Korea's nuclear capabilities are important, and Part Two of this book will show how different technology leaps and milestones have helped Kim Jong Un with specific parts of his deterrent. But we have seen above that deterrence is just as dependent upon perception as reality. The key question for understanding the nuclear threat posed by Kim Jong Un is not "What, technically, can North Korea do with its nuclear weapons?", but rather "Why did North Korea acquire nuclear weapons?", "When would North Korea use its nuclear weapons?", "What kind of nuclear posture will North Korea adopt?", and "What objectives will North Korea pursue now that it has nuclear weapons?" All of these concerns boil down to one core question: what does deterrence mean to Kim Jong Un?

The issue of understanding North Korean intentions is critical yet, unfortunately, not particularly in vogue within U.S. and allied governments. The causes of this are understandable, if unpersuasive. North Korea, to this day, is viewed as an obsessively secretive and 'unknowable' state. Among journalists with experience reporting on North Korea, this reputation is captured in the clichéd reference by generalist reporters to a "rare glimpse" inside this odd, modern Stalinist dystopia, whenever photographs emerge from inside the country. But outside of these tired clichés, North Korea is surprisingly transparent about its intentions—particularly where its nuclear weapons are concerned. All things considered, this makes sense: there is no point in a deterrent that nobody knows you have, or if nobody understands how you might use it.

A whole corpus of coordinated comments from a range of North Korean officials and state media reports offer insight into the country's thinking about the nuclear deterrent, while the carefully coordinated propaganda imagery of significant missile and nuclear test events has also conveyed important information about its likely deployment. We can also establish a richer texture on the regime's strategy from the years of diplomatic interactions between North Korean officials and other countries. If we draw from these sources, and grant North Korea the assumption of rationality as a self-interested state actor looking to survive and deter, it is possible to paint a picture of Kim Jong Un's emerging posture—of what it is he's trying to deter, and how.

For much of its independent history, North Korea has not felt particularly secure in its neighborhood. South of the DMZ, it faces an opponent twice its size in population, an order of magnitude wealthier, and long allied with the world's foremost military superpower, the United States. During the Cold War, between 1958 and 1991, the United States balanced against what remained of North Korea's military advantage in numbers against the South by basing tactical nuclear weapons on South Korean soil. While Pyongyang has one military ally of its own in the form of China, the basis of that partnership has come into question with North

Korea's transition to nuclear status. Kim Il Sung's 1961 mutual defense agreement with Beijing still stands, but Pyongyang's emergence as a nuclear power in the 2000s was likely the end of any assurances that Beijing would come to its aid in practice. Ever committed to self-reliance, North Korea today maintains its chronic sense of insecurity, but with nuclear weapons to ensure its survival in what it sees as a rough neighborhood.

While survival is the strategic end-goal that North Korea seeks, the role of nuclear weapons in enabling the strategy is more complex. Here arise questions of North Korea's nuclear *posture*, or what role its nuclear arsenal might play in the execution of its national strategy. Essentially, emerging nuclear powers like North Korea have a small menu of three nuclear postures to select from. These postures were codified by political scientist Vipin Narang as *assured retaliation*, *asymmetric escalation*, and a *catalytic strategy*.[6] One of these postures speaks for itself: *assured retaliation*. This strategy signals to adversaries and to the world that an actor will use nuclear weapons to deter any nuclear attacks or coercion; what makes this posture credible and able to function is the possession of capabilities that are survivable and could withstand a first-strike attack by an adversary—for example, submarine-launched missiles that would not be affected if vessels were at sea while land-based capabilities were destroyed. Countries such as China and India today employ this sort of posture. China has since 1964 held to an unqualified pledge of nuclear No First Use,[7] whereby it would only use nuclear weapons after its own territory had come under nuclear attack; Beijing has sought to make this credible to the United States by storing nuclear warheads separately from ballistic missiles in peacetime, and running military exercises simulating a chaotic, post-nuclear attack environment. However, given North Korea's compact geography and serious resource constraints, the regime has never adopted an assured retaliation posture, and is unlikely to do so anytime in the future.

A *catalytic* posture, according to Narang, is one of maximizing ambiguity around an actor's capabilities and intentions: escalating threat perception or conflict in a crisis, in order to draw in a reliable and powerful patron to intervene on its behalf, diplomatically or militarily. South Africa's short-lived nuclear program relied on this posture, as did Pakistan during the latter years of the Cold War and through much of the 1990s.[8] The Kim Jong Il era (1994–2011), when North Korea had broken out as a nuclear power but still had nothing close to a secure second strike capability—or even a robust first-use capability—would have been a propitious time for this posture. China, North Korea's major third-party patron in this period, would have had an interest in preventing regime collapse in Pyongyang or eruption of a massive humanitarian disaster, resulting in refugee flows across the border; or in averting the outbreak of war on the Peninsula during the U.S.—North Korea crises of the 1990s and early 2000s, since its mutual defense obligations would have pressured Beijing to join the conflict. However, given the lack of open sources and our inexact knowledge of the timeline of North Korean nuclear weapon development, it is unclear what sorts of assurances China was privately willing to give North Korea at this time.

Beijing was never quite moved to intervene internationally on Pyongyang's behalf during crises in the same way that a proliferation-averse United States was prompted to act on behalf of Pakistan and South Africa. Ultimately, a catalytic posture only works when your patron is motivated to intervene, and as the North Korean nuclear program progressed, Beijing was increasingly weighing the costs of being tied to an unreliable client like Pyongyang—whatever the 1961 friendship treaty said. In 2011, Chinese President Hu Jintao reportedly sent an envoy to Pyongyang with a frank message for Kim Jong Il: "If North Korea would first attack South Korea and, as a result, there were full-scale arms clashes, China wouldn't aid North Korea."[9] In any case, given Kim Jong Un's major nuclear and ballistic testing campaign, his self-declaration as a nuclear power, and his announcement that his deterrent is complete, 'strategic ambiguity' is clearly not his plan.

So this leaves one final option, the most compelling explanation of North Korea's nuclear strategy: Pyongyang has almost certainly settled on an *asymmetric escalation* posture. This is appealing for a specific kind of small, insecure nuclear state and North Korea fits the bill well. Asymmetric escalation seeks to deter any conventional aggression against one's territory, including conventional (non-nuclear) attacks by a neighbor-adversary who is superior in numbers or quality of forces. Before the Kim Jong Un era, Pakistan was the most infamous adoptee of this posture. With victory elusive after four wars against a conventionally superior India in 1947, 1965, and 1971, Pakistan broke out as a nuclear power in 1998 alongside India. Today, it signals the early use of nuclear weapons against Indian conventional military formations to make New Delhi think twice about using its military might to attack or seize Pakistani territory. Like North Korea, Pakistan suffers from chronic insecurity and harbors fears about its territorial sovereignty becoming irreversibly compromised as it was when it lost its eastern territory (now Bangladesh) in the 1971 war. Similar to some readings of North Korean objectives, Pakistan holds revisionist territorial goals too, having fought multiple conflicts with India to integrate the Muslim-majority region of Kashmir since Partition in 1947.

Researchers have found that coercion and nuclear weapons do not generally go hand in hand,[10] but Pakistan is nevertheless an instructive parallel. Even if Kim Jong Un is not seeking to coercively unify the Peninsula using nuclear weapons, he can learn from Islamabad's methods of using nuclear weapons to blunt New Delhi's ability to retaliate with conventional weapons. The

1999 limited war between India and Pakistan, and Islamabad's subsequent use of sub-conventional forces, including terrorist groups, is commonly cited as an example of what scholar Glenn Snyder has labeled a 'stability—instability' paradox: vulnerability to nuclear weapons on both sides prevents the breakout of a full-fledged war, but enables the weaker state to pursue lower-level conventional aggression under the nuclear overhang.[11]

With the U.S.—South Korea alliance on its doorstep, Pyongyang is just as worried about attempts at unification, invasion, or 'regime change' from the other side of the DMZ, and looks to hold at risk allied military targets across South Korea, Japan, and elsewhere in the Western Pacific to ward off this kind of action. Kim will look for signs of the United States and its allies preparing to carry out an invasion of its territory, such as amassing forces, jamming or disabling North Korean communications, or evacuating American civilians from South Korea and Japan. Since the end of the Korean War in 1953, the Korean People's Army has been preparing for a resumption of full-scale hostilities with the United States. To this end, just as American strategists do with the U.S.'s adversaries, North Korean planners have carefully studied how Washington fights its wars. For North Korea, one of the areas of particular interest is how the United States—unparalleled today in its ability to project force worldwide—prosecutes wars with grand revisionist objectives in far-flung places. Luckily for North Korea, there is no shortage of data to mine here. Once it was Cold War-era examples like the U.S. war in Vietnam and the invasion of Grenada, and for Kim Jong Un today it is the United States' more recent misadventures in the Gulf War of 1990–91, Iraq in 2003, and Libya in 2011. North Korean propaganda alludes to these campaigns regularly.

Whatever the North Koreans learned from the demise of Hussein and Gadhafi, perhaps the greatest takeaway is simply that the path Pyongyang has chosen—to acquire nuclear weapons, no matter the cost and no matter the disarmament plan on offer—is the right one for their country, lest Kim Jong Un meet a similar fate. "The Saddam Hussein regime in Iraq and the Gadhafi regime in Libya could not escape the fate of destruction after being deprived of their foundations for nuclear development," a North Korean state media editorial put it once. It was this same sentiment that helped explain why, during 2018, a year of diplomacy, North Korea reacted sharply to U.S. references to disarmament or the "Libya model" (see Part Three). Beyond these precedents, many of North Korea's assumptions about how the United States and South Korea would fight a joint war against it are informed by more than speculation: in 2016, Pyongyang's hackers successfully stole war plans from the South—including plans for an allied "decapitation" strike on Kim.[12]

The form of Kim Jong Un's nuclear strategy has also been shaped by observations of how the U.S. Department of Defense mobilizes forces: with a tremendous quantity of logistical support. According to former U.S. officials, the North Koreans "vowed never to let the United States turn their country into another Iraq," and, to make sure of it, studied U.S. military operations carefully.[13] For the 2003 invasion of Iraq, the U.S. Navy was tasked with transporting some "56 million square feet of combat cargo" and "4.8 billion gallons" in fuel,[14] on top of the need to bring in the actual instruments of war—aircraft, warships, aircraft carriers, and infantry. These activities amount to transaction costs associated with an American decision to wage war on the ground. Using nuclear weapons to disrupt these processes, therefore, is a good way to prevent, or at least seriously complicate, American success in a regime change mission. Neither Hussein nor Gadhafi had been able to stem American mobilization efforts, which were the spark that lit the fuse for the eventual collapse of their regimes. Kim Jong Un is determined to be smarter.

For this form of nuclear deterrence to work—to deter an American expeditionary force build-up in the first place—North Korea would have to convey a willingness to introduce nuclear weapons early and before any *actual use of force* against it by the United States and its allies. If Kim waits for his territory to be struck first, it may be too late: the allies might be capable of destroying most of his nuclear warheads or missiles, leaving him completely vulnerable. He will quickly begin to face "use-or-lose" pressures. Kim knows that to have a chance at survival, North Korea would need to go first and go big. The terrifying consequence of this posture is that Kim Jong Un finds himself in the position of *rationally* favoring nuclear first use. The option of using nuclear weapons is not *good* for North Korea: in any situation where it has to contemplate first use, the situation in its neighborhood will have deteriorated to a total crisis. But, faced with decades of inherited fear about resumed hostilities on the Peninsula, and the United States' known inclination toward regime change, Kim sees nuclear weapons as his best bet.

The calculation might look something like this: *My enemies are preparing to invade. If I do not use my nuclear weapons now, I might lose them entirely to offensive strikes by stealth fighters my air defense radars cannot see. Even if my missiles are not destroyed, advanced American cyber and electronic warfare might sever me from my ability to command my nuclear forces. So I should ready my short-, medium-, and intermediate-range ballistic missiles, mate them with nuclear warheads, and prioritize valuable military targets.* These would likely include the U.S. Air Force Base on Guam, U.S. Forces Japan headquarters at Yokosuka, and the U.S. THAAD missile defense battery in South Korea's Seongju county, among many others.

The strategic logic of this sort of nuclear weapons use was apparent to Kim's grandfather, long before North Korea's nuclear capabilities were close to being realized. In the final days of the

Korean War, American military officers reflected on the potential damage that a Soviet nuclear bomber strike could do to U.S. operations across the Korean Peninsula. In part, it was this observation that prevented the United States itself from introducing nuclear weapons into that war. General Joseph Collins, on March 27, 1953, reflected on this (emphasis added):

> Before we use them [nuclear weapons] we had better look to our air defense. Right now we *present ideal targets for atomic weapons* in Pusan and Inchon. An *atomic weapon in Pusan harbor could do serious damage to our military position in Korea.* We would again present an ideal target if we should undertake a major amphibious operation. An amphibious landing fleet would be a perfect target for an atomic weapon at the time when it was putting the troops ashore.[15]

While much has changed between the Korean War and Kim Jong Un's time, the basic geographic requirements for massive American expeditionary conventional operations on the Korean Peninsula have not. Under Kim Jong Un, statements released after ballistic missile tests have alluded to the ability of North Korean nuclear weapons to degrade allied warfighting capability. After a July 2016 test launch of short- and medium-range missiles, for example, the North Koreans gave the purpose of the exercise as simulating "preemptive strikes on the ports and airfields in the operational theater of South Korea through which nuclear war equipment of the U.S. imperialists are brought in." The exercise was explicitly designed to validate operational parameters for nuclear weapons use.[16]

These targets close to home are important for Kim's deterrent, as we will see in Chapter Five; but they are not enough on their own. For a regional nuclear state, North Korea faces the unique and demanding deterrence challenge of holding at risk not only territory adjacent to itself (South Korea) and nearby in the Pacific (Japan and Guam), but also the U.S. homeland on the other side of the globe. For years, North Korea's chosen nuclear posture was left incomplete until it developed the capabilities to strike at American cities, for even if Kim Jong Un were to successfully strike at the military targets it sought to hold at risk in South Korea, Japan, and the Pacific, there would be little standing in the way of a full court allied press on its territory—one that would assuredly remove Kim from power. This is why the Kim Jong Un era has opened a new chapter in the nuclear story: this is the age of the North Korean intercontinental-range ballistic missile. With three flight tests in 2017, Kim demonstrated that he had at least two separate missile designs capable of credibly threatening nuclear destruction of valuable American targets from San Diego to New York to Trump's Mar-a-Lago retreat in Florida.

Returning to the scenario where Kim has chosen to employ nuclear weapons to forestall an invasion of his territory, he would likely count on holding his ICBMs in reserve. After nuclear strikes had presumably successfully deteriorated the ability of the United States and its allies to continue a robust military campaign against North Korea, Washington might then find itself unable to disarm Kim of his ICBMs. Moreover, were Kim to possess additional warheads beyond his initial attacks, he could also choose to hold regional metropolises like Seoul and Tokyo at risk. While, in reality, the odds of the United States standing down after a nuclear attack against military targets in Northeast Asia is low, Kim's calculation proceeds *probabilistically*. If an invasion is imminent and he does not use nuclear weapons, the chances of survival for him and his regime are effectively zero. If there is a chance that an American president might balk at the risk of nuclear use against an American city— or the Greater Tokyo and Greater Seoul areas, home to some 65 million people put together—then his probability of survival is higher than zero.

In March 2013, Kim Jong Un made all this clear by offering the outside world a glimpse at his nuclear targets: both those within realistic reach at the time and the more aspirational ones. State media released a photograph of Kim sitting at a large glossy wooden desk, surrounded by four men in military uniforms and presiding over an "urgent operation meeting" for the KPA Strategic Rocket Force. Behind him, in the top left, a large map annotated with the words "U.S. Mainland Strike Plan," showed four trajectory lines from the Korean Peninsula. The targets of these trajectories were Hawaii, the headquarters of U.S. Pacific Command; San Diego, home to the U.S. Pacific Fleet; Washington, D.C., the nation's capital and a mainstay in previous North Korean threats; and a final target, obscured by one of Kim's men in uniform, which some analysts have suggested as Barksdale Air Force Base in Louisiana—home to the U.S. Air Force Global Strike Command, which is charged with long-range strategic bomber operations. This "map of death," as it came to be called among analysts, outlined Kim's strategic logic: to really deter a war on North Korea, these were the targets that he wanted to bring into range.[17] It would only be a little over four years after the image was published before he did.

Nuclear Weapons at the Center of National Defense

While these scenarios are immensely grim in their implications for Northeast Asia, the fact remains that Kim seeks to rely on deterrence, and not striking out in anger. None of the above is ever meant to transpire, as long as his capabilities are perceived to be credible. For Kim, nuclear weapons serve as a bulwark against attempts at forcible regime change or outside interference in North Korean decision-making, whether this might look something like Iraq and Libya in the twenty-first century, or like Korea itself in 1905, when the Peninsula came under Japanese colonial control.[18] Nuclear weapons, according to the North Korean view, are the ultimate enablers of national self-determination. By developing robust and credible capabilities to inflict unacceptable damage if his regime is threatened, Kim hopes to seed in the minds of policymakers and publics in the United States, South Korea, and Japan the fears of what might result should nuclear deterrence fail; this is the "balance of terror" he seeks.

Should he succeed, the ultimate result would be that the United States and its allies would never contemplate even preparing for a preemptive war of aggression against North Korea: the risks would be too great. By posturing to escalate asymmetrically, Kim's chances of survival are maximized. What's more, a wedge is driven between the United States and its allies in Kim's backyard. In the late 1950s and early 1960s, European leaders began to wonder: would the White House really risk Boston for Bonn, Portland for Paris? Just as France in the 1960s decided Washington would not come to the aid of French cities against a Soviet nuclear attack, breaking with NATO Integrated Military Command and seeking its own independent deterrent, so—Kim hopes—debates about nuclear proliferation in Seoul and Tokyo might snowball into a political decision in those capitals that the U.S. alliance is no longer reliable enough. By increasing the costliness of allied assurance for Washington, Kim seeks to realize a longstanding North Korean strategic objective in Northeast Asia: the eviction of the United States whose presence is made manifest by forward-based military forces, from the region.

Strategy involves the matching of means to desired end-states, under conditions of material scarcity. While North Korea's basic nuclear strategy may have well been apparent to Kim Il Sung decades ago, getting there would not be cheap. Pyongyang persisted, seemingly bearing any cost to get there. For years, North Korean nuclear developments—from weapon fuel production onwards—has been singularly focused on the broader strategic goals of deterrence for survival. There have been five key items on the "shopping list" for Pyongyang to fully realize its nuclear strategy:

1. *Indigenous production of fissile material.* There are two possible fuel sources for nuclear weapons: plutonium or highly enriched uranium. Ideally, a nuclear power will have access to both—and in plentiful amounts. Without this, little else is possible.

2. *Design and manufacture.* Once fissile material is available in sufficiently large quantities, a "nuclear weapons complex" is needed, to manufacture the nuclear fuel into weaponized packages that can be tested for safe detonation. This requires nuclear knowledge and technical expertise. The next chapter explores North Korea's journey, from 1948 to 2017, toward mastery of these first two steps, which together constitute 'the bomb.'

3. *Delivery.* Even once you have the bomb, it needs to get to its target. In North Korea's case, this means you need a ballistic missile to carry it; this makes it possible to hit military targets south of the DMZ, and as far on the other side of the globe as the contiguous United States. Chapters Five through Eight chart this long road to deterrence, culminating in Kim Jong Un's 2017 triumph with the ICBM.

4. *Launch and reentry.* Ballistic missiles with nuclear weapons on them, even if they are headed for the United States, are of no use if they cannot be relied on in a conflict. What are they being launched from, can they successfully reenter the earth's atmosphere over their target, and can they hit that target accurately? Kim Jong Un's likely future plans for refinement of his launch and reentry systems are explored in Chapter Eight.

5. *Command and control.* Kim Jong Un may now have the fuel to build nuclear bombs, and the missiles and launchers to deliver them to target, but now he will have to consider the infrastructure, military setup and politics that such a capability demands. How to make sure his nukes will always be ready for his command, but never launched without his authoriza-

tion? What do the uncertainties about this mean for the rest of the world? This final component, without which no nuclear force is complete, is the subject of Chapter Nine; but it is worth having a look now at the risks surrounding Kim's nuclear decision-making.

Risk and Uncertainty

This chapter's discussion of Kim Jong Un's nuclear posture and deterrence strategy is heavily based on assumptions about his rationality. But what makes North Korea's possession of nuclear weapons today so dangerous is not that Kim might behave irrationally, but the strong chance that he might have to make decisions about nuclear use under considerable uncertainty, based on imperfect information. This means that we must also resist the impulse to hyper-rationalize Kim's calculus. He will not randomly blow up a U.S. city for no good reason, but we should not sit back in a complacent assumption that he knows exactly what he is doing, either. No policymaker has the luxury of making decisions about war and peace in an environment of perfect information, and North Korea's choices about its nuclear posture are made particularly dangerous by several capability gaps outside its nuclear force.

For instance, given that Kim's decision to employ nuclear weapons in a crisis hinges upon a North Korean assessment of U.S. and allied intentions, a good decision there will rely upon intelligence, surveillance, and reconnaissance capabilities. Part of North Korea's chronic sense of insecurity—and particularly why Pyongyang bristles at the use of advanced aerial stealth platforms, including bombers and fighters—is the fact that the country's early warning systems are rudimentary. North Korean state media, for instance, pushes back on allied activities on the basis of South Korean and American news reports. In some instances, foreign misreporting on military activities has been interpreted by North Korea as reality. In April 2017, for instance, U.S. Pacific Command suggested that the USS *Carl Vinson* carrier strike group was off the Korean Peninsula when it was actually several thousand kilometers away, in the Tsunda Strait. The North Korean Ministry of Foreign Affairs reacted with an aggressive complaint before the truth of the matter was clarified.[19] In South Korea and Japan, North Korea is also thought to rely on a network of scores of human spies to gather first-hand information where possible on unusual military movements near and around U.S. bases.[20] The risks of such sources are obvious.

The inherent limitations on North Korea's ability to precisely understand American and South Korean intentions is also a driver of its discomfort with major joint military exercises—especially those with a live-fire and mass mobilization component. Pyongyang has long feared that these exercises could be used by the alliance as a ruse to initiate a preemptive war under otherwise peaceful conditions. In these sorts of circumstances—an exceptionally large mass mobilization exercise—Kim's strongly ingrained "use-or-lose" incentives for his nuclear weapons would be particularly acute, and the chances for a serious miscalculation would rise. The tensions around joint military exercises were demonstrated with one Cold War nuclear near-miss in September 1983. Amid the lead-up to the massive NATO Able Archer exercise, a Soviet early warning alarm system glitched out due to a rare atmospheric anomaly. It issued an alert that nuclear missiles were inbound. The receiving Soviet lieutenant trusted his "gut," as he later would recount, and did not respond. Would his North Korean counterpart keep his cool in the same scenario, given Pyongyang's rudimentary early warning capabilities, high threat perceptions, and offensive nuclear strategy?

We should also be modest in our understanding of North Korean thinking on nuclear weapons; some choices do not necessarily accord with publicly stated postures. For instance, as of 2020, North Korea has shown little interest in developing low-yield nuclear weapons that might be employed on the battlefield to create uncertainty about possible nuclear escalation—the route Pakistan has taken in the face of a very similar combination of strategic challenges. Not only has North Korea not taken this step yet, but its command and control choices appear sub-optimal for its strategy. As we will see in more detail in Chapter Nine, Kim Jong Un has chosen to exercise assertive control over his nuclear weapons, and has not authorized or predelegated launch authority in peacetime. North Korea may be a particularly strong case of dynamic command and control procedures, whereby posture shifts based on crisis indicators—for instance, if Kim had reason to fear an imminent regime change war, he could have incentives to become an "early crisis delegator."[21] But the fact that this system is not yet in place shows that Kim still has a long way to go in rounding out the command and control structures that will actually determine any use of his nuclear deterrent in the future. This is not good news for the prospects of nuclear war.

While Kim Jong Un has not shown himself willing to test South Korean resolve to retaliate by launching low-yield nuclear weapons over the border, he may choose other non-conventional options. Where Pakistan has used proxy terrorist groups, there is major concern in South Korea that Pyongyang might seek to use its considerable cyber capabilities to attack business in the South with impunity and even initiative-limited conventional skirmishes—in other words, the 'stability–instability' paradox might manifest on the Korean Peninsula. Given the already expansive international sanctions against Pyongyang, the cost-benefit calculation for these kinds of actions would be straightforward. Should Kim find himself indefinitely stuck under the sanctions regime against him, with an ever-more-advanced nuclear force at his disposal, he may adjust his risk tolerance and strategies in favor of greater conventional adventurism, boxing in the United States and South Korea with the nuclear deterrent. Kim Jong Un may reign over North Korea as a nuclear weapon-wielding leader for decades to come, and we can expect that the balance of risks for the world will continue to evolve.

North Korea has a well-defined, minimally capable, and organized nuclear force, which continues to grow both in qualitative and quantitative terms, absent any agreement to cap its arsenal. Under Kim Jong Un, the country's national defense strategy has been squarely positioned around nuclear weapons. These are relied upon to deter invasion and regime change at the hands of hostile foreign forces, via a threat of pre-emptive first use whose threshold is ambiguous. Kim hopes to leave the option of a war of choice against his regime unthinkable, for the United States, South Korea, and Japan. So now that we know what he wants, we can turn to how he has gathered these tools in his box—in full knowledge of the immense risks they represent.

PART TWO

TESTING, TESTING

4

BUILDING THE BOMB

The terrifying destructive effects of nuclear weapons stand at the core of what allows them to deter. The etymology of the word *deterrence* itself reveals the mechanism embedded within, from the earliest days of the nuclear age: it originates from the Latin *terrere*, or to frighten. In explosive terms, nuclear weapons yield several orders of magnitude more energy than their conventional counterparts. In the U.S. arsenal today, the very largest conventional (non-nuclear) explosive yields just 11 tons of TNT equivalent in explosive force. The arsenal's smallest nuclear yield, by contrast, is 300 tons.[1] Moreover, while the former weighs in at 8,500 kg and can only be delivered by heavy bomber, the latter weighs just 320 kg and can be carried by fighter aircraft: tremendous terror in a compact package. For a country like North Korea that counts on ballistic missiles to bring its opponents into range, nuclear weapons also have value in compensating for imprecise targeting, even at the vast ranges required to hold the United States homeland at risk: a conventional ballistic missile without some degree of precision is of dubious military use, but a nuclear-tipped missile can even the balance by wiping out a much greater target area.

For the nation's founder Kim Il Sung, while the Korean People's Army's conventional weaponry successfully deterred an invasion from the south by promising to wreak destruction on the urban megalopolis that is Seoul, nuclear weapons would provide a more elegant solution. Certainly, if North Korea was ever to fully deter the United States, nuclear weapons—deliverable by long-range missile—were the only solution. Beyond their tremendous explosive effects, nuclear weapons come with several other unique characteristics. While conventional and nuclear explosives result in blast waves to release energy, nuclear weapons have a considerably higher release of thermal (heat) energy—in the moments after the explosion, the thermal release produces temperatures as hot as the Sun, generating a high-pressure wave that dissipates outward, causing a sharp rise in atmospheric pressure, and which can flatten and pulverize surrounding structures. The heat of the initial flash can also scald and destroy human skin, and even initiate devastating firestorms over great distances, greatly multiplying damage to life and property from the initial blast wave. At the moment of explosion, a flash of light occurs that surpasses the Sun's luminosity as viewed from earth by several orders of magnitude. This initial flash can blind any humans unfortunate enough to look straight at the explosion.

Moreover, these weapons cause a massive release of nuclear radiation, adding to their environmental destructiveness potential. Nuclear fallout—particles rendered radioactive as a result of a nuclear explosion—can amplify these hazards and spread them over great distances. Nuclear weapons can even be engineered specifically to maximize fallout, if so desired. The amount of fallout can vary depending on the yield of the weapon in question and the altitude at which it detonates. Nuclear weapons generally are detonated either as "air bursts"—whereby the detonation takes place at altitude and the nuclear fireball does not reach the surface, relying primarily on the thermal release—or "surface bursts," whereby the explosion occurs near the earth's surface. The latter produces considerably greater nuclear fallout. More exotic weapons have included earth-penetrators, designed to cause a nuclear detonation several meters under the earth's surface, and underwater nuclear explosives, including mines. For North Korea and its chosen delivery method of ballistic missiles, either air or surface bursts would do fine. If the ballistic missiles were to be the hilt of Kim Jong Un's "treasured sword," nuclear weaponry would become the finely-honed blade. What benefit could Kim hope to gain from brandishing his sword if he did not have a well-honed blade at hand?

Fueling Kim's Weapons

The physical constraints of designing nuclear weapons themselves applied in North Korea as they did everywhere else in the world. Kim Jong Un could not claim to have his bomb today without the country first having having access to fissile material suitable for use in a nuclear weapon. Weapons-grade nuclear materials thankfully cannot just be mined out of the earth, but the road to acquiring these materials begins there. Natural uranium is plentiful in North Korea and serves as the primary input into North Korea's nuclear weapons complex. While it serves as an input, the processes involved in getting to weapons-grade fissile material are complex.

For weapons use, uranium is useless unless it can sustain a chain reaction of nuclear fission. This quality in uranium was discovered by German scientists some nine months before the start of the Second World War, in 1938. In January 1939, American scientists at Columbia University recreated that fission experiment, observing that the nuclear fission phenomenon produces an epic amount of energy as mass is converted into energy. By August 1939—on the eve of the breakout of war—two Hungarian emigré physicists,

Leó Szilárd and Eugene Wigner, prepared a letter that would be signed by Albert Einstein for the eyes of the U.S. president, Franklin D. Roosevelt, claiming that the discoveries around nuclear fission would allow for the development of "extremely powerful bombs of a new type." They continued:

> A single bomb of this type, carried by boat and exploded in a port, might very well destroy the whole port together with some of the surrounding territory. However, such bombs might very well prove to be too heavy for transportation by air.

Many physicists at the time were skeptical about weaponizing fission,[2] but Roosevelt took these claims seriously. He convened a three-man committee to investigate nuclear fission and uranium, including the two Hungarians. The committee concluded that uranium "would provide a possible source of bombs with a destructiveness vastly greater than anything now known." By 1942, Roosevelt had initiated the Manhattan Project in the United States to master the destructive potential of the atom. The first experiment to provoke a self-sustaining nuclear chain reaction was conducted in late 1942 under a shroud of secrecy, using the following coded phrase to signal success in a daring experiment that some had worried might spiral out of control and accidentally produce an explosion: "the Italian navigator has just landed in the New World."[3]

As we know, the Manhattan Project was successful, leading to the first detonation of a nuclear weapon on July 16, 1945. The discovery of the fissile qualities of uranium was key to this effort. The American experiments had established that uranium has two naturally occurring isotopes (variants of an element) that can serve as fuel for a fission chain reaction phenomenon. One is uranium-235, but it comprises less than 1 per cent of uranium found in the earth. So Manhattan Project scientists also worked on a second path toward the bomb: plutonium. This element occurs naturally in infinitesimally small amounts, but metallurgists and chemists worked to chemically separate it from uranium-238, which is abundant in nature. It was plutonium-239 that powered the first nuclear detonation on July 16, 1945. While the world has changed greatly since the days of the Manhattan Project, the physics of basic nuclear weapons design have not.

For North Korea, fuel for nuclear weaponry—uranium-235 and plutonium-239—would be the basis on which its nuclear ambitions would live or die. To ensure progress in these areas, it would need to invest in nuclear science—and it did. North Korean scientists and engineers worked over decades to master the nuclear fuel cycle, eventually working to indigenize every stage of the process, starting with the extraction of natural uranium from the earth at facilities like the Pyongsan Uranium Mine and Concentration Plant. By 2019, North Korea was sitting on an estimated sixty-five weapons' worth of plutonium and uranium, according to U.S. intelligence assessments based on multiple sources.[4] Between its plutonium and highly enriched uranium output, U.S. estimates were that North Korea was producing as much as twelve warheads' worth of weapons-grade fissile material annually.[5] Under Kim Jong Un, North Korea not only emerged as a nuclear weapons power, but as a self-sufficient country in the realm of fissile material production—even if it did not have the resources to scale out a large, nuclear power infrastructure.[6]

Yongbyon and its Secrets

As long as the United States and South Korea have had concerns about North Korean nuclear activities, they have been interested in the Yongbyon Nuclear Research Center. A sprawling complex of more than 400 structures some 95 kilometers from the national capital, Yongbyon is the beating heart of North Korea's nuclear complex. Or at least it was made to be so over the course of decades—by the North Koreans and the outside world alike.

Today North Korea's production of nuclear material, including for weapons, has long spilled past Yongbyon's frontiers, but as the sole site containing *declared* facilities for production of nuclear fuel to this day, the complex has often been seen as the prize to be won in any negotiated settlement of the nuclear problem in North Korea, from the 1994 Agreed Framework with the United States, which focused on disabling, monitoring, and freezing facilities there, to the Six-Party Talks in the 2000s, to the February 2019 summit between Kim Jong Un and Donald J. Trump.

Yongbyon's origins date to the 1960s, when its initial facilities were completed—a delayed consequence of the founding of North Korea's Atomic Energy Research Institute in 1952. From that time, the complex began to grow in parallel with North Korea's nuclear ambitions. Today, it encompasses some of the best known and most scrutinized nuclear facilities in North Korea, hence its salience in denuclearization diplomacy to the present day. The first notable nuclear facility at the site was a small research reactor provided by the Soviet Union, known as the IRT-2000. This allowed North Korean scientists to acquaint themselves practically with nuclear materials and research, but it was never going to be the cornerstone of a weapons program. It operated on highly enriched uranium, which at the time the North Koreans needed to replenish from their Soviet benefactors. While Moscow was a major patron of Kim Il Sung, it did not actively encourage North Korean nuclear weaponization efforts, so a small research reactor was seen as the most practical way to proceed. But that did not cap North Korean curiosity.

According to a North Korean declaration given years later, in 1975, nuclear scientists in the country had successfully separated a very small amount of plutonium—just grams, far too little for any weapon—at the IRT-2000 research reactor.[7] This effort took place just two years before the International Atomic Energy Agency safeguarded the facility in 1977.[8] By the 1980s, North

Korea had embarked on a major indigenous effort outside of the IRT-2000.[9] Along the bank of the Kuryong River, North Korean scientists had overseen the construction of an indigenous nuclear reactor with an estimated 5 megawatt (electric) capacity. Frustrated by Soviet refusal to supply fuel for this reactor, the North Koreans set up their own fuel fabrication facilities at Yongbyon, capable of processing natural uranium into fuel rods. In 1986, the indigenous reactor began operating for the first time, one year after Kim Il Sung had been pressured by the Soviets to sign and ratify the Treaty on the Nonproliferation of Nuclear Weapons (NPT).

This indigenous reactor—largely modeled on the United Kingdom's first-ever commercial reactor at Calder Hall—had several advantages for North Korean purposes. First, for fuel it used not enriched uranium but natural uranium, which is abundant in North Korea as in many other countries. Second, the reactor would produce plentiful amounts of spent fuel, which can be reprocessed in order to make nuclear weapons. When U.S. intelligence agencies detected the construction of an apparent reprocessing facility near the reactor in 1988, concerns spiked about Kim Il Sung's plans. As far as the United States was concerned, extracting weapons-usable plutonium by reprocessing the spent fuel rods was the only plausible purpose for such a facility. By 1990, the reprocessing plant was operational, and construction promptly began on two more reactors, both significantly larger than the existing one. Together, if these sites were to reach completion and begin operations, North Korea would have more spent fuel than it would know what to do with. For a burgeoning nuclear weapons program, however, there would be plenty of material for reprocessing into plutonium for use in a bomb.

The 1994 Agreed Framework with the Clinton administration froze North Korea's plutonium production, and for the agreement's duration, the two unfinished reactors fell into a state of disrepair. In 2004, after the accord had collapsed, the visiting American nuclear scientist Siegfried Hecker observed that the new, larger reactor at Yongbyon was multiple years away from completion—not one year away as North Korean officials had claimed in the 1990s.[10] Ultimately, construction never finished, and the lone 5 MWe reactor remained the center of focus at Yongbyon. North Korean technicians didn't let their talents go to waste, however; in September 2007, the the Israeli Air Force struck and destroyed an apparent nuclear reactor in eastern Syria over concerns that Syrian President Bashar al-Assad was seeking nuclear weapons. The suspected reactor was of "similar size and technology" to the Yongbyon 5 MWe reactor, according to then CIA Director Michael Hayden. With its existing reactor, North Korea has "enough plutonium for one or two weapons per year," Hayden added.[11]

The Yongbyon reactor has been on-again, off-again, on-again, off-again, and on-again. The United States and the international community succeeded in limiting the reactor's operation until they did not. As with the Agreed Framework of the 1990s, the Six-Party Talks process also led to a halting of activities in 2008, with the North Koreans staging a major goodwill demolition of the cooling tower at the facility, with international media watching. However, the processes supposedly dismantled by this demolition were soon restarted covertly. In April 2013, under Kim Jong Un, the North Koreans announced that the disabled reactor would be brought up to its former glory and restarted—a development that took place in September that year, under Kim Jong Un.

Today, the United States has more to worry about than the lone Yongbyon reactor, which is likely nearing the end of its life after more than three decades of intermittent plutonium production. By the time of Kim Jong Il's death in 2011, North Korea had set up multiple centrifuge facilities to enrich uranium indigenously, opening up the second path to the bomb denied to Kim Il Sung by his Soviet patrons. North Korea had been mining and milling uranium at four sites it had declared in 1992 to the International Atomic Energy Agency, but its enrichment program was developed covertly. By 2010, North Korea had converted its old fuel fabrication facility at Yongbyon to an operational uranium enrichment facility, known internally in North Korea as the 63 Project Office.[12] But how had Pyongyang managed to make this leap in building the bomb?

From AQ Khan to Self-Sufficiency

> We ... believe Pyongyang is pursuing a production-scale uranium enrichment program based on technology provided by AQ Khan, which would give North Korea an alternative route to nuclear weapons.
>
> CIA Director George Tenet, congressional testimony in
> February 2004

Kim Jong Un would have had to wait significantly longer for North Korea's emergence as a self-sufficient nuclear weapons possessor had it not been for the role played by Abdul Qadeer (AQ) Khan, the father of Pakistan's nuclear weapons program and the man at the center of the world's most notorious known proliferation network. For years, analysts have tried to understand the origins, underpinnings, and full extent of this network, which became public knowledge after his public confessions in 2004.[13] While mysteries persist about Khan's activities and the precise machinery that allowed his network to persist for as long as it did, what is clear is that without AQ Khan, North Korea's nuclear weapons program would not be what it is today. Of his three known customers—Iran, Libya, and North Korea—and one unknown fourth customer, only Pyongyang has been able to fully capitalize on this foreign assistance and to break out as a nuclear power.

AQ Khan began life as a subject of British India. After independence, his family was among the millions dislocated in the trauma of the subcontinent's partition. Khan wound up in Europe, where he burnished his academic credentials as a metallurgist. Metallurgy had played a central role in the development of a range of technologies in the twentieth century, including nuclear weapons and long-range missiles. In 1972, Khan's foundations in this field eventually landed him a job at a Dutch research laboratory that subcontracted for the Urenco Group, a multinational nuclear fuel company. This allowed him to become well acquainted with uranium enrichment centrifuges, which by this time were well known and coveted as the most efficient form of separating the useful fissile isotope uranium-235 from the more naturally abundant uranium-238.

The previous year, in 1971, Pakistan had suffered a military defeat to India, resulting in territorial changes which included the creation of Bangladesh. This singular trauma disturbed Khan to his core and would be mentioned by him in the 2000s as a motivator for his interest in Pakistan's national defense.[14] He wrote to then Pakistani Prime Minister Zulfikar Ali Bhutto, underscoring the importance of a Pakistani national uranium enrichment program.[15] Bhutto had famously declared in the mid-1960s: "If India builds the bomb, we will eat grass or leaves, even go hungry, but we will get one of our own. We have no alternative."[16] The reason why this was so important was that India's conventional military forces were superior to Pakistan's—a nuclear arsenal was the only way to even the score. (As we saw in the previous chapter, this is evocative of Pyongyang's own predicament versus South Korea.)

From 1971 to 1975, Khan transformed from patriotic metallurgist to the world's most notorious nuclear smuggler and proliferator. He used his perch at the Dutch lab to pilfer information on the design and manufacture of uranium enrichment centrifuges. In 1974, he was spurred on even further by India's detonation of a nonweaponized nuclear device—what New Delhi euphemistically called a "Peaceful Nuclear Explosion" carried out under the aegis of the equally docile-sounding Operation Smiling Buddha. CIA and Dutch intelligence were tracking his activities, but did not pick him up—possibly because they had "hopes of learning more about Pakistan's nuclear-smuggling network" through continued surveillance.[17] Khan returned to Pakistan a free man, with a treasure trove of information in tow that secured him a hallowed sinecure atop Islamabad's weapons program by 1976. From there, he slowly began moving in a direction that would reverberate decades later on the Korean Peninsula.

In a 2009 television interview, Khan remarked that "we had achieved 90 per cent result in the enrichment program by the early 1983,"[18] and Pakistan was "two screwdriver turns" away from a bomb by 1986.[19] Although the Reagan administration was concerned with Pakistani and Indian breakout at the time, Cold War impulses—specifically, Pakistan's critical status as a partner in Afghanistan, then under Soviet occupation—prevented the nuclear issue from rising to the top of the U.S.—Pakistan agenda. Having built the bomb unchecked, Khan now "started marketing his nuclear expertise abroad," from direct resources and knowledge to his extensive network of contacts.[20]

North Korea was not Khan's first port of call. Of his three known customers, his immediate outreach in the 1980s was toward Libya and Iran. Ultimately, though, North Korea was a more compelling customer, if not for Khan's pocketbook then for Pakistan's broader national priorities. As we will see in Chapter Five, by the late 1980s, North Korea had flight-tested and made considerable progress in domestically reverse-engineering Soviet designs of short-range, liquid-fueled missile. By this same time, North Korea is also thought to have started taking an interest in uranium enrichment centrifuges, both for civilian power and nuclear weapons applications.

While the precise nature of Khan's interactions with Pyongyang over the years remains subject to debate—particularly given the unreliability of Khan's own testimony about his activities, and self-interested testimony by other Pakistani officials—what is clear is that centrifuges resembling Pakistani designs have been seen in North Korea and, in turn, ballistic missiles resembling North Korea's Nodong remain in use in Pakistan. Despite former Pakistani President Pervez Musharraf's claim in his memoir that Khan's efforts represented a "a one-man act and that neither the government of Pakistan nor the army was involved," there is a body of evidence that the quid pro quo drew in other parts of the Pakistani state.[21] In 1993, Pakistani Prime Minister Benazir Bhutto visited Pyongyang to discuss missile cooperation, among other things; Khan has said in an interview that he discussed Pakistani's need for long-range missiles with Bhutto herself, and that Bhutto said she would pursue cooperation with Pyongyang if her chief of staff approved.[22]

AQ Khan's assistance to North Korea's program was critical in the late 1990s, with Pyongyang eventually transitioning to self-sufficiency in centrifuge technology. This led to the first nuclear test in 2006, and prompted UN Security Council resolution 1718 to try and deny Pyongyang access to the foreign components it would need to continue manufacturing centrifuges for uranium; the hope was that this would limit its nuclear fuel program to plutonium, where severe material constraints would restrict the country's supply of fissile material. In a matter of years, however, that effort turned out to be in vain.[23] In 2013, two independent experts presented research based on open source information that found that North Korea had likely transitioned from relying on foreign sourcing of critical centrifuge components to having mastered production entirely within its own borders.[24] In less than twenty years, North Korea had fully capitalized on the opportunity AQ Khan had presented. There was no going back.

BUILDING THE BOMB

The Covert Enrichment Sites

> *Let us dash forward in the spirit of Chollima!*
>
> North Korean slogan from the Chollima Movement in the late 1950s.

It has long been thought that sites relating to North Korea's production of fissile materials exist outside of the Yongbyon complex. True, North Korea declared its facilities at Yongbyon to the International Atomic Energy Agency, but, especially after the collapse of the Agreed Framework in October 2002, suspicions grew about how and where North Korea might have started constructing facilities related to the uranium enrichment program. In 2002, the United States alleged that North Korea was violating the spirit, if not the letter, of the Agreed Framework, which had stipulated the freezing of its plutonium production capabilities at Yongbyon. This intelligence was not based on a specific site that had been discovered. Rather, North Korea had been persistently procuring specialized equipment in quantities great enough to allow U.S. intelligence agencies to assess, with a high level of confidence, that it was seeking an alternative path to the bomb by pursuing a uranium enrichment capability. The centrifuges had not started spinning at the time of the Agreed Framework's collapse, but Kim Jong Il had evinced a clear interest in indigenous uranium enrichment, as opposed to the plutonium production banned under the agreement.

By the time the American nuclear scientist Siegfried S. Hecker traveled to North Korea in November 2010, having taken up an invitation to view a fully assembled uranium enrichment plant at Yongbyon, much had changed. "Quite frankly, I was expecting not much, sort of a couple of dozen centrifuges," he later said. Instead, he had found a state-of-the-art facility at Yongbyon with six centrifuge cascades. Hecker's impression at the time was that this may not have been the North Koreans' first experience with such an enrichment plant. He remarked on the cleanliness and what struck him as the world-class nature of the Yongbyon facility. "We were also told that this facility was constructed and operated strictly with indigenous resources and talent," Hecker wrote in his report.[25]

Shortly after Hecker's visit, an unnamed South Korean intelligence official told the *Chosun Ilbo* newspaper that Washington and Seoul suspected as many as "three or four locations" in addition to Yongbyon as possible enrichment sites.[26] Today we know for certain that, starting in the early 2000s, North Korea had begun construction on at least two facilities now known to the U.S. intelligence community as covert uranium enrichment sites. The location of one remains unknown, but in 2018, a collaboration (of which I was part) between *The Diplomat* and a team of open source researchers from the Middlebury Institute of International Studies at Monterey publicly revealed the location of the other secret facility—a cluster of buildings known to U.S. intelligence as Kangson,[27] "first described by a North Korean defector."[28] A source with knowledge of U.S. intelligence assessments about North Korea's nuclear complex confirmed to me—along with coordinates—that this was the site the United States regarded with a high degree of confidence as a covert uranium enrichment site.

Starting in 2001 or very early 2002—around the time of North Korea's suspected serious investment in an alternative path to the bomb—construction teams broke ground at a nondescript compound, on the eastern limits of Chollima, a well-known industrial town named for the East Asian mythological equivalent of the Pegasus, a winged horse creature. Beginning in the era of Japanese colonial occupation, Chollima—then still known as Kangson—became home to a major steel mill complex.[29] In the years following the Korean War armistice in 1953, the Kangson Steel Works were identified as a post-war rehabilitative priority. In the late

1950s, Kim Il Sung called on the steelworkers to significantly increase their industrial output as part of his Chollima Movement, which called for a rapid period of economic modernization.[30] The workers responded with an efficiency that was subsequently mythologized: Kim "called on the workers of Kangson near Pyongyang to produce 10,000 tons more steel and in response they turned out 120,000 tons from a blooming mill with a supposed capacity of only 60,000 tons."[31] Those steelworkers at Kangson then became the heart and exemplar of the Chollima Movement, resulting in the renaming of the town itself, which retains its status as a prized industrial center to this day.[32] Kim Jong Il, recalling this history, may have chosen Kangson as the site of this covert enrichment site for symbolic reasons—perhaps hoping that a new generation of workers at Kangson might turn out miraculous quantities of highly enriched uranium!

Chollima is not far from the North Korean capital, Pyongyang. In fact, the covert enrichment site is just a little more than 5 kilometers away from the city's Mangyongdae neighborhood, which is mythologized in state propaganda as North Korean founder and Kim Jong Un's grandfather Kim Il Sung's birthplace. So, for more than a decade, North Korea has been enriching uranium in what is effectively a Pyongyang suburb, on the doorstep of Kim Il Sung's apocryphal birthplace. What's more, the entrance to the compound is hardly 1 kilometer off the expressway, which is accessible to foreigners and diplomats based in the capital. When the existence of the site finally became public in 2018, some experts were taken a back at this curious choice of location. A *Washington Post* report published earlier that year had incorrectly suggested the site was an underground facility,[33] presumably located as far as possible from existing road networks and nearly imperceptible to satellite imagery analysts but for a small opening in a mountainside. Many such sites do exist in North Korea and their purposes often remain shrouded in secrecy, but Kangson was not one of these. As a North Korean site of national defense importance, Kangson was hidden in plain sight—at least until 2018.

What was in some ways remarkable about Kangson is just how long it took for North Korea's secret to come out into the open. It is not clear when North Korea first broke ground on the site, but at least one satellite image taken in April 2002 shows a well-established foundation for the main enrichment hall, indicating that construction was well underway by that point. In 2018, a U.S. intelligence source noted that the United States "didn't suspect a nuclear role [for the Kangson facility] until 2010."[34] In other words, the U.S. assessments in 2002 that North Korea had broken with the spirit of the Agreed Framework's plutonium freeze, seeking a second path to the bomb, were not based on specific intelligence about this site. By 2007, when a new, Six-Party Talks agreement was concluded, the United States had discovered the construction at Kangson, but still did not know its purpose: the then chief U.S. intelligence officer for North Korea told Congress that there was "high confidence" within the U.S. intelligence community that North Korea had accumulated sufficient materials to pursue this second path to the bomb, but only "mid-confidence" that such a program actually existed.[35]

In hindsight, it was clear that the United States had a good idea of what North Korea was trying to do, but not where exactly it was doing it or how far it had got. South Korea was similarly in the dark, its lead negotiator in the Six-Party Talks commenting as late as 2009, "Nobody seems to believe that they have an enrichment plant up and running, but I cannot tell you how far North Korea's enrichment program has evolved."[36] All of this stood in sharp contrast to President Bush's confident declaration in November 2002 that North Korea had started enrichment: "contrary to an agreement they had with the United States, they're enriching uranium, with a desire of developing a weapon."[37] Bush is remembered today for bending American intelligence assessments to facilitate the disastrous invasion of Iraq in 2003, but the collapse of the Clinton-era Agreed Framework was similarly enabled by a dishonest portrayal of what the U.S. intelligence community was willing to commit to the page with high confidence. To this day, accounts of the collapse of the Agreed Framework disingenuously cite North Korea's pursuit of covert enrichment "activity," as if it had already started occurring by 2002.

Today, Kangson is easily visible to anyone with access to commercial satellite imagery. As you read, you might navigate to the coordinates 38°57'25.5"N 125°36'43.3"E to have a look yourself. What immediately jumps out is the single, large building at the center of the compound, with easily the largest square footage in the entire town of Chollima. Here we might expect North Korea to house its centrifuge cascades, which output highly enriched uranium suitable for use in nuclear weapons. The entire site, including the main hall, the long entryway road, and the associated support buildings, is surrounded by a one-kilometer-long perimeter wall; and there appears to be a cluster of residential multi-story buildings—all of which suggests that Kangson is a high-security area. The configuration of the site suggested it had a sensitive national defense role. Another notable feature of the site that highlights a probable special purpose is the existence of an obelisk and what appears to be a propaganda mural, both erected in the Kim Jong Il era—features commonly seen at important and sensitive military-industrial sites to commemorate received visits from the North Korean leadership. Our investigation actually found that the Kangson site was the sole large industrial facility in the Chollima that was *not* shown in regime propaganda to have received a visit from Kim Jong Il or Kim Jong Un, further highlighting its potential sensitivity.

As for Kangson's potential purpose, the investigative team identified satellite imagery from the winter months of December 2017 and January 2018, showing that while the surrounding area was covered in snow, including the rooftops of nearby buildings, the large main hall at Kangson was not, suggesting internal heat generation and year-round operations. One explanation could be multiple gas centrifuge cascades operating within, producing highly enriched uranium. The current U.S. assessment is that Kangson had likely first served as North Korea's first major centrifuge facility, allowing the country's nuclear scientists to experiment with initial gas centrifuge cascades before setting up the facility at Yongbyon, knowing that the latter would one day be shown to foreign scientists and offered up as a concession in international diplomacy.

After the 2002 collapse of the U.S.—North Korea Agreed Framework—over U.S. accusations of covert uranium enrichment—in January 2003, North Korea announced its withdrawal from the Nuclear Nonproliferation Treaty. Jump forward to the 2019 Trump–Kim summit in Hanoi, and the importance of Kangson in nuclear diplomacy was clear. That meeting ended without any deal, and Trump openly explained that the sites North Korea had offered were insufficient. When asked by a reporter whether the "second uranium enrichment plant" was something the United States wanted in addition to the facilities at Yongbyon, Trump responded "Exactly." U.S. Secretary of State Mike Pompeo added that even after dismantlement at Yongbyon, that "still [would leave] missiles, still leaves warheads and weapons systems."[38] A U.S. intelligence source told me at the time of reporting, meanwhile, that the latest U.S. estimates around July 2018 were that Kangson's output of highly enriched uranium was twice that of Yongbyon.[39] Even without Yongbyon, Kangson would output plenty of fissile material for nuclear weapons. With the establishment of Kangson, the first item on the

North Korean checklist for becoming a nuclear power—indigenous production of nuclear material—was in place.

North Korea's Six Nuclear Tests

With nuclear fuel production underway, North Korea turned to its next priority: the development of nuclear bombs themselves. To the outside world, North Korea's six nuclear tests between 2006 and 2017 were a reminder of Pyongyang's pariah status—it remains the only country to have detonated nuclear weapons for any purpose in the twenty-first century—but for Kim Jong Il and Kim Jong Un, the tests were a crucial demonstration of capability, bringing ever-closer the final objective of a perfected nuclear deterrent. Since the dawn of the nuclear age, nuclear testing has been carried out at more than sixty sites by nine countries—the vast majority of the more than 2,000 detonations having been conducted by the United States and the Soviet Union during the Cold War. France alone conducted more than 200 tests between 1960 and 1996. With the exception of North Korea, an informal global nuclear testing moratorium has been in place for more than two decades since Pakistan's final nuclear test in May 1998, shortly after India's own weaponized tests that same month. Such tests can be underground, atmospheric (detonation in the open air), outside the Earth's atmosphere, or underwater, depending on exactly what you want to study; and of course Hiroshima and Nagasaki provided unique information in 1945 on how nuclear weapons affect human beings and structures in real world use. North Korea opted to conduct all of its nuclear tests through 2017 underground.

Beginning in the early 1980s and through the early 2000s, North Korea conducted several dozen high explosives tests, initially at Yongbyon before moving to Punggye-ri for full-yield nuclear testing.[40] The aim of the initial tests at Yongbyon was thought to have been the development of the precise conventional explosives used as the trigger for certain kinds of nuclear weapons. The later Punggye-ri tests were likely related to implementing and developing the kind of seismic instrumentation that might be necessary to measure the eventual yield of nuclear tests, the first of which would come in 2006. Without the proper instrumentation and measurement, the scientific value of a nuclear test would be lost and all that North Korea would gain would be international opprobrium and economic sanctions. As a result, testing had to be careful, calibrated, and useful. October 2006 marked the first nuclear weapons test, and September 2017 saw the last to date, according to the regime a two-stage thermonuclear weapon test that generated the largest nuclear yield on Earth since 1992.[41]

Kim-1: October 9, 2006

By the first days of October 2006, North Korea was preparing to cross a point of no return. On October 3, Kim Jong Il's Ministry of Foreign Affairs issued a statement that immediately sparked concern around the world: "The DPRK will in the future conduct a nuclear test under the condition where safety is firmly guaranteed."[42] This was the first time North Korea had publicly stated its intention to carry out nuclear testing, the ultimate manifestation of the *physical* demonstration that had obsessed North Korean scientists up to that moment. *The New York Times* observed that "A successful test would confirm North Korea as the eighth declared nuclear power, following the steps of the United States, Russia, Britain, France, China, India and Pakistan."[43] At the time, U.S. and South Korean intelligence were agreed that Pyongyang had the capability to conduct a nuclear test if it so chose.[44] All that was needed was for Kim Jong Il to give the order.

The U.S. intelligence community had been watching North Korea make preparations at a site known as Punggye near a village in the country's northeast. Punggye had been known to American and South Korean intelligence for years; tunneling at the site had started in the late 1990s.[45] Now, cables were being delivered that the United States assessed would be used for instrumentation, monitoring, and data collection on an underground nuclear test. On October 9, 2006, at 10:35 a.m., a 4.2 magnitude seismic event occurred near the village. North Korea had conducted the first nuclear test of the twenty-first century, at what would come to be known as the Punggye-ri nuclear test site. The test was conducted underground, using the East Tunnel at the site. U.S. intelligence quickly concluded that the explosion at the Punggye-ri site had indeed been nuclear in nature, but was of a low yield of less than 1 kiloton (the target had been 4).[46]

The test seized global headlines and immediately sparked concern. The UN Security Council convened shortly after and set in place the bedrock resolution of the sanctions regime against Pyongyang that is still in place today: resolution 1718. Chinese reports said that Pyongyang had given officials in Beijing notice of the test just twenty minutes before it was to take place. There was great fear in Japan and South Korea that the test could have "vented" massive amounts of radioactive material into the atmosphere. While the United States did collect air samples with radioactive debris, authorities in the two Northeast Asian countries ultimately reported no signs of unusual radiation—but the fear had been very real.[47]

This first nuclear test of the twenty-first century appeared to have had a modest, but critical objective: to demonstrate North Korea's seriousness about becoming a nuclear power. Even though the yield of the test was low, this was a litmus test moment for the global nonproliferation regime: North Korea had just become the first country to have exited the NPT and tested a nuclear device. While official rhetoric around the world implied that a nuclear-armed North Korea would be intolerable, the test did not result in any retaliatory attack on Pyongyang. Such a reaction, of course, would have come with major costs. But, if there was a moment when the world deliberated and—perhaps subconsciously—determined that it could, in fact, tolerate or maybe even coexist with a nuclear North Korea, it came in October 2006. There was no going back now—for Pyongyang. Diplomatic efforts, however, continued.

Kim-2: May 25, 2009

In the years following the first nuclear test, the two Koreas had been coming closer together, with the second-ever inter-Korean leaders' summit in 2007 under progressive South Korean President Roh Moo-hyun,[48] and in 2008, North Korea had successfully disabled eleven sites identified as critical to its plutonium program. But the tide turned with two new arrivals in office: Kim Jong Il did not welcome the arrival of the Obama administration in 2009, nor the hardline Lee Myung-bak government that began in South Korea in 2008. Following the deterioration of the Six-Party Talks process later that year—especially after Kim suffered a stroke in August—North Korea hunkered down. The limited and hard-won diplomatic progress under the 2005 Six-Party declaration was crumbling. In January 2009, the month of Obama's inauguration, Pyongyang withdrew from all inter-Korean agreements concluded under the progressive Roh,[49] and in April, the International Atomic Energy Agency was evicted from North Korea; it has not since returned.

After all this, North Korea's decision to test a second nuclear device on May 25, 2009, was not entirely a surprise to U.S. officials, especially given that intelligence agencies had observed the maintenance and expansion of the Punggye-ri site after the first test in 2006.[50] While the first test had been either a fizzle or total failure, this new attempt in 2009 "helped satisfactorily settle the scientific and technological problems arising in further increasing the power of nuclear weapons and steadily developing nuclear technology," as KCNA claimed. North Korean scientists placed the device under Mount Mantap at Punggye-ri, using the site's North portal this time. The weapon was thought to be plutonium-based, and most experts presumed that North Korea had tested an implosion fission design this time, intending to use that as the basis of its warhead designs going forward. Kim Jong Il had likely not given orders to begin serially producing even a small number of nuclear warheads based on the unproven design tested in 2006.

International interpretations of this second test were divergent. By mid-June, the United States had assessed seismic data from the blast and gave the explosion yield as "approximately a few kilotons," while the early Russian estimate was the considerably higher 20 kilotons. Estimating underground explosive yields is a challenge, particularly without strong knowledge of the test site's geology or good assumptions about the depth at which the nuclear device was buried. In reality, the test successfully produced some 4 to 7 kilotons in nuclear yield. Political reasoning around the timing of the test also varied. The CIA suggested that Kim Jong Il, concerned about his health and age, wanted to see one more nuclear test before he died. Others simply saw it as North Korea's way of signaling the final nail in the coffin of the Six-Party Talks process.

Whatever the case, one thing was clear: Pyongyang was making progress toward the bomb. In 2012, after Kim Jong Il's death, the words "nuclear-armed state" were added into the preamble of the North Korean constitution.[51] The following year, the Workers' Party adopted a law codifying that nuclear status and identifying Kim Jong Un—the "Supreme Commander of the

Korean People's Army"—as the person with the power to issue an order for nuclear launch.

Kim-3: February 12, 2013

In the two years since Kim Jong Il's death, Kim Jong Un had scuttled a short-lived deal with the Obama administration and overseen two satellite launches in 2012. On January 24, 2013, after a new round of UN sanctions in response to the December 2012 satellite launch, the North Koreans made an official announcement of plans to conduct a nuclear test in the near future. A few minutes before noon local time on February 12— days before what would have been Kim's father's seventy-second birthday—Mount Mantap shook again, registering a magnitude 4.9 event on the U.S. Geological Survey's tracker. Kim Jong Un had ordered his first nuclear test, North Korea's third. This time the technicians had chosen the West Tunnel at Punggye-ri for the test, and the Korean Central News Agency (KCNA), the state news portal, claimed that the device was "miniaturized and lighter" in comparison with previous tests, and "did not pose any negative impact on the surrounding ecological environment," despite having "greater explosive force." The yield for this third test was generally estimated to have been in the range of 6 to 16 kilotons, clearly building on the 2009 results.

KCNA's statement criticized the United States and particularly Washington's refusal to accept a legitimate space program in the country—this had been a sticking point throughout 2012. As with the two previous tests, Kim's initiative that February met with widespread condemnation, including from the United States, Russia, and China. President Obama called for "further swift and credible action by the international community" against North Korea, and the test sparked the start of a broader period of U.S.— North Korea tensions that extended into March and April, when the United States and South Korea carried out joint exercises. At the same time, however, in April the U.S. postponed a planned intercontinental ballistic missile test amid concerns that North Korea would see it as provocative—even though the test was not set to occur anywhere near the Korean Peninsula.[52] The world was taking this nuclear testing campaign seriously.

Kim-4: January 6, 2016

At 10 a.m. local time on January 6, 2016, the U.S. Geological Survey recorded a shallow 5.1 magnitude tremor near the Punggye-ri site. Just as North Korea's third nuclear test had been timed around Kim Jong Il's birthday, Kim Jong Un conducted this fourth nuclear test just two days before his own—January 8. The yield did not appear to be far off from the third test, with most assessments placing the detonation's strength between 7 to 17 kilotons; the U.S. Air Force Technical Applications Center, or AFTAC, eventually settled on 13.[53] However, the test was not an empty gesture to mark a birthday. The North Koreans were making a very serious technical claim about their advancing nuclear capabilities. For the first time, they professed to have tested a "hydrogen bomb." The United States disputed the notion that this was a fully staged hydrogen bomb, but lacked important data in the form of radioactive debris; North Korea had apparently been successful in its bid to prevent the "venting" of the test site.

Once again, the world remained united in its criticism of the North Korean test. In the United States, it came amid heated Republican and Democratic presidential primary races, giving candidates in both parties a forum to opine on the Obama administration's management of North Korea. In South Korea, the test—combined with another satellite launch one month later—led to a significant measure to sanction the North: the closure of the Kaesong Industrial Park, an inter-Korean special administrative region on North Korean territory where South Korean firms leveraged cheap North Korean manufacturing labor. Seoul's ruling conservative government concluded that positive inducements needed to be pulled back to condition North Korean behavior. UN Security Council sanctions also followed. As for North Korea itself, its official statement on the test focused on deterrence, stating that the tested weapon would enhance Pyongyang's ability to hold at bay the United States, which was described as "the chieftain of aggression" and a "gang of cruel robbers."

The North Koreans also hinted at their drive for status on the international stage—long a secondary motivator for the nuclear program—with a state television broadcast declaring that the "complete success" of the test pushed North Korea into the "rank of advanced nuclear states." While few took the claim of a hydrogen bomb seriously at the time, successful testing of one would certainly justify such a boast—hydrogen bombs are only known to be available to the five NPT-recognized nuclear powers: the United States, Russia, China, France, and the United Kingdom. And Kim would offer more insight on this question in due time.

The 'Disco Ball', or Kim-5: September 9, 2016

The heightened pace of testing under Kim Jong Un had only escalated by 2016, the first year in North Korean history to see more than one nuclear weapons test. At 9:00 a.m. local time on September 9—the founding anniversary of North Korea—yet another nuclear device was detonated under Mount Mantap at Punggye-ri. The official political rationale offered for this double-whammy in one year was a protest against the sanctions that had followed the January test and the February satellite launch. The technical claims after this fifth test, however, were of greater interest to most analysts. For the first time, North Korea claimed to have tested a nuclear weapon design that was compact, standardized, and apparently suitable for mounting on ballistic missiles. If true, this would have marked the accomplishment of an objective for North Korean nuclear development dating back to the time of Kim's grandfather.

The test was not fully unanticipated; 2016 had marked an unprecedented flurry of ballistic missile testing, including several tests of the medium-range Hwasong-10, which was at the time the longest-range-capable ballistic missile ever flown by North Korea, as well as launches into Japan's exclusive economic zone. Kim Jong Un was stepping up his antics and provoking his neighbors and the United States. Meanwhile, reports from within the country as early as May 2016 had hinted at Workers' Party political planning for a possible fifth nuclear test.[54] The preceding summer, North Korea had strongly protested South Korea's decision to accede to deployment on its soil of the United States' THAAD missile defense system. Finally, the year's U.S.—South Korea Ulchi-Freedom Guardian joint military exercises had concluded a month earlier, in the first days of August. As in previous years, Pyongyang bristled at these exercises. Politically, the stage had been more than set for a demonstrative test to coincide with the sixty-eighth anniversary of North Korea's founding.

According to the North Korean release that followed, the test "finally examined and confirmed the structure and ... movement of a nuclear warhead that has been standardized to be able to be mounted on strategic ballistic rockets ... The standardization of the nuclear warhead will enable [North Korea] to produce at will and as many as it wants a variety of [such weapons.]" In other words, the North Koreans were indicating that the design tested was ready for mass production and operational use. This was no longer an experimental device, but a real weapon destined for the "strategic ballistic rockets of the Hwasong artillery units of the Strategic Force of the Korean People's Army." The sharp edge of North Korea's so-called treasured sword was being honed.

North Korea might have hoped that this would settle the years-old "miniaturization" debate raging in the United States about its nuclear capabilities. Without any real knowledge about the specific design choices for its fission bomb, based solely on knowledge of the country's ballistic missile technology, experts and laypeople alike felt confident in asserting that there was no way that North Korea's nuclear weapons engineers had crossed the all-important threshold of shrinking a nuclear weapon to the point where it could be accommodated by its known arsenal of ballistic missiles. Indeed, the task was not a trivial one. The earliest nuclear devices were almost comically large by the standards required to fit weapons within a ballistic missile warhead. The challenge is to create the lightest and most compact "physics package" possible—this Cold War military jargon describes the essential components that allow a nuclear weapon to function.

Slowly but surely, North Korea in the Kim Jong Un years had begun making claims about its progress on developing a compact warhead. This was part of Kim's years-long campaign of carefully polished propaganda directed at an external audience, to convey that the country was inching closer to its long-sought goal of a credible nuclear deterrent. Now, in September 2016, the regime claimed to have fulfilled this ambition. But what was the famous "standardized" miniature warhead? After the September test, the U.S. Geological Survey had registered a magnitude 5.3 seismic event, the highest of any North Korean test so far, and the explosive yield was also the largest yet, with most estimates measuring the explosive yield at somewhere between 15 and 30 kilotons. Beyond this, however, details about the precise type of weapon that had been detonated were concealed from U.S. intelligence: North Korea had successfully prevented any venting of radioactive material.

A clue had come earlier in the year on March 9, when KCNA released undated images that would instantly become iconic and shock the world. They showed Kim, surrounded by advisors, inspecting a shiny, metallic sphere. In one image, Kim had his left hand raised above the device—as if to bless it—and his right in his overcoat's pocket. With this carefully chosen outfit comprising a fur hat and a brown trench coat with a fur trim, the supreme leader had dressed to resemble his revered grandfather, Kim Il Sung. The choice to imitate his grandfather was fitting. Not only had Kim's choice of the *byungjin* strategic line borrowed from Kim Il Sung's policy guidance, but he had broken with his father's military-first policy to assert the central authority enjoyed by his grandfather by favoring the Workers' Party over the Korean People's Army in national affairs.

But the outfit was not what was important; it was the shiny object before Kim. The sphere's surface was covered in small circular reflective bits resembling compact disks. The object, per the state media report accompanying the images, was North Korea's standardized fission bomb. In an instant, Kim Jong Un had contributed a classic image to the annals of the second nuclear age. The headline was clear: "Kim Jong Un Guides Work for Mounting Nuclear Warheads on Ballistic Rockets." The object needed a name, and North Korea had declined to give it one. Western nuclear weapons analysts, always in the mood to inject dark moments with levity, agreed on a shorthand: the 'Disco Ball.' (A pedant might quibble that this was not a ball or a sphere at all; the shape was technically a chamfered icosahedron.)[55]

Though KCNA was dutiful in not revealing the Disco Ball's location, the released imagery and video footage gave away enough for open source researchers to pinpoint the site: the Chamjin Missile Factory, not far from Pyongyang. As is typical for these types of guidance visits, Kim was accompanied by a coterie of high-level Worker's Party functionaries and senior officers of the Korean People's Army Strategic Force. Present at the visit—but invisible in the pictures—was his younger sister, Kim Yo Jong, the deputy director of the Propaganda and Agitation Department. This indicated the momentousness of the occasion, and the point that this disco ball was intended for real ballistic missiles was underscored by the presence of three other important figures: General Kim Rak Gyom, the commander of the KPA Strategic Force and a mainstay at North Korean missile events; Hong Yong Chil, the deputy director of the Workers' Party Machine-Build Industry Department (MBID); and Hong Sung Mu, head of the department's Nuclear Bureau.

As if all this was not clear enough, North Korean media gave an explicit punchline: Kim had been there to hear about "research conducted to tip various type tactical and strategic ballistic missiles with nuclear warheads." He further "acquainted himself with the specifications and mechanism of the *miniaturized* powerful nuclear warheads." The pageantry of the event was grand and designed to allow even those observers outside the country without an eye for subtlety—or for the prose stylings of KCNA—a glimpse at what North Korea had achieved. In one shot, taken further away from Kim's position during the inspection of the mocked-up weapon, the reentry vehicle of a KN14/ Hwasong-13 mod 2 intercontinental-range ballistic missile was visible. Kim is then seen walking over from the mocked-up physics package to the missile's warhead. The sequence of images had a logic: *this* goes inside *that*. Also in view in KCNA's image release were what looked like guidance electronics and an arming, fuzing and firing system, all designed to communicate that this was credible.

Finally, the state media release carried Kim's own words underlining that, whether the United States liked it or not,

North Korea's march toward a real, missile-deliverable nuclear capability was inexorable. "We have a firm guarantee for making a breakthrough in the drive for economic construction and improving the people's standard of living on the basis of the powerful nuclear deterrent," Kim said, foreshadowing what would become the regime's standard line on its nuclear capability by 2018. "The [byungjin] line of simultaneously developing the two fronts is not a temporary counter-action for coping with the rapidly changing situation, but a strategic line to be permanently held fast to as long as the imperialists' nuclear threat and arbitrary practices persist." The unveiling of the Disco Ball had a clear message: Kim Jong Un now had the ultimate weapon, and he intended to keep it.

The exact date when North Korea mastered the design it was now showing off was unclear: in December 2017, low-resolution video footage of the 8th Conference of the Munitions Industry—a conference to celebrate the great accomplishments for Kim Jong Un's nuclear forces that year—would feature a large painting on a wall of Kim's father, who died in 2011, standing next to an apparently similar fission bomb design, with his hand outstretched over it in a similar manner to his son's in the Disco Ball pictures.[56] If the device tested in September 2016 was indeed the Disco Ball, then it was a good one, in design terms. But it would take until July 2017 for multiple U.S. intelligence agencies to agree with high confidence that this was the case; that North Korea's nuclear warheads had been successfully made compact enough to fit atop its ballistic missiles.

With the Disco Ball, then, Kim Jong Un had a tried and tested, standardized nuclear physics package, ready for serial production—another fundamental building block for North Korea's burgeoning nuclear force. The KCNA statement released after the test, attributed to the North Korean Nuclear Weapons Institute, concluded by issuing an ominous warning that the country would "take further measures to bolster the state nuclear force in quality and quantity for safeguarding its dignity." Sure enough, North Korea would soon follow through on this boast.

'The Peanut', or Kim-6: September 3, 2017

August 2017 was not a cheerful time for North Korea's relationship with the United States. First, Kim Jong Un had made a show of reviewing plans prepared for him by the KPA Strategic Rocket Force to launch four intermediate-range ballistic missiles into the waters around the U.S. territory of Guam. In response to that demonstration, U.S. President Donald J. Trump, speaking off the cuff, threatened Pyongyang with "fire and fury." At the same time, the United States and South Korea embarked on their annual late-summer computerized command post military exercise, Ulchi-Freedom Guardian. On August 28, Kim Jong Un oversaw and guided a Hwasong-12 launch that overflew Japan— marking the first time North Korea had launched a ballistic missile designed to carry a nuclear warhead over Japanese territory. Finally, in the early hours of September 3, 2017, KCNA dispatched photographs showing Kim Jong Un giving "guidance to nuclear weaponization." Kim was seen inspecting a peanut-shaped metallic device—an apparent thermonuclear weapon. He was in a well-lit room that had never previously been seen in any North Korean imagery, surrounded by civilian officials, including a former director of the Yongbyon Nuclear Research Center and a top figure from the Workers' Party Munitions Industry Department.[57] True to form for the Kim Jong Un era, scientists received great prominence in this propaganda event—but the star of the show was the object itself.

The peanut-shaped, "physics package" portion of the device sat on a set of green metallic supports as Kim pointed at it. Behind it, on a metal table, sat what appeared to be an arming and fuzing unit—the part of the weapon that would appropriately initiate a detonation. Just like the March 2016 photos of a mocked-up fission bomb, this was meant to be convincing. According to KCNA, Kim had been "greeted by senior officials of the Department of Munitions Industry ... and scientists of the Nuclear Weapons Institute" and given a briefing on their recent success "in making a more developed nuke, true to the strategic intention of the [Party] for bringing about a signal turn in nuclear weaponization."[58] The photograph and accompanying article were undated, as is practice for most North Korean reports on Kim Jong Un's activities. One U.S. intelligence analyst suggested that the image may have been taken in April 2017, when the United States had a high degree of expectation for the sixth North Korean nuclear test.[59] Whatever the date of the events, the report of them grabbed attention around the world on its release.

The significance of this release was immediately apparent: the North Koreans were claiming to have developed a two-stage thermonuclear weapon. If that was true, then Kim's ability to deliver nuclear payloads in the range of megatons to the United States could soon be in reach. This was precisely what the North Koreans sought to convey with this latest report. The North Koreans had made matters less-than-subtle in the photos of Kim's inspection visit: a reentry vehicle and apparent ICBM shroud were visible, as was a display board showing exactly how the nuclear device in front of Kim would be mounted. Once again, Kim was saying: This goes into that. Just days earlier, Gen. Paul Selva, the vice chairman of the U.S. Joint Chiefs of Staff, had issued a statement that North Korea still had not shown the "requisite technology and capability to actually target and strike the United States with a nuclear weapon."[60]

Within a few short hours of these images being released to the world, international seismic monitoring stations picked up a tremendous tremor emerging from the Punggye-ri nuclear test site.

The U.S. Geological Survey reported a magnitude 5.2 event initially, revising it upward to 6.3. That revision was unsettling: in the moment magnitude scale (a successor to the Richter scale), the difference between a 5.2 and a 6.3 event is vast. The Japan Meteorological Agency and the Russian Academy of Sciences also quickly concluded that a 6+ magnitude event had taken place. Whatever the North Koreans had detonated at Punggye-ri was apparently considerably more powerful than even the combined yield output of the first five nuclear tests put together. This was a massive explosion, in other words, and its effects could be seen from space: radar imagery before and after the test showed that Mount Mantap had measurably subsided after the blast.[61] The message was clear. Kim Jong Un had responded decisively to Trump's threat less than a month prior that North Korea would experience "fire and fury like the world has never seen" were he to continue his threats against the United States. The sixth North Korean nuclear detonation marked the largest explosion on Earth in some twenty-five years.

Like all its tests after the first, North Korea succeeded in preventing the venting of radioactive debris from this massive test. This meant that U.S. surveillance aircraft like the WC-135C Constant Phoenix were unable to gather information that would allow for insight into the design choices North Korea had made. It was possible that tritium and/or lithium-6 might have been incorporated into the device—isotopes useful in boosting nuclear weapons and making the use of weapons-grade nuclear fuel more efficient. For North Korea, producing and maintaining domestic stores of tritium and lithium-6 was not a trivial task. With a half-life of 12.9 years, Tritium decays, causing problems for the long-term storage and maintenance of nuclear weapons, for instance. These 'booster' isotopes are only a feature of advanced nuclear weapons designs, like the U.S. W88 warhead and are designed to improve efficiencies.

Research and development work around lithium-6, tritium, and other hydrogen isotopes is thought to have taken place in North Korea for decades—probably in the IRT-2000 research reactor. Experts believe that North Korea set up indigenous lithium-6 production facilities at the Hungnam Chemical Complex, on the country's east coast, including a research reactor.[62] Some analysts see this reactor as fully sufficient for North Korea's tritium needs today,[63] and the North Korean side at the Trump—Kim Hanoi summit in 2019 was reportedly shocked by U.S. demands for concessions on tritium production sites.[64] Ending indigenous tritium production would mean that, over time, it would be very difficult to maintain Kim's most advanced thermonuclear weapons to their original design specification—including the probable two-stage thermonuclear weapon that shook Mount Mantap in September 2017.[65]

While the sixth test represented a grave advancement in North Korean capabilities, Pyongyang made one final claim that appeared tailored for a very specific audience in the United States. The KCNA release declared that this new thermonuclear weapon was suitable for detonation "at high altitudes for superpowerful [electromagnetic pulse, or EMP] attack according to strategic goals."[66] That was likely an exaggeration intended to cause a panic in the United States, where a particularly determined and paranoid coterie remains concerned about secondary EMP effects from nuclear detonations. Given North Korea's acute warhead constraints, it would be highly unlikely that it would choose to expend a precious nuclear warhead in an actual conflict on a mere secondary effect like a high-altitude EMP burst. Pyongyang's strategic needs would be best met by ensuring a successful airburst nuclear detonation over an American city. But the sixth test's seismic signature was convincing enough to the outside world. Within days, U.S. intelligence analysis concluded that this was no ordinary fission weapon, but an "advanced nuclear device"—most likely a two-stage thermonuclear weapon, as the North Koreans had claimed.[67] With the knowledge acquired that day, the North could likely build even higher-yield nuclear weapons if it desired.

The September 2017 nuclear test of the "Peanut" came just a little more than two months after Kim Jong Un oversaw North Korea's first-ever ICBM flight test. The higher nuclear yield demonstrated in this sixth and, to date, final weapons test quickly changed the conversation about the precision requirements for his ballistic missiles. Given that Kim's strategic objective with his long-range missiles is to hold U.S. cities at risk, a larger nuclear yield can compensate for what would likely be poor accuracy and precision in the country's first-generation ICBMs. This was the most important testing milestone for North Korea—so much so that within eight months, in April 2018, Kim Jong Un announced a unilateral moratorium on nuclear testing and ordered the dismantlement of the Punggye-ri nuclear test site, declaring that his scientists and engineers had accrued sufficient design data over the six tests to complete a nuclear deterrent. The six tests were enough, as Kim would soon announce, and North Korea had the bomb.

The End of Testing?

In his April 2018 address, Kim proffered a set of directives on the future of nuclear and ballistic missile testing. Per state media's reporting of the speech:

> He said that no nuclear test and intermediate-range and inter-continental ballistic rocket test-fire are necessary for the DPRK now, given that the work for mounting nuclear warheads on ballistic rockets was finished as [were] the whole processes of developing nuclear weapons ... the mission of the northern nuclear test ground has thus come to an end. ... the discontinuance of the nuclear test is an important

process for the worldwide disarmament, and the DPRK will join the international desire and efforts for the total halt to the nuclear test. ... the DPRK will never use nuclear weapons nor transfer nuclear weapons or nuclear technology under any circumstances unless there are nuclear threat and nuclear provocation against the DPRK.

This resolution came at an opportune moment. Kim had declared his deterrent complete and was turning toward diplomacy with the United States and South Korea. Just seven days after delivering this message, he would meet with South Korean President Moon Jae-in for their first-ever summit meeting.

Announcing the end of nuclear testing was a low-cost, high-payoff gesture. Ahead of the Trump—Kim summit in June 2018, the North Korean leader made sure to follow up on his promise to dismantle Punggye-ri. Journalists were invited to witness the demolition, which U.S. intelligence quickly deemed would take a matter of weeks to reverse—the North Koreans had simply blown up the tunnel entrances with shallow explosions, while much of the underground tunnel network's infrastructure would remain in place.[68] One analyst noted also that it would have been fairly trivial for the North Koreans to preidentify a second candidate nuclear-testing site before offering up Punggye-ri; given how adept North Korean engineers had grown over the years at rapidly building tunnels and underground facilities, such a site could be constituted in a matter of months and prepared for use based on the experience gained over more than a decade of testing.[69] The State Department noted in August 2019 that "So far, the P'unggye Nuclear Test Site is the only *assessed* underground nuclear test site in North Korea,"[70] and we certainly cannot rule out an alternative future site in light of Kim's resolution referring to Punggye-ri as the "northern" test site.

Furthermore, full-yield tests like those detailed above—where the nuclear weapon package detonates as designed, producing the maximum release of energy—are not the only kind of nuclear test. Sub-critical tests are deliberately designed to validate aspects of a weapon's physical design *without* generating the full explosive yield, either by using substitute materials or by using fissile material at an insufficient level (below critical mass). In April 2018, the same month as his declaration of the nuclear testing moratorium, Kim Jong Un acknowledged sub-critical testing as a facet of North Korea's development work for the first time. Analysts of Kim's nuclear weapons program had already been assuming that Pyongyang had likely conducted such experiments, but Kim's choice to mention it at a particularly high-profile moment for his nuclear intentions—just as he announced the closure of the Punggye-ri site—may have shown particular intent for the future.

Such speculation in 2018 was accompanied throughout the year's diplomatic process by signs that Kim was not quite ready to let go of Punggye-ri, either. The North Koreans dangled an offer for some form of external verification at the site, only to pull it back U.S. National Security Council Senior Director for Asian Affairs Matthew Pottinger, on a conference call, told administration surrogates that: "Secretary [of State Mike] Pompeo and the South Korean government were both promised that experts would be invited to verify today's demolition and to do some advance work there."[71] In October 2018, when Pompeo returned to Pyongyang for a largely unproductive visit, the one major concession he walked out with was yet again a promise that inspectors would be allowed into Punggye-ri—in other words, something the United States had already obtained.[72] Inspector access at the site never took place; the Trump administration failed to make it a priority at his 2019 meetings with Kim. Access to the test site would have had limited value and the demolition was easily reversible, but Pyongyang could have used inspector access as a gesture of sincerity—it was telling that it chose not to do so.

In 2019, cracks began to appear in the moratorium on nuclear testing, raising the possibility that North Korea may choose to resume activity at its Punggye-ri test site should its interests demand so—especially if Kim deems that he needs small-diameter, low-yield nuclear weapons for use on short-range, tactical weapons, which would be very helpful for North Korea's aggressive, first-use-oriented nuclear strategy. To date, Pyongyang had not conducted any tests of a low-yield device. That determination appears to not yet have been made, but in August, as the United States and South Korea prepared to begin toned-down joint military exercises, the North Korean Ministry of Foreign Affairs warned that the 2018 moratorium was a measure of "goodwill and consideration for (sic) dialogue partner." That was a far cry from Kim Jong Un's original announcement that nuclear testing was no longer necessary for technical reasons. This Foreign Ministry statement was particularly concerning against the backdrop of a spate of testing for several new North Korean missiles and artillery systems that make promising candidates for battlefield nuclear weapons. Finally, after months of signalling that North Korea would take a hard line in its national policy going into 2020, in December 2019, Kim publicly announced that he was ending the moratorium.[73]

In other words, as early as 2019, the moratorium had appeared far from watertight and the only thing keeping it in place had been North Korea's own will; the moment that will dissipated, nuclear testing could resume with minimal refurbishment of the facilities at Punggye-ri. The signs point to the possibility of future development and testing of low-yield nuclear weapons designed to fit a package with a diameter as small as potentially 300 or 400 mm. Kim may well further sharpen his "treasured sword" in the years to come, but by the end of 2017, Pyongyang had conducted enough nuclear testing to be satisfied that it now had its bomb. But building the bomb is only half of the story when it comes to Kim Jong Un completing his deterrent. Parallel with this weapons development journey has been an equally significant feat: building the missiles to deliver them.

5

DETERRENCE CLOSE TO HOME

Having nuclear weapons would have been no use to Kim Jong Un without a means of delivering them. Over the course of Part Two, we will see how his country has endeavored to pass a series of 'missile milestones,' each one ticking off a specific set of targets on Pyongyang's list and each ranging further than the last. The start of this story takes us right back to the Kim Il Sung era, when North Korea first began its pursuit of short-range ballistic missiles that could threaten targets south of the 38th parallel.

Beginnings of a Missile Power

The fundamental building block of North Korea's missile force—and of its large-scale liquid-fueled rocket technology—was the Soviet Union's R-17 missile, better known by its NATO reporting name, Scud. The Scud is the most widely proliferated short-range ballistic missile worldwide and became particularly iconic during the Cold War. Moscow exported the Scud widely to a range of Warsaw Pact-aligned and nonaligned countries alike. For the first time, the Scud and its variants gave militaries an important capability to hurl conventional payloads further than ever before, without the use of aircraft. This ground-based missile saw widespread operational use during the Yom Kippur War, the Iran-Iraq War, the first Gulf War, the Afghan Civil War, the Chechen Wars, and the Libyan Civil War. More recently, variants of the Scud have seen use in the Yemeni Civil War and the Syrian Civil War. All in all, the Scud and its variants have seen the most operational use of any ballistic missile since Nazi Germany's V-2, the world's first guided ballistic missile.[1]

Not long after the Cuban Missile Crisis, Kim Il Sung had announced the parallel directive emphasizing simultaneous development of both the economy and self-reliant national defense. By the time North Korea established a Second Machine Industry Ministry in 1966,[2] U.S. tactical nuclear weapons had been present on South Korean soil for some eight years, helping balance South Korea's then military weakness against the North. Kim Il Sung "had probably made the political decision to establish an indigenous missile production capability after the Soviets rebuffed his request for ballistic missiles."[3] According to one account by a senior North Korean regime defector, delivered in a 1997 testimony before U.S. lawmakers, Kim also decided in 1965 to "develop rockets and missiles to hit U.S. forces inside Japan."[4] It was around this time, too, that the Soviet Union ramped up its delivery of shorter-range and tactical systems including surface-to-air missiles, coastal defense and anti-ship missiles, and unguided battlefield-range rocket artillery systems.

Kim Il Sung's strategic aspirations had coalesced around the value of a large ballistic missile force, and although North Korea's pathway to realizing and deploying such a force would take decades, this process was now underway. The Soviet artillery rockets were an important entry point into the world of surface-to-surface missiles. They were transferred under two agreements with the Soviet Union in 1965 and 1967, along with a handful of launch vehicles and associated support equipment, possibly in 1968.[5] This would turn out to be a particularly charged year between Pyongyang and Washington, as North Korean forces captured a U.S. Navy intelligence ship, the USS *Pueblo*, and its crew in the Sea of Japan. Fifteen years after the armistice that ended the Korean War, a resumption of full-scale hostilities was not outside the realm of possibility.

By the 1970s, however, North Korea's prospects for ballistic missile procurement were looking somewhat mixed. Following Khrushchev's departure from office and Leonid Brezhnev's ascent to the Soviet leadership, Soviet—North Korean relations soured. In the late 1960s, Brezhnev had counseled Kim Il Sung to moderate his provocations toward the United States—advice that was roundly ignored, as crystallized by the seizure of the *Pueblo*. Indeed, even earlier, Kim had regarded Soviet internal changes under Khrushchev, who had notably criticized Stalin's personality cult, as an implicit threat to the similar mode of governance he himself practiced in North Korea.[6] On the whole, Soviet—North Korean ties were cooler by the end of the 1960s, setting up a renewed period of North Korean outreach to China in the 1970s.

In September 1971—some ten years after the Sino—North Korean friendship treaty was signed and the same month that North and South Korea held the talks that would lead to their first ever joint statement in July 1972—China and North Korea concluded a military agreement for Beijing to sell Pyongyang a range of missiles it had reverse-engineered and some that it had designed. Many of these weapons remain in North Korea's arsenal to this day. The agreement also included provisions for North Korean scientists to become involved in the design and production of ballistic missiles themselves.[7] According to international security expert Daniel Pinkston, the agreement's real return on investment for North Korea, insofar as ballistic missile knowhow was concerned, came some years later, in 1977, when North

Korean "engineers participated in a joint development program for the DF-61 [Dong Feng 61]." The missile in question was a Chinese short-range, liquid-fueled ballistic missile, similar to a Soviet Scud-C in performance.[8] But, even with this cooperation and the special relationship with China, Beijing would ultimately provide little of note to North Korea. The Soviet Union was soon back in the picture.

The First Scuds

While we are still unclear on the details and exact timing of North Korea's first acquisition of Soviet-made Scuds, the generally accepted account since the 2000s is that it received a small batch from Egypt, who had procured them directly from Moscow.[9] North Korea has maintained a close, special relationship with Egypt for decades. The Scud transfer was a long-delayed payment of gratitude for North Korean assistance in the 1973 Yom Kippur War, when the Korean People's Army provided training for the Egyptian military in North Korea and sent around thirty pilots and technicians to Egypt.[10] North Korea had also exported arms to Egypt during the 1967 Six-Day War. The Scud delivery was a useful way for Cairo to maintain close ties with Pyongyang, and Egypt would remain a reliable partner for Kim Il Sung; it was only after his death in 1994 that Egypt granted diplomatic recognition to South Korea in 1995 and Seoul and Cairo exchanged ambassadors.[11]

This first shipment represented the primordial soup from whence North Korea's indigenous missile forces would emerge. The timing of the initial delivery is thought to have been in the late 1970s, but possibly as late as 1981 or even 1982. Ultimately, this would allow the proliferation story to come full circle: an August 2019 UN report suggested that Egypt was one of three countries, including Iran and Syria, where North Korean technicians were "establishing a complete supply chain" for the production of ballistic missiles far more advanced than the Scuds that came from Cairo during the Cold War.[12] This all began with the few Scuds that North Korea received from the Egyptians. They were enough—probably with considerable foreign technical assistance—to set up production lines for North Korea's first indigenous ballistic missile, the Hwasong (or Mars)-5.

On October 11, 1984, the U.S. National Photographic Interpretation Center, then the primary agency tasked with imagery intelligence analysis, put out an important assessment: for the first time, a "Scud (SS-1C) tactical surface-to-surface missile" was identified in North Korea, at a site on the east coast astride the Sea of Japan called "No Dong" by the U.S. intelligence community. The equipment in question was limited, but suggestive of the fact that North Korea had successfully procured at least one usable Scud. Also identified were what appeared to be a "partially canvas-covered/camouflaged" launch vehicle for the missile, procured from the Byelorussian Soviet Socialist Republic, and numerous other vehicles were present too—indicating possible preparations for a launch. It is suspected that the first tests of the Hwasong-5 took place in early 1984, with the missile reported to have flown to around 300 to 320 kilometers.[13]

Four years later, a September 1988 U.S. National Intelligence Estimate listed North Korea among "at least 15 developing countries" that would have an ability to produce or build ballistic missiles. (The rest were Argentina, Brazil, Egypt, India, Indonesia, Iran, Iraq, Israel, Libya, Pakistan, South Africa, South Korea, Syria, and Taiwan.) It added that while North Korea had started manufacturing missiles based on "foreign designs," its program would not be significantly affected should foreign assistance from the Soviet Union or China decrease. However, the report reassured that there would be limited military utility to these initially developed ballistic missiles in North Korea and other developing countries, making the prescient observation that accuracy would be a great challenge—guidance, control and eventually reentry for longer-range missiles would indeed take North Korea decades to address.[14] Critically, while the report observed that ballistic missiles could destabilize the military balance across a range of regions, it did not express particular concern about the situation on the Korean Peninsula. Instead, the greatest areas of concern at the time were in the Middle East and in South Asia. The CIA had identified something of an arms race throughout the 1980s on the Indian subcontinent, with both India and Pakistan covertly racing to weaponize their nuclear capabilities.

Yet, on May 18, 1989, William H. Webster, then the director of the CIA, testified to the U.S. Congress that North Korea had started to serially produce the Scud-B ballistic missile, making the fact public and amplifying concerns in the early 1990s about Pyongyang's pursuit of a plutonium path to a nuclear weapon. By the mid-1990s, North Korea's ballistic missile proficiency and industrial capacity had grown considerably. A 1997 U.S. intelligence assessment noted that the country had "progressed from producing Scud missiles to establishing a broad-based missile industry, developing and producing a variety of missiles both for its own use and for export."[15] The assessment added that these missiles were capable of carrying weapons of mass destruction, and that several longer-range systems, some based on Scud technologies, were also under development. All this was being observed more than two years into implementation of the 1994 Agreed Framework, which had curtailed North Korea's plutonium path to the bomb, but had not addressed other topics, including ballistic missiles. At the time, the primary U.S. concern over North Korean missiles was not their use for a domestic nuclear program, but their proliferation; Pyongyang exported or attempted to export Scuds and other missiles to at least eight countries, including Egypt, Iraq, Syria, Libya, Yemen, Iran, the United Arab Emirates, and Pakistan.[16]

By the mid-2000s, North Korean missile proliferation activity had decreased, due to a range of factors including external forces and a shift in Pyongyang's priorities. However, in December 2002, two months after the United States had initiated Operation Enduring Freedom–Horn of Africa, its NATO ally Spain received an apparently routine request for assistance in the eastern Indian Ocean, near the mouth of the Gulf of Aden. An unflagged freighter had drawn the attention of U.S. military intelligence in the region. The United States had reason to believe that the vessel was involved in arms trafficking near NATO-monitored waters. The Spanish Navy, with the assistance of aerial surveillance, managed to identify the vessel. It turned out to be part of the coalition's database of suspicious ships and was identifiable as the North Korean *So San*. After its interception, fifteen Scuds were found on board, with the presumption that they were bound for Yemen. The *So San* incident, among others, sparked the creation of the U.S.-led international Proliferation Security Initiative, a multilateral effort to interdict shipments of missiles and weapons of mass destruction.[17] By the Kim Jong Un era, North Korean proliferation practices had moved away from shipping wholesale systems overseas to largely providing some old partners—notably Syria and Iran—with access to knowhow and technical assistance on ballistic missiles and even chemical weapons. In the Syrian case, as we saw in the previous chapter, North Korean technicians were even involved with efforts to set up a Yongbyon-like nuclear reactor.

The Limitations of North Korea's First Short-Range Missiles

Today, North Korea's large arsenal of short-range ballistic missiles remains in place, but their military utility on the Korean Peninsula likely remains limited, especially in terms of what they add to Pyongyang's ability to deter an all-out attack, given its expansive conventional long-range artillery and multiple rocket launch systems. In particular, U.S. and South Korean missile defense technology against short-range missiles like the Scud or Hwasong-5 has come a long way since Pyongyang first dispersed them across the southern reaches of the country in the 1990s. Back then, the American Patriot missile defense systems in Israel famously failed to intercept any of Iraq's own variant of the Scud. North Korea would have ways of getting around the limitations of these missiles.[18]

Even today, however, a simple solution to advanced missile defense is for North Korea to win the "numbers game," mastering simultaneous salvo-style launches and thus saturating the ability of allied battle management software to cope with multiple missile targets at once. Salvo tests took place in March and July 2016, demonstrating synchronicity between multiple missile launch crews across as many as three launch vehicles. In March 2017, Kim Jong Un oversaw a salvo test launch coordinated between five extended-range Scud launch vehicles.[19] This was the first time the North Koreans had used an auto control system to coordinate launches.[20] In wartime, the Korean People's Army might attempt multiple such salvos from several launch sites, presenting a serious challenge to South Korea-based missile defense systems.

Even with this rebuttal to missile defense, Scuds or their North Korean equivalents were only ever going to be a first stepping stone for Pyongyang on the path to more advanced missiles. Scuds, by their very nature, require a preparatory period before they can be used. At North Korea's missile operating bases—all of which would be under heavy scrutiny by U.S. space-based assets in the lead-up to a conflict, or during a major crisis—units would have to load missiles on to their road-mobile launchers, disperse the launchers sufficiently to avoid destruction of multiple launchers in any counter-battery barrages or stealth fighter strikes by the enemy, fuel the missiles once in place, mount nuclear warheads where available, and then launch. The "transaction costs" of actually using Scuds in a conflict are not cheap for North Korea and the window for South Korea or the United States to destroy them before launch is obvious.

To make matters worse, Kim Jong Un possesses more missiles than he does transporter-erector-launchers, incurring a further time penalty during reloading and exposing the missiles to enemy detection due to the presence of support vehicles required to fuel a liquid-propellant missile in the field. The KPA has therefore likely chosen another option for operating Scuds in wartime: leaving them fueled in storage (possibly for as long as a year), which cuts down the wait between flushing out and firing missiles. But this comes with problems too: rolling missiles out of their operating bases fully fueled is risky if the liquid rocket propellants (such as kerosene fuel) have been poorly maintained—and the North Korean nuclear program is known to have laxer standards in peacetime. Premature combustion of the missile's fuel could cause a major accident, with the launch vehicle, missile, and possibly crew lost in a fiery explosion.

Even if we overlook these obstacles and assume that North Korea manages to launch large numbers of Scuds, the military utility of these older missiles is most seriously limited by their imprecision and inaccuracy. This is illustrated by the historical experience of countries that have used them in battle. A 1993 independent analysis of Iraqi Scud use during the first Gulf War against targets in Israel and Saudi Arabia found that damage was relatively limited due to the missile's inaccuracy, a high "dud rate" (roughly 10 per cent warheads failing to detonate), and the ability of U.S. satellites to offer post-launch warnings, allowing civilians to take shelter. Missile defenses played a marginal role, if any, and the Israeli and Saudi civilians who faced the wrath of Iraqi Scuds mostly got lucky: the missiles either missed any useful targets, or the civilians had ample warning time to take cover. "The widely held belief that ballistic missiles are themselves weapons of mass destruction is simply incorrect, as demonstrated by this as well as past episodes," the authors concluded.[21]

This is an important observation. Missiles—particularly less precise ones—require powerful warheads and precision to serve reliably as lethal weapons. This has been demonstrated recently by the Houthi movement in Yemen, which has been using short-range ballistic missiles against a variety of Saudi targets since 2015, hitting little of note due to the low precision of these missiles. But increased precision can make conventional missiles deadly and damaging; Iran's strike against Iraq's Al-Asad Air Base in January 2020 used precise conventional ballistic missiles, successfully destroying several important base facilities and injuring more than fifty U.S. personnel, who suffered traumatic brain injuries associated with the blasts.[22]

Launching unsophisticated, short-range ballistic missiles is a roll of the dice, and there is simply no way to reliably use a Scud as a precision tool in warfare. Its best use from Pyongyang's perspective would be against densely packed urban areas in South Korea, hoping to inflict damage against civilian populations in an effort to cause South Korea and the United States to stand down. Here Scuds could deliver high explosive and even chemical or biological payloads to terrorize urban populations. But so long as Pyongyang's stock of warheads remains relatively limited, we can assume that most would be preserved for arming the more critical, longer-range missiles designed to reach U.S. regional bases and the U.S. homeland. Few would be left over for short-range units.

Modernization in North Korea: Beyond the Scud

None of these many limitations of the Scud would have been unknown to North Korean engineers and military planners. But by the 2000s, North Korea was an experienced operator and producer of these short-range, liquid-fueled missiles—not to mention a proliferator and marketer. Such is the country's expertise under Kim Jong Un that he has begun turning its attention toward improving their suitability for military campaigns on the Korean Peninsula. The fruits of these efforts have been a second, more precise generation of indigenously modified North Korean Scuds, and other short-range missiles.

At a military parade in April 2017, North Korea showed off a new variant of its Hwasong-6, appearing on a new launcher chassis that bore almost no resemblance to the launch vehicles previously seen in North Korea. For analysts watching the parade live through North Korea's Korean Central Television feed, it was quickly apparent that this was no ordinary old Hwasong-5 or Hwasong-6, both of which had made several parade appearances in the past. This new missile was a redesign, evoking precision and aerodynamic maneuverability, an upgrade of an earlier attempt at a redesign that was abandoned in 2014.[23] A little more than a month later, this new "ultra-precision" missile would see action, as Kim Jong Un supervised its first test at the end of May 2017.

The missile, launched from the new and improved integrated launch vehicle, was said by state media to contain a "precision control guidance system" and to have a "markedly" shorter "launching time." It flew to a range of 450 kilometers, according to South Korea's Joint Chiefs of Staff, and splashed down in the disputed exclusive economic zone around the Liancourt Rocks, administered by South Korea as Dokdo and claimed by Japan as Takeshima. This became a brief point of contention between Seoul and Tokyo as Japan's Chief Cabinet Secretary Yoshihide Suga quickly issued a statement claiming that North Korea had launched a missile into Japan's EEZ. Disputed territory aside, with its first outing this modernized Scud had already addressed two of the main shortcomings of its Cold War predecessors: greater precision and higher survivability.

The official North Korean claim about the precision performance of the new modernized Scud was impressive, but likely exaggerated—especially given the inability of North Korean ground crews to precisely observe and measure the missile's final warhead impact, landing as it did in non-North Korean waters.[24] The timing of the test was significant, however: Kim Jong Un had demonstrated this new modernized Scud just weeks after the first U.S. THAAD missile defense battery had arrived in South Korea. THAAD, unlike many other such systems, has a robust record of testing successes, and is well suited to defend against short-range ballistic missiles like the Scud in the terminal phase of their flight, such as in cases when the warheads have descended toward their targets. This makes improving short-range missile maneuverability even more important for Kim; the state news agency KCNA has referred to testing for the "feature of evading interception."

Efforts to modify and improve Scuds continued through the summer of 2017, with three short-range ballistic missiles launched on August 26 (the second exploded in flight). U.S. intelligence quickly assessed that these were a new type of North Korean missile: more maneuverable variants of the Hwasong-5, North Korea's oldest ballistic missile.[25] Even if the performance of these newly modernized Scuds was imperfect, the overall trajectory of North Korean arms development was clear: an ongoing modernization effort to render the short-range ballistic arsenal militarily useful was underway. Scuds were not the only focus of this program.

* * *

In mid-January 2018, as North and South Korea were laying the groundwork for a year of diplomacy, U.S. intelligence detected North Korean telemetry checks out of a facility on the country's east coast, likely for a new missile.[26] On February 8, one day before the opening of the PyeongChang Winter Olympic Games in South Korea, Kim Jong Un held another military parade. This was effectively a celebration of the end of his *byungjin* missile testing campaign, following his triumphant New Year's Day announcement that the nuclear deterrent was complete. In addition to the mock-ups of its first flight-tested ICBMs (see Chapter Eight), another new arrival in North Korea's arsenal made its first public appearance that day, and it raised eyebrows immediately. There, rolling through Kim Il Sung Square atop a launch vehicle, were multiple missiles that closely resembled the Russian short-range Iskander-M—a ballistic missile system feared by NATO countries for its impressive precision, ability to evade radar, and dual conventional/nuclear payload capabilities.[27]

Had it not been for the positive inter-Korean diplomatic trajectory in the lead-up to the Winter Olympics, the new missile could have seen its first test that February. But months passed without another glimpse of it as North Korea chose to maintain a low profile during Kim Jong Un's whirlwind year of diplomacy. With the exception of an unpublicized conventional "tactical" weapons test in November 2018—possibly to test how Washington would react to renewed testing amid diplomatic efforts[28]—Kim kept his fingers off the testing trigger. That restraint ended not long after the disappointing outcome at the Hanoi summit in February 2019, where Kim asked for sanctions relief and was refused by Trump. In April came what North Korea called, without elaborating, a "tactical weapons test", and on the morning of May 4, an alert went out from the South Korean Joint Chiefs of Staff that North Korea had launched a short-range ballistic missile. This ended the 522-day testing hiatus, the longest to date in the Kim Jong Un era.

The next day, the North Korean party newspaper referred to this new weapon only as a "tactical guided weapon"—North

Korea did not offer up a new Hwasong designation publicly.[29] This phrase, "tactical guided weapon", had been used in the past to describe testing of a short-range ballistic missile called the Toksa, the North Korean variant of the Soviet Tochka, which had been in North Korea's possession since at least the early 1990s; Toksa testing and engine manufacture had begun in the mid-2000s, under Kim Jong Il.[30] The repeat of this language in May 2019 strongly implied that the new missile was a modernized Toksa. As far back as March 2007, the then commander of U.S. Forces Korea had testified to the House Armed Services Committee that the Toksa "can be deployed more flexibly and rapidly than the existing system ... in a much shorter preparation period."[31] Testing of the original Toksa, which circumvented the 1999 Berlin Agreement's moratorium on long-range missile testing, had allowed North Korea to get its feet wet in the world of guided solid-fueled missiles. In theory, solid-fueled missiles are usable as field commanders need them, without the time loss and vulnerability of fueling at launch that hamper the Scud and the Hwasong-5, because solid-propellant missiles have their fuel cast into the airframe casing at the time of manufacture. Unsurprisingly, they have become a major focus in Kim Jong Un's continued development of North Korea's nuclear forces.

The official Party newspaper reported Kim's satisfaction with the May 4, 2019 test flight, with an emphasis on the promptness of operations and the demonstration of "fire readiness." The crews had been asked to conduct the exercise seemingly at the drop of a hat by Kim Jong Un, who expressed "great satisfaction with the rapid response ability" they had demonstrated. Just days later, Kim would repeat this trick from the other side of the country. On May 9, North Korea once again carried out a long-range artillery drill, and yet again launched two of the apparent Toksa successors, with one flying to 420 kilometers. The missiles had been launched from near the city of Kusong in an easterly direction, overflying much of North Korea on their way to the Sea of Japan. The launches were reported to have taken place ten minutes apart from each other, likely from the same launch vehicle. This matched what had been seen at the February 2018 parade, which had shown the system with two missiles side-by-side on the launch vehicle.

Down to its deep forest green color, the modernized Toksa's similarities to the Russian Iskander-M jumped out to numerous analysts, some of whom suggested that the most likely explanation for the sudden appearance of this new short-range missile was proliferation activity by Russian entities or individuals—likely without official sanction from Moscow. That remains a hypothesis: U.S. intelligence did not have a definite assessment of the missile's provenance after its public debut at the parade, leaving open the possibility that it was largely indigenous.[32] This would suggest considerable growth in North Korea's indigenous solid fuel production infrastructure, in the Hamhung-Hungnam area along the country's east coast. But the modernized Toksa's early successes and perfect flight record across seven initial tests raised questions about how exactly Pyongyang had pulled this off. For instance, developing an airframe to fly and maneuver at the hypersonic speeds exhibited by these test flights would be difficult without a hypersonic wind tunnel. North Korea is not known to possess a facility like this.

The new missile's resemblance to the Iskander went beyond performance-related choices. It seemed to have been designed with the express intention of conveying to outside observers: *Yes, you should think of Russia's highly precise Iskander missile when you look at this new weapon we have just introduced—and yes, it is a modernization of our older Toksa.* The similarities did not go unnoticed by South Korea and the U.S. as further test flights were carried out in 2019.[33] North Korea released images of a test conducted that August showing one of the missiles striking a target island off the country's east coast. The missile could be seen glowing red from apparent aerodynamic heating. The image, apparently taken from a drone, was meant to underscore the precision that Pyongyang had achieved with the modernized Toksa: this missile did not just look like an Iskander, it largely performed like one too. Official South Korean data on the missile's flight performance said that it flew at speeds of Mach 6.9—or 6.9 times the speed of sound—while within the earth's atmosphere.[34]

Given these observations, the KN23, as it was dubbed by U.S. intelligence, is more than a simple iterative modernization of the old Toksa. To go by the images North Korea released, and the assessments of South Korean and official U.S. sources, it represents a serious battlefield capability. First, the KN23 has continued a trend of the Kim Jong Un era: solid-propellant missiles capable of delivering a large payload at significant range. It has been shown to fly under certain conditions to 600 kilometers, further than the officially stated range of the Russian Iskander, which was nominally designed to be compliant with the range restrictions of the Intermediate-Range Nuclear Forces Treaty—a 1987 arms agreement that prohibited Moscow and Washington from possessing ground-launched cruise and ballistic missiles with ranges between 500 and 5,500 kilometers.

This North Korean improvement on the Soviet Iskander's range has important implications. The KN23 may have carried a conventional payload in 2019, and all official North Korean state media coverage has been careful to omit any hint of a nuclear capability, but U.S. assessments have suggested that it could in the future be modified to serve as a nuclear delivery platform for targets based on the Korean Peninsula.[35] Given that Pyongyang never acknowledged the departure of U.S. tactical nuclear weapons from South Korea in December 1991, if it chose to nuclearize the KN23, it could seek to justify this based on the pretense of a tit-for-tat deployment. One piece of evidence supporting this possibility is the fact that the KN23 made its debut in the February 2018 military parade, where Kim showed off his most threatening nuclear missiles to date, but it did not appear in a further parade that September, which only featured conventional weapons systems.

North Korea's lack of boasts about a nuclear future for the KN23 are not a source of reassurance on this matter: after all, without a formal acknowledgement from Kim that the 2018 diplomatic process was over, threatening the South with nuclear attack would have been overly aggressive—certainly disproportionate if the test was primarily designed to punish Seoul and Washington for their resumed springtime military exercises. This may even have been the reason for the exclusion of the nuclear arsenal from the parade that September, a time when Kim was hosting senior foreign dignitaries for North Korea's seventieth founding anniversary, and was about to enter into a third summit with South Korean President Moon. Weeks before the first KN23 test in April 2019, Kim had been given the expansive title of "supreme representative of all the Korean people."[36] Following that designation up with a nuclear threat to the *minjok* (Korean people), the majority of whom live south of the Military Demarcation Line, would have been unwise.

North Korea's intentions for the KN23 are ambiguous, but even short of nuclearization, the missile presents a formidable challenge to U.S. and South Korean defense planners. Its inauguration fills a gap in Pyongyang's arsenal, being Kim's first responsive, short-range, precise weapon, capable of delivering large conventional payloads to ranges between 200 and 500 kilometers. This is very significant given what North Korea is up against. In April 2017 South Korea had tested a new extended-range variant of its own Hyunmoo-2 short-range ballistic missile, with a range of 800 kilometers.[37] This was an important capability for South Korea that would enable retaliatory precision strikes on North Korean targets under the Korea Massive Punishment and Retaliation plan, should Pyongyang initiate an attack. Those 800 kilometers would allow the South Korean launchers to keep out of range of North Korean artillery. This enhanced Hyunmoo-2C is also envisioned to play a role in South Korea's Kill Chain strategy, whereby ballistic missile units would rapidly mobilize in the event of a North Korean mobilization for an invasion or a strike.

North Korea's 2019 unveiling of an apparent new generation of solid-fueled missiles and rockets were a new stress on the missile defense capabilities of South Korea and the United States. We have already seen that, in 2016 and 2017, Pyongyang had bristled at the arrival on South Korean territory of the U.S.-operated THAAD missile defense system, which was deployed on a golf course in Seongju county despite South Korean public resistance. But THAAD had been introduced to the Korean Peninsula precisely in response to growing concerns about Kim Jong Un's short- and medium-range ballistic missile capabilities. The 2019 introduction of the KN23 and two multiple rocket launch systems was a serious advance far beyond anything the old Scuds had to offer. The quasi-ballistic KN23 flies too low for any available missile interceptors, including THAAD, to intercept it easily.

Making matters worse, this low-flying altitude seemed to allow the new systems to evade detection from Seoul, which relies on ground- and sea-based sensors to track North Korean missile launches (unlike the U.S., which has space-based missile detection assets). For years—and certainly through Kim Jong Un's intense missile testing in 2016–17—the South Korean Joint Chiefs of Staff immediately announced detected launches, which would then promptly be reported to the world by the dominant Yonhap News Agency. But on July 31, 2019, when Kim conducted the inaugural launch of a new multiple rocket launch system, the first reports came from the United States. It would be hours before the South Korean side reported the launch—suggesting that Seoul's sensors had missed it entirely. Within weeks, a statement attributed to South Korea's director-general of American affairs pointed out that Seoul had become a "global laughing stock" because it had "failed to calculate properly the range of the power demonstration firing of our army."[38] Though many of these low-flying launches were incapable of ranging Japanese territory, Tokyo's land- and sea-based sensors had the same trouble tracking some of them.[39]

In 2017, Kim Jong Un's inaugural test of his clumsily modernized Hwasong-6 constituted a lackluster tit-for-tat. South Korea's solid-fuel Hyunmoo-2C was a much more impressive missile. But where the Hwasong-6 fell short, the KN23 does not. While the newer missile's launch system resembles the Russian Iskander, the missile itself appears externally similar to the Hyunmoo-2 series. This led one analyst to humorously dub the KN23 the 'Hyunmoo-too': a sign from Kim to South Korea that Pyongyang could keep up in a peninsular missile race.[40] The resemblance was indeed noted in South Korea, where at least one conservative lawmaker demanded answers from the Moon government regarding the possibility that North Korea had stolen design schematics from South Korea's Agency for Defense Development. After the KN23's inaugural appearance at the February 2018 military parade, Rep. Chung Jin-suk of the conservative Liberty Korea Party expressed outrage to then South Korean Defense Minister Song Young-moo that "Our Hyunmoo missile appeared at the center of North Korea's military parade."[41] "It is like North Korea introducing an advanced version of Hyunmoo missile and holding a military parade to mock us," he added.

Even if Rep. Chung's insinuation of design theft was not borne out by any evidence, his analysis of the message being sent was apt. This "keeping up with the Joneses" dynamic to Kim's missile modernization was further underscored by yet another new short-range, solid-fuel missile first tested in August 2019, this time bearing a strong resemblance to the United States' MGM-140 system. It just so happened that the MGM-140 and the Hyunmoo-2 had both been deployed by the United States and South Korea in 2017 when they conducted rapid response drills to North Korean missile launches. Just two years later, Kim Jong Un was sending a warning of his own: Pyongyang's short-range missile modernization is rapidly narrowing the performance gap.

Ranging Beyond the Peninsula

Concurrent with North Korea's work on short-range missiles pointed at South Korea, the country has also been honing the ability to reach other targets close to home: notably, Japan and U.S. air bases in and around the region. From the late years of Kim Il Sung's rule, engineering attention was turned toward developing intermediate-range ballistic missiles that could carry a large payload of at least 1,000 to 1,500 kilograms. It would take North Korea a long time to get there, until Kim Jong Un's triumphant test flights in 2017, but he could not have crossed the finishing line without building upon earlier development efforts under his father and grandfather.

In May 1990, U.S. satellites detected an interesting development at the closely-watched missile base at Musudan-ri, in northeastern North Korea. Evidence of a large explosion was apparent on a known launch area that now bore a 'scar.' Whatever the device being tested was, it was probably not just a simple Scud. Indeed, it was North Korea's first medium-range surface-to-surface ballistic missile, which would come to be known as the Nodong-1.[42]

Simply put, the Nodong was a perplexing missile. One of the biggest puzzles was just how sparse its flight-testing was before

North Korea began selling the thing to interested customers—notably Iran, Pakistan, and Syria.[43] To this day, this is a sharp source of divergence among researchers and analysts, informing their fundamental assumptions about North Korea's expertise and domestic production capabilities. One prominent theory, which continues to receive credence, was that this was not the first major homebrewed North Korean missile design at all, but a previously unknown Soviet-era design that had never found its way from the drawing board to the production lines during the Cold War. Pyongyang could not have developed the missile itself, because, if that were the case, where were the hundreds of engine tests and scores of flight tests that the Soviet Union or other nuclear states would have conducted before going public?[44] For a handful of Western rocket scientists who operate their analysis on this basis, not only the Nodong, but even the missiles developed under Kim Jong Un, can only have been achieved with considerable foreign assistance.

Another hypothesis, the one now preferred by U.S. intelligence, is that the Nodong was not the result of one-way foreign assistance, but of partnership, most likely with Iran and Pakistan: scientists of the three countries sharing testing and development information. U.S. assessments suggested that this outsourcing would reduce pressure on North Korea internally. According to *The Telegraph*, Iran may even have conducted a surrogate test of another North Korean intermediate-range missile before it had ever been flight tested in North Korea itself.[45] It can certainly be said that the Nodong enjoys an extensive and infamous international profile. In the 1990s, it sat atop a family of proliferated missiles based on its basic design: the Shahab-3 and Ghadr-110 missiles in Iran, as well as the Ghauri-I and Ghauri-II in Pakistan. These missiles were not *exactly* the Nodong, but bore a strong resemblance.

In the 1990s, the Nodong was the largest known North Korean ballistic missile, and the most promising candidate yet for a nuclear delivery role should the country construct a handful of nuclear warheads. It is no longer a prominent fixture in North Korea's missile arsenal, given the development and production of far more capable systems under Kim Jong Un, but it marked an important milestone, as Pyongyang's first attempt at an intermediate-range ballistic missile that could threaten regional targets. Before North Korea could think about holding the continental United States at risk, it had long set its eyes on a closer prize. The U.S. territory of Guam, the largest island of the Mariana archipelago, vexed Pyongyang like little else in the Pacific Ocean. Guam was home to Andersen, a major USAF strategic bomber base. The bombers responsible for the August 1945 nuclear attacks on Hiroshima and Nagasaki had taken off from another island in the Northern Marianas. Though the United States would not launch nuclear-armed cruise missiles at North Korea from Guam's bombers out of the blue, Pyongyang's planning has to consider this scenario. Under Kim Jong Un, the Korean Central News Agency has evocatively described these bomber planes as the "air pirates of Guam."

Guam's distance from North Korean territory would pose a challenge for Pyongyang, however. Guam was more than 3,000 kilometers from North Korean soil. Getting there would require a ballistic missile more capable than anything North Korea had tested through the 1990s and 2000s. In the 1990s (and right into the Kim Jong Un era), the answer looked like it might be the Hwasong-10—the North Korean variant of a Soviet liquid-fueled missile in North Korea's possession, known as the R-27 Zyb.

* * *

In 1992, a group of Russian men—somewhere between fifty and sixty of them—were apprehended at Moscow's Sheremetyevo international airport. They were all missile scientists and technicians with a common resumé line at V.P. Makayev OKB, the former Soviet Union's major submarine-launched ballistic missile bureau, which had produced the original R-27 Zyb SLBM.[46] They had been bound for North Korea, likely to engage in mercenary work for the benefit of Kim Il Sung's ballistic missile aspirations. Some accounts suggest that the men had been at the airport with their families, ready for a lengthy relocation to Pyongyang. Following the collapse of the Soviet Union, the priorities of the newly independent Russian Federation in the 1990s focused on economic stability, with scarce opportunities for nuclear and missile engineers. One landmark study from 2001 found that more than 62 per cent of these experts were earning less than $50 per month and many had taken on additional work to support themselves. A particularly shocking finding was that 89 per cent of the experts surveyed had reported a decline in their living conditions after Soviet collapse.[47]

The Makayev experts who had attempted to enter North Korea in 1992 were ahead of the curve, seeking to take matters into their own hands. Back then, North Korea's poor economic destiny was less apparent and a foreign missile expert might have expected a decent—if not glamorous—lifestyle. The most unsettling implication of the interception of these Soviet scientists was what it said about all those who may not have been caught. For instance, Makayev specialists were thought to have assisted North Koreans in the late 1980s with the scaling up of the Scud into the abortive intermediate-range Nodong-1.[48] As for the Hwasong-10, on which hopes of threatening Guam were now pinned, in May 1992 the general director of Makayev's Engineer Design Office "went to Pyongyang to sign a $3 million contract," with the stated purpose of sending Russian experts to teach in North Korea.[49] This contract had the assent of Russian authorities, who may have taken its stated purpose at face value.

In September 2003, shortly after the Six-Party Talks had started, North Korea had mooted parading an early prototype of the Hwasong-10 through Pyongyang for the first time to commemorate the fifty-fifth anniversary of its founding. Although the missiles were not shown off then, American spy satellites were nevertheless able to detect their presence at the Mirim Parade Training Grounds, outside the capital. In 2009, a year before the Hwasong-10 would finally be revealed to the world, American analysts had come to "expect both the new [Hwasong-10] intermediate-range ballistic missile (IRBM) and the solid-propellant Toksa short-range ballistic missile (SRBM) to be fielded in the coming years."[51] This assessment added that the Hwasong-10 "represents a substantial advance in North Korea's liquid propellant technology"—a long stride away from the primordial Scud. The assessment at this time suggested that the Hwasong-10 would be capable of delivering a 500 kilogram payload to a range of 4,000 kilometers—enough to deliver a reasonable, compact nuclear payload to Guam.

The Russians were less sure about this capability: according to a U.S. State Department cable, defense official Evgeny Zudin told a State Department delegation that "the widespread claims about North Korea's achievements in the missile area are dubious," citing the lack of "reliable sources" and of "successful tests of this missile," either in North Korea itself or in Iran. It was indeed curious that, despite being a subject of great interest outside of North Korea for years prior, and seemingly having actually been deployed in the 2000s—taking on an emergency use status[51]—there were no known flight tests of the Hwasong-10 before the mid-2010s. The reason for the system's deployment under Kim Jong Il is unknown to this day, but it likely had more to do with Kim's profound state of paranoia after the 2002 collapse of the Agreed Framework and the 2003 U.S. invasion of Iraq, rather than having a basis in any evidence that the system was performing well and would become a crucial part of Pyongyang's intermediate-range arsenal. In fact, the lack of flight testing at that time may well be evidence that North Korean engineers were simply not ready to begin tests.

Like the Nodong, then, this second potential medium-range missile was a mystery. Three years after its first public appearance at a military parade in October 2010, an unclassified public report by the U.S. National Air and Space Intelligence Center concluded that North Korea had "fewer than 50" of these missiles in its inventory.[52] Just how real was this North Korean program?

Ultimately, Evgeny Zudin was proven right. It would become clear in subsequent years—particularly with testing—that the Hwasong-10's performance had been overestimated. Starting in April 2016, the Korean People's Army tested the missile eight times, with seven unambiguous failures and just one success. U.S. intelligence assessed in 2017 that one third of the pre-2016 launch vehicles compatible with the Hwasong-10 had been damaged over the course of multiple failures.[53] In particular, two failed tests in October 2016 were so catastrophic that the launch vehicles involved were deemed irrecoverable for at least one year.[54] South Korean media reported that Kim Jong Un, apparently enraged and deeply suspicious, ordered an internal inquiry in the belief that the United States and South Korea had sabotaged his missile efforts somehow.[55] Kim Heung-kwang, a South Korea-based North Korean escapee, said that a "special investigation team" had been put together to probe the scientists and engineers who had worked on the Hwasong-10: "Officials and workers who engaged in the launches of the missiles are now banned from traveling and their mobiles phones are confiscated to check their conversation records." The outcome of that North Korean investigation remains unknown.

Hopes had been high for the Hwasong-10: Kim had launched its final test on the night of the third presidential debate between U.S. presidential candidates Donald J. Trump and Hillary Rodham Clinton, hoping to elevate himself onto the agenda. We now know that the Hwasong-10's real threat was not to Guam; even its one successful test flight had fallen short of the required range, by a few hundred kilometers. Following its last presumed failure in October 2016, it made no more public appearances; given that it was succeeded only a year later by a far superior successor, the Hwasong-12 (see Chapter Seven), it is likely to be fundamentally redesigned at best, and retired at worst. But it still turned out to be an important milestone for North Korea's nuclear program. The Hwasong-10's ultimate value lay in the technology underlying it, which would go on to make multiple appearances elsewhere in North Korea's advanced nuclear program, including the burgeoning ICBM and space launch programs (see Chapter Eight).

The elusive stories of the Nodong and Hwasong-10 disappointments are still important despite their ultimate failure to achieve the dream of threatening Guam and Japan. Both the North Korean ambition that these projects revealed, and the level of international concern and debate around their potential, shows that Pyongyang's nuclear program was marching forward, and its ability to credibly deter was growing. With his intensified testing efforts, Kim Jong Un would soon crack the intermediate-range challenge.

6

FIRE FROM THE SEA

Early in the Cold War, both the United States and the Soviet Union quickly discovered that the marriage of a then new technology—the long-range ballistic missile—and the submarine made for a potent combination. Instead of basing nuclear weapons in vulnerable silos in the ground, at operating bases, or on road-mobile launchers, they could be hidden beneath the waves. The advent of naval nuclear propulsion would later make the ballistic missile submarine even more deadly, as deployments of practically unlimited duration—restricted only by the endurance of the crews—became a reality. As we saw in Chapter Three, for nuclear strategists, ballistic missile submarines have long been the most promising *survivable second strike* platform, making first use of nuclear weapons all but unthinkable for one's adversaries, given the high probability of nuclear retaliation from under the sea. For instance, even if a Soviet surprise attack were to have destroyed all of the United States' land-based nuclear missiles and bombers, lurking U.S. submarines with sufficient nuclear warheads could flatten several Soviet cities in retaliation.

Submarines are a familiar technology to North Korea. Even with its relative resource constraints compared to its military rivals in Northeast Asia, Pyongyang maintains the world's largest submarine force. Some of these submarines were procured from China in the early 1970s, and others assembled indigenously.[1] All of them, however, are obsolete and highly vulnerable to modern anti-submarine warfare, with their tiny, noisy propellers, and inelegant hulls. This massive fleet is comprised entirely of conventionally (not nuclear-) powered systems. Many of the submarines are classified as mini—or "midgets," to use the less politically correct appellation—weighing less than 150 tons; they are not built for long-endurance missions, and are only flushed out from their ports when needed for specific missions. It was one of these kinds of submarines that, in 2010, sank the South Korean naval ship ROKS *Cheonan*, killing 46 sailors and nearly reigniting war between the two Koreas.[2] For the Korean People's Navy, what the submarine force does offer in wartime is something of a concept of operations built around strength in numbers: flushing out enough submarines to cause serious planning complications for its enemies.

Choosing to develop even a simple ballistic missile submarine was always going to be a tall order for North Korea. Submarines present unique challenges as a launch platform. Firstly, while land-based launch vehicles can adjust in position, the natural movements of a submarine out at sea can introduce a tremendous source of targeting error (tens of kilometers), rendering the missile nearly useless. So a mitigation mechanism must be developed to counteract this. Secondly, the safest way to launch from a submarine is a "cold launch," where the missile's motor only ignites once in the air—but this system is more sophisticated, and complicated to assemble. The easier alternative is a "hot launch" (igniting the missile within its launch cell), and this can save important seconds of engagement time; for example if the missile is meant to intercept an incoming ballistic or cruise missile—U.S. Navy surface ships' interceptor missiles are equipped for hot launch for this reason. But the downside is a big one: catastrophic failure during or shortly after motor ignition—while the missile is still on board the submarine—could result in the loss of the entire vessel.

Thirdly, it must be decided whether the missile will launch while the submarine is submerged, or whether it will need to surface first—which would negate the stealth benefits of the submarine. If submerged launch is required, then a missile system must be designed to work this way. Even with such a system in place, there are a whole host of other dilemmas associated with undersea launch, including the chance that the missile can be crushed—or otherwise structurally affected—by water pressure; the need to ensure reliable underwater ignition of the missile's motors (if hot launching); and the possible effect on the missile's ascent and the submarine's viability if water enters an open missile launch tube.[3]

Fourthly, should North Korea use liquid fuel for its submarine-launched missiles, as the Soviets had early on, or should it use solid fuel, which is much less risky? We have already seen the hazards of liquid propellants on land, and the task of safely storing a liquid-propellant ballistic missile within a submarine hull, with human crews in close proximity, is an even greater challenge. Even after the launch mechanism has been developed and tested at land, sea-trials that avoid fuel leakage are a further hurdle. The stakes are high: nitric acid for example, produces serious chemical burns on skin contact, and can react explosively with a range of organic compounds. The tragedy that struck a Soviet ballistic missile submarine in October 1986 illustrates the challenges. After some fifteen years' operation without incident, a small explosion and fire in a launch tube allowed salty sea water to penetrate one of the missiles on board. The seawater reacted with fuel residue in the launch tube, producing an explosion that immediately killed two sailors on board. A third succumbed to poisoning from inhaling the toxic fumes that penetrated the submarine's living quarters. Matters only worsened from there, with a second, larger explosion causing the hull to rupture, allowing in more seawater and causing the entire submarine to sink.[4] After a frenzied attempt by the crew to save the vessel, it was lost on the North Atlantic sea floor.

Like decision-makers in Washington and Moscow decades before him, Kim Jong Un has been faced with these sorts of problems before even beginning to consider a realistic submarine-launched ballistic missile capability. Kim was not going to flinch in the face of this technical challenge. In June 2014, KCNA released undated images of him inspecting the KPN's Naval Unit 167.[5] The leader could be seen variously standing on a submarine's conning tower, peering through a submarine's periscope on board, inspecting a submarine's torpedo room, and posing with officers and sailors. While the release made no reference to nuclear weapons, strategic deterrence, or a nascent SLBM program, it gave clear prominence to the Korean People's Navy's undersea capabilities—and Kim's interest in their development.[6]

Realizing the North Korean 'Polaris'

That same year, U.S. intelligence agencies tracked static, on-land SLBM tests in North Korea. This is the normal way to begin SLBM testing, in order to validate performance of launch mechanisms without risking a submarine.[7] In October, a "new test stand at the ... Sinpo South Shipyard" on the east coast was spotted.[8] This was indication of serious intent: why build a test stand if not to pop out a dummy missile? South Korean Defense Ministry officials had also confirmed in September that Pyongyang was developing both its first ballistic missile submarine and a missile to go with it: the solid-fuel, intermediate-range Pukguksong-1.[9] *Pukguksong*, incidentally, is Korean for North Star, or, in effect, Polaris—the name of the U.S. Navy's own first series of SLBM, in service from 1961 through 1996.

The 2014 static ejection tests at Sinpo were to test a "cold launch" mechanism: the safer but more technically complex option. In addition, the submarine for the Pukguksong-1 was being designed to remain under the surface as it launched a missile—a superior form of attack, but open to serious challenges.[10] In other words, although Pyongyang had learnt the lesson of Soviet liquid-fueled SLBMs and opted for solid fuel, North Korea's first real foray into submarine-launched nuclear missiles was going in at the deep end.

The following year, the new submarine was revealed to the world, and North Korea was ready to begin at-sea testing for its first SLBM. Two such tests were successfully conducted in January and April of 2015, but neither was publicized by the North Koreans.[11] The third test took place less than three weeks after the second and marked the country's official unveiling of the Pukguksong-1 to the outside world. North Korea was seeking to showcase that its undersea deterrent had at least reached the level of sophistication required for submerged launch—the bare minimum for some degree of usefulness in the age of advanced anti-submarine warfare techniques. On May 8, Kim Jong Un traveled to Sinpo to witness the test. On May 9, North Korea announced the test, and KCNA's reporting revealed that smoke and mirrors were going to be part and parcel of the North Korean SLBM program.

We have seen the many technical challenges that liquid fuel poses in SLBM development, and, as we know, North Korea had chosen to fuel the Pukguksong-1 with solid propellant. Yet the footage of this first public at-sea test suggested to the world that North Korea had apparently already mastered liquid-fueled

SLBMs: analysts could see that the plume at the bottom of the missile was burning clear, whereas a solid propellant would be expected to leave a billowing cloud of smoke in its wake. The North Koreans had digitally inserted the plume from a liquid-fueled rocket into the photos of the Pukguksong test. The official images also showed that the missile appeared to be at too much of an angle with the surface of the sea, suggesting that it had been ejected successfully, but may have been captured falling back toward the water without any engine ignition; or that the ejection angle had been off.

There was a further deception underway, too. KCNA reported that, after Kim had given the order to begin the test, "the strategic submarine ... submerged up to a depth for firing the ballistic missile."[12] That claim stood out at the time. It would be unusual for any country to attempt its first submerged ejection test out of a live submarine, let alone a country with just a single operating ballistic missile submarine. There is considerable evidence across the years of North Korean engineers playing fast and loose with safety standards and testing schedules for its land-based missiles, but, at sea, it would only take one major accident to lose the vessel, effectively setting back the SLBM program years while another submarine hull was laid down. Yet Pyongyang had claimed publicly that its first-ever SLBM test was not only conducted from a "strategic submarine," but that it had been "fully" successful; Kim was paraphrased in the report as having likened the day's technical accomplishment to that of a satellite launch—high praise indeed.

Once again, Pyongyang's claims would turn out to be exaggerated. In the days following the test, U.S. intelligence sources told reporters that the test had taken place off a submerged barge—a much more likely testing precaution.[13] Google Earth imagery of the Sinpo site plainly showed a submersible barge just south of the submarine itself, which North Korea had apparently towed to the site of the launch. This sleight of hand was perhaps at Kim's own direction—given the comparison made with a satellite launch, perhaps acknowledging the barge would have been a little bit too unimpressive. Analysts working with North Korea's own images and footage of the test found the evidence that gave the game away: while most shots had been tightly cropped around the site of the launch, one that had not clearly showed the tugboat that had towed the submarine.[14]

The extensive—if poor—attempts at deception around this first public SLBM test may seem like an embarrassing tale of technical limitations, but they also speak to the ambition of North Korea's submarine-launched missile program. The intentions for sophisticated future systems were clear, and the test had been conducted with one eye on the global reaction. North Korea had taken proper precautions, given the nascent state of its SLBM program, and had conducted a successful third ejection test, this time at sea—it had just botched the effort to doctor the official narrative of a submarine launch. Despite the propaganda slip-up, Kim Jong Un had Western analysts debating the meaning of a North Korean SLBM capability for weeks and months. The strategic communications purpose of the test had been served. The event of the first-ever North Korean SLBM test was rendered additionally dramatic by a public assessment put out by the head of the North American Aerospace Defense Command stating that North Korea now had "the ability to put a nuclear weapon on [a long-range missile] and shoot it at the homeland."[15]

However, matters took a turn for the worse with the Pukguksong-1 program. Two subsequent flight-test attempts that year would fail. The first, on November 28, 2015, was, as expected, an attempt to apply the lessons of the May test to a true submarine launch, but while the missile ejected, it failed to "soar from the waters," according to one anonymous South Korean official.[16] It is unclear if the missile encountered catastrophic failure after launch, or if its engine failed to ignite following ejection from the launch tube. In any case, North Korea, as usual, did not acknowledge the failed test and moved on. Kim Jong Un's determination to realize an undersea nuclear deterrent and reach his regional targets was unperturbed. North Korean shipbuilders at Sinpo were able to repair the submarine after the botched test a little more than three weeks later.

On December 21, North Korea tried again. The submarine was in no state to see testing again so soon, so this time a barge was used. Shortly after the engine's ignition, the missile suffered a catastrophic failure. Nevertheless, North Korea claimed the test as another major milestone for the program and released video footage of the launch in January 2016. The delay between the test event and the public release was odd, but the reason why would become clear in due time: the video of the test-flight had been doctored again, splicing in footage from a successful short-range ballistic missile test just seconds before the aerial explosion of the medium-range Pukguksong-1.[17] But these winter failures were not entirely unsurprising: the problem seemed to be the missile's all-new solid-fuel engine, and this was North Korea's first foray into long-range solid-fueled missiles. Using the SLBM program to explore and innovate in this area was sensible: a solid-fuel SLBM would be more reliable, safer, and, as China had learned with the JL-1 SLBM, a useful base technology for land-based missiles too. Some bumps in the road were to be expected, but victory was close at hand.

In 2016, a year of rapid testing for Kim Jong Un, the Pukguksong-1 program accelerated and the SLBM was one of the important achievements reached by the year's end. North Korea conducted two successful tests on April 23 and August 23. The April test, according to U.S. intelligence, was the first successful submarine-borne ejection and partial flight-test of the Pukguksong-1, finally accomplishing for real what North Korean state media had claimed with the inaugural flight test a year earlier. Further testing was still needed, though, as the missile only flew to around 30 kilometers. Finally, in late August, as the United States and South Korea conducted their annual late-summer joint military exercises, Ulchi-Freedom Guardian, the Pukguksong-1 would truly arrive. For the first time, the SLBM was launched on a "lofted" (steep) trajectory, which allowed the entirety of its fuel to burn out without physically demonstrating the missile's full range—which would have meant overflying Japan.

Instead the missile entered Japan's Air Defense Identification Zone, drawing a sharp reaction from Tokyo. North Korea did not acknowledge any intention of threatening Japan, officially announcing that the "test-fire was successfully carried out without any adverse impact on neighboring countries."[18] State media also observed that Kim had "noted with pride" that, with this test, North Korea had "joined the front rank of the military powers fully equipped with nuclear attack capability."[19] After so many efforts to enhance the program's apparent performance for the benefit of an international audience, North Korea had finally truly demonstrated a capability that few countries possessed. An undersea deterrent and a medium-range missile system were key components of Kim's nuclear strategy, but it was also a momentous accomplishment for national prestige and status.

Toward Quiet Modernization

In the landmark year of 2017, even as Kim undertook the final flourishes in "completing" his nuclear forces, the submarine-launched program remained mostly under wraps. There were no flight tests this year and when Kim did return to Sinpo, it was to observe other missile tests (see Chapter Seven). However, there was a reason why the Pukguksong-1 did not make any further appearances in testing: it appeared that North Korea was already moving toward a successor missile. Analysts disagreed regarding Pyongyang's motivations for leaving behind a missile design that had experienced its first fully successful flight test just a year prior. Regardless, U.S. intelligence agencies tracked heavy activity around the static ejection test stand at Sinpo, with one test on May 30 and three others following in the summer (on July 18, 25 and 30).[20]

Later in the year, Kim hinted at what was to come. In August 2017, exactly one year after the last flight test of the Pukguksong-1, Kim Jong Un visited a facility described as the Chemical Material Institute of the Academy of Defense Science. There, he viewed a range of components and materials related to the assembly of advanced ballistic missiles, especially those using solid fuel like the Pukguksong-1 and the land-based Pukguksong-2. One of the assembled pieces of equipment on show was a partially finished missile casing that clearly showed the use of comparatively advanced manufacturing technologies, promising one day to facilitate the development of both larger solid-fueled missiles and better-performing liquid-fueled missiles. There was a second hint, too: a high-resolution photograph of Kim's visit released by KCNA showed off a poster describing a solid-fueled, submarine-launched missile known as the Pukguksong-3. Coupled with the ongoing, low-profile land testing that the U.S. had picked up at Sinpo, it seems unlikely that this was another misleading or deceptive ploy for the attention of foreign observers. This was the clearest public evidence yet that Kim's undersea missile ambitions had not stopped with the first SLBM.

The Pukguksong-3 was placed on the backburner while Kim pivoted to diplomacy in 2018–19, and it would be more than two years between this first glimpse and the second-generation SLBM making its debut. There was plenty of work to do in the meantime. On October 2, 2019, just days before U.S.—North Korea working-level negotiations were set to open in Stockholm,

North Korean scientists oversaw a launch marking the next step in the missile's development. This was North Korea's first firing of an unambiguously nuclear-capable missile since the November 2017 firing of the Hwasong-15 ICBM (see Chapter Eight), and a clear reminder to the United States that it was not about to submit to nuclear disarmament, regardless of how many talks were held between the two countries.

That said, North Korean state media underlined that Kim was not present at the launch, having instead sent his congratulations; this was a major departure from normal practice for major missile tests, where Kim is usually prominently on show. For him to sit out the inaugural flight-test of a new SLBM was highly unusual. A closer look at the imagery released after the test suggested that Kim may indeed have been present, but his presence was obscured through photo manipulation and staging.[21] Perhaps the North Korean leader was dissociating himself with testing ahead of talks with the United States—or perhaps he was simply adopting a more assured posture as the leader of a nuclear state, no longer needing to portray his personal involvement in every move.

As with its previous long-range missile tests under Kim Jong Un, North Korea lofted the missile. Even so, it covered 450 kilometers of the earth's surface, splashing down inside Japan's exclusive economic zone. With that trajectory, the Pukguksong-3 had instantly demonstrated a range capability of nearly 2,000 kilometers, and possibly more: this was the longest-range solid-propellant missile that had ever been seen in North Korea. As with the intensive 2017 testing campaign, a camera on the missile's reentry vehicle beamed back images of the Sea of Japan from space. This new SLBM was an ominous sign of what lay ahead, not just for Kim's undersea deterrent, but also his land-based nuclear forces. Just as the Pukguskong-2 followed the -1 on land, so too could a more capable land-based Pukguksong-4 emerge.

The Pukguksong-3 was not the only at-sea nuclear deterrent project to start up during the 'quiet,' test-free year of 2017. U.S. intelligence was also tracking with interest the expansion of North Korea's ballistic missile submarine fleet. For decades, the U.S.—South Korea alliance has made extensive preparations in anti-submarine warfare, given concerns about the Korean People's Navy's extensive submarine inventory, which is one of the world's largest with between sixty to ninety submarines. The 2010 sinking of the South Korean *Cheonan* corvette had made clear the dangers of even technologically obsolete submarines in sufficient numbers, and North Korean agents have also used submarines for infiltration missions across the inter-Korean maritime boundary. But it seems the danger is only set to grow: under Kim Jong Un, the extensive work on the SLBM program has signaled the future direction of the national submarine forces.

Despite the clear indicators from the regime that it seeks to operationalize an undersea deterrent with its SLBM program, for most of Kim's tenure, a single submarine has represented the entirety of North Korea's at-sea strategic nuclear launch capability, the diesel-electric *Gorae*. Its endurance is relatively short—it has yet to sail far from North Korean shores—and it has been involved only in limited testing to date, without many live launches. As we have seen with the Pukguksong-1, the fact that the *Gorae* was the sole viable seaworthy launch platform precluded frequent live launches in SLBM testing. In short, it does not represent the ideal launch vehicle for North Korea's sea-based nuclear deterrent.

Historically, North Korea has demonstrated some interest in naval nuclear propulsion technology for its submarines. Under Kim Jong Il, the country's Nuclear Weapons Institute established a special office, known internally as the 912 Project Office, to study this prospect. According to one Central Intelligence Agency assessment, North Korea began pursuing this line of inquiry because such technology was permitted under the Treaty on the Non-Proliferation of Nuclear Weapons [NPT].[22] The 912 Project was cancelled in 2015 under Kim Jong Un, having led to little in the way of promising advances. By the time of the program's termination, the CIA assessed that North Korean nuclear-powered subs could not even begin sea trials before 2030.[23]

Instead, North Korea's efforts at new ballistic missile submarines have zeroed in on its conventional diesel-electric vessels. The existence of a successor to the *Gorae* was first reported in October 2017. The U.S. Defense Intelligence Agency assessed that the new submarine was likely the largest vessel assembled for the Korean People's Navy since the 1970s. There were also signs that year that the KPN was studying long-range shore-to-sea communications with its *Romeo* submarines; in August, U.S. intelligence had detected "highly unusual and unprecedented" submarine deployments from Sinpo, including two *Romeo*-class vessels, later confirmed as exercises to test communications performance.[24] One of the *Romeo*s had ventured out of North Korea's traditional maritime exclusion zone, a move that was interpreted by U.S. intelligence analysts as a warning.[25]

On July 23, 2019—a little more than four years after the first underwater ejection test of the Pukguksong-1—Kim Jong Un "inspected a newly built submarine," which indeed appeared to be a modified *Romeo*, and was labelled by the U.S. intelligence community as the *Sinpo-C*. Significantly, this July visit marked Kim's first formal review of a military system designed explicitly for nuclear-capable missiles since the November 2017 ICBM launch (see Chapter Eight); in contrast with his official absence from the Pukguksong-3 test flight, this time the recent memory of a historic summit with President Trump three weeks prior was not stopping Kim from openly signaling North Korea's self-reliance in national defense, both domestically and internationally.

For the first time, Kim had offered a glimpse at what a future North Korean at-sea deterrent might look like. The publicity around and recent nature of the *Gorae*'s debut in Pukguksong-1 testing had led some observers to expect a modified *Gorae* to expand the nuclear deterrent fleet, but Kim now appeared to have an entirely new design up his sleeve instead. The Korean People's Navy was known to have twenty *Romeo* submarines, imported directly from China in the Mao era or assembled with parts supplied from China over a few decades. These aging vessels were ungainly and highly vulnerable to undersea acoustic detection of the sort that might be used by U.S.-allied sub-hunters. But what they did bring to the table that suited North Korea's needs was their size: 2019's new *Sinpo-C* appeared to have been modified to accommodate as many as three launch tubes, most likely for the Pukguksong-3. While Kim's public visit was to Sinpo, this successor submarine could also be built and deployed on the country's western coast, at Nampo, for instance—giving Pyongyang one on each side.

By early autumn 2019, satellite imagery demonstrated what appeared to be a concealment structure at the Sinpo shipyard's submarine basin, suggesting that Kim was getting close to launching his first non-experimental ballistic missile submarine.[26] A truly complete sea-based deterrent would require more than just this: as we will see in Chapter Nine, it will be crucial for Kim to ensure that he retains command and control over his at-sea nuclear weapons, now that he has begun producing them. But, by the final months of 2019, it was clear that North Korea's underwater nuclear deterrent was here to stay, with Japan in range. The *Gorae* and the Pukguksong-1 represent the first generation of this intermediate-range deterrent, with a potential new *Romeo*-class variant for the Pukguksong-3 soon to follow.

7

TO GUAM AND BEYOND

By the end of 2016, Kim Jong Un was happy—but not fully satisfied. His nuclear strategy was coming together, but obstacles remained for his intermediate-range deterrent. His submarine-launched program was yet to achieve success at this point. On land, the Hwasong-10 had turned out to be a disappointment, no matter how hard his engineers scrambled to sustain an unusually high-tempo testing campaign. The missile meant to hold Guam at risk could barely hold itself together a few seconds into flight. Not all the news from 2016 was bad, however: that year was the first to see two North Korean nuclear weapons tests, in January and September. The second was presumed to be the 'Disco Ball' test, the data from which allowed North Korean scientists to standardize their fission bomb design for mass production and mating with ballistic missiles.

The prospect of threatening Guam was closer than ever before. But before a land-based intermediate-range missile could succeed, Kim Jong Un was going to need two key ingredients: a new launch vehicle, and a new engine. His ostentatious pursuit of these prizes in 2017 elicited alarm on the part of his enemies;

before the year's end they would lead Kim to a victorious full package: a true 'Guam-killer.'

Kim's Building Blocks

It was a time of change for Pyongyang's adversaries. In November 2016, shortly after Trump had been elected, the North Korean Ministry of Foreign Affairs released an incredibly lengthy memorandum, amounting to an official North Korean history of relations with Washington in the Obama years. The message for the incoming Trump administration was clear: *change course, or get nowhere, just like your predecessor.* In the meantime, as 2016 came to a close, South Korea erupted in a political scandal that sent hundreds of thousands onto the streets of Seoul and would, months later, lead to the impeachment of the hardline right-wing president, Park Geun-hye, daughter of the late South Korean autocrat Park Chung-hee. Through November, December, and January, the Korean People's Army quietly carried on with its regular winter training cycle. But this pause on high-profile missile launches came to an abrupt end with a spectacular missile test on February 12, 2017—three weeks after Trump's inauguration.

With this February test, Kim Jong Un kicked off the most eventful ten months of missile-testing in North Korean history. By the time he was done, the Northeast Asian security environment would be transformed. The missile launch came during the first high-profile leader-level summit of the Trump administration. Japanese Prime Minister Shinzo Abe was in the United States and he and Trump had wrapped up a mostly successful White House summit with a trip to Trump's estate at Mar-a-Lago, in West Palm Beach, Florida. On what was supposed to be an evening of relaxed bilateral interaction, Abe and Trump were rudely interrupted by the news that North Korea had launched a ballistic missile, its first of the New Year, ending the nearly four-month-long break during the U.S. presidential transition.

On the other side of the world, it was morning. A few minutes before the clock struck 8 a.m., Kim Jong Un was in position for the test of a new medium-range ballistic missile, with a cup of tea. He had a representative map of the planned trajectory in front of him, and a set of computer monitors to his right, designed to show him live data from the missile's flight. The missile soared off into the skies, reaching an altitude of 550 kilometers before splashing down 500 kilometers off the eastern shore. As with previous launches of longer-range missiles, North Korea had "lofted" the missile, sharpening its trajectory angle to allow a full demonstration of its performance without overflying—or hitting—someone else's territory (in this case, probably Japan). The missile in question was the Pukguksong-2, for all intents and purposes a modified version of the sea-based Pukguksong-1—in a similar cold-launch canister, and stuck on top of a new launch vehicle rather than a submarine. The KCNA release confirmed this design heritage: "our People's Army is capable of performing its strategic duties most accurately and rapidly in any space: under waters or on the land."[1]

The success of the Pukguksong-2 was an important evolution in North Korea's burgeoning nuclear strike forces, being the country's largest land-based solid-fueled missile yet. But the real significance of its arrival was its new, odd-looking launcher, which drew the attention of U.S. and South Korean military intelligence; the early conclusion was that this was a new indigenous design.[2] With its tank treads rather than wheels, it seemed designed to go off-road—a risky undertaking with fragile solid-fuel rocket casings, but important in a country with compact geography and very limited paved road networks. Off-roading would also allow for concealment in underground facilities or shelters carved into North Korea's naturally mountainous terrain, making a disarming first strike attack much more difficult for the United States and South Korea.

These benefits were made clear with a further test flight on May 21. On that clear, sunny afternoon, Kim Jong Un grinned through his binoculars as he watched the Pukguksong-2 fly into the Sea of Japan for a second time, and was photographed smiling gleefully and pointing at a nearby monitor showing the reentry vehicle's beamed-back picture of Earth; in one image, the Yellow Sea was discernible. U.S. intelligence confirmed a few days later that these images were authentic.[3] But the point of this second test was its location: the new launch vehicle had been driven off the road and into the damp banks of Lake Yonphung, its tracks leaving a clear trail in their wake. This set-up conveyed a simple message to the United States, South Korea, and Japan: this missile launcher could go where the older ones could not. No longer would operating crews be tied to pre-paved launch pads, which could be monitored in peacetime and added to hostile target lists.

After this second successful flight-test, Kim Jong Un celebrated the missile's "perfect" results and called for its "deployment ... for action," ordering both the Pukguksong-2 and its impressive new launch vehicle to be "rapidly mass-produced in a serial way to arm the KPA Strategic Force."[4] Mass production of the missiles did not immediately follow, but production of the heavy launch vehicles began soon after and continued through 2018, while Kim Jong Un traveled abroad to meet with foreign leaders, including Chinese President Xi Jinping, South Korean President Moon Jae-in, and U.S. President Donald J. Trump. In June 2018, just days after the first-ever U.S.—North Korea leaders' summit in Singapore, U.S. military intelligence confirmed that North Korea had continued to produce the launchers. By mid-2019, North Korea had dispersed Pukguksong-2 launchers to bases in the northern part of the country. In August 2019, a UN report on

North Korean capabilities observed that these missiles had been deployed.[5] The Pukguksong had come ashore on the Korean Peninsula, and it could now launch toward regional targets from more or less anywhere on North Korea's terrain. But it still wasn't enough to range the U.S. territory of Guam.

* * *

Kim Jong Un's new launch vehicle for long-range missiles was a raging success; even better, in the same time period he had also found his new engine. On March 18, 2017, Kim traveled to the static rocket engine test stand near the Sohae Satellite Launching Center, where Kim's missile men had something special in store for him. U.S. intelligence has only observed a handful of static engine tests in North Korea over the years, despite careful observation of its known test sites for rocket engines, so this was obviously a special occasion. Kim was there for the test of a previously unseen North Korean engine, to ensure its proper functioning before mounting it at the bottom end of missiles. And it went off without a hitch.

KCNA reported that Kim had declared the day's accomplishment the "March 18 Revolution," and "the birth of the [indigenous] rocket industry." Ominously, he also reportedly warned, "The whole world will soon witness what eventful significance the great victory won today carries."[6] U.S. Air Force intelligence later concluded that the engine was indeed an indigenized variant of a Soviet-made series—but "codeveloped" with Iran, according to one analyst (there was no high-confidence assessment on that at the time).[7] At the very least, U.S. and South Korean intelligence traced North Korean procurement of several components thought to have been used in the new engine to manufacture in Belarus, Japan, and Russia. In April 2018, the CIA underscored that North Korean inability to procure these components in sufficient amounts was log-jamming production of the new engine, slowing down the production of Hwasong-12 and Hwasong-15 missiles.[8]

The 'March 18 Revolution' took place during the then U.S. Secretary of State Rex Tillerson's inaugural visit to China, where he planned to discuss North Korea among other issues. Kim Jong Un had big plans for this engine. If it performed as he was led to believe after this test, it would hold the key to realizing that long-sought component of his nuclear posture: an intermediate-range ballistic missile that could threaten the U.S. air base on Guam. He knew the world was watching.

Hwasong-12: The Future 'Guam-Killer'

On April 4, 2017, Kim traveled to the Sinpo coastal testing site to view a launch of the new intermediate-range missile intended to benefit from the "March 18 Revolution" engine: the Hwasong-12. This test was scheduled for the day before Trump's first summit meeting with Chinese President Xi Jinping. It was reported by South Korean and U.S. military authorities as a failure—the missile had flown for a little less than nine minutes to a very short range—but it gave the world a glimpse of what Kim had in store. The April 15 military parade through Kim Il Sung Square, commemorating the 105th anniversary of his grandfather's birth, was one for the ages. It included a range of impressive new ballistic missiles and launchers, including the new submarine-launched Pukguksong-1. In the final moments of the parade's main procession, out came a previously unseen missile, looking like a possible successor to the failed Hwasong-10. Kim simply let the new offering roll on by, as foreign journalists present were permitted to take close-up photographs of the system. Analysts scratched their heads, wondering what this new missile could be.

Kim wasted little time answering their questions. The next day, he returned to Sinpo for a second test of the Hwasong-12, which failed: the missile "flopped" out, according to one U.S. official, who described the event as a launch unlike any other they could recall in North Korea. It seems that the crews probably successfully prepared the missile for testing, but after its engines ignited, it briefly rose and collapsed in a fiery heap, causing significant damage to the precious launch vehicle in the process.[9] The only useful data obtained was that a catastrophic explosion of a large liquid-fueled ballistic missile would ruin most everything near it in a fireball. Yet the careful timing of the Hwasong-12 tests against the international geopolitical agenda was having an impact. Back in the United States, the Trump administration had completed its policy review on North Korea. Trump had taken a particular interest in Kim Jong Un's capabilities; outgoing U.S. President Barack Obama had told him that North Korea would be the most serious foreign policy challenge his administration would face. Kim Jong Un's repeated launches were making clear that Obama was right: this was a problem that Trump could not ignore.

The White House was convinced that its policy approach—what was dubbed "maximum pressure and engagement"—was the right one.[10] The United States launched an international campaign to convince partners, allies, and even adversaries, that North Korea needed to be choked of the resources that allowed it to continue its pursuit of weapons of mass destruction. At the same time, murmurs would grow in the halls of the White House that the window for a military solution might soon close, as North Korea continued to advance its capabilities. On April 28, Kim's scientists conducted a third test of the Hwasong-12, this time at the Pukchang Airfield, in South Pyongan province—a short drive from Pyongyang. This change of scene from the two failed launches reflected Kim's hopes for success on the third try, but he was disappointed yet again. *Is the Hwasong-12 another dud like the Hwasong-10? When will my March 18 Revolution materialize? Will I ever be able to hold Guam at risk?*

Desperation can be a dangerous thing. This third test of the Hwasong-12 did tell us something important about Kim's nuclear program—but nothing that bodes well. When it failed shortly after launch, the missile crashed in the Chongsin-dong area of the city of Tokchon, provoking a large explosion upon impact and causing considerable damage to a complex of industrial or agricultural buildings. This was a worrying episode in an overall trend of Kim diversifying his launch sites in the mammoth testing years of 2016 and 2017, moving away from the relatively safe seaside location of Sinpo and using previously unused areas, notably including airfields, to store and launch even developmental missiles. Later in 2017, Kim also oversaw ballistic missile launches from a restricted area at Pyongyang's Sunan Airport, the entry point for most non-Chinese foreign visitors to North Korea. The potential for accidents in populated regions remains high, especially with untested systems and with liquid-fuel missiles like the Hwasong-12. But this does not seem to give Kim pause for thought: during his 2019 testing campaign, North Korean state media acknowledged that short-range ballistic missiles had even overflown Pyongyang in a coast-to-coast flight demonstration.[11] South Korean sources told reporters that one short-range missile from this campaign had failed its test-flight and landed inland.

To be sure, the Chongsin-dong explosion was far from the world's first tragedy involving rocketry near a civilian area. In February 1996, a Chinese satellite launch vehicle failed shortly after launch from the Xichang Satellite Launch Center in Sichuan, exploding near a populated area and causing immense damage in addition to loss of life. To launch at range, North Korea, given its small size, would need to launch over the territory of other countries—most notably Japan. In August 2017, North Korea started launching ballistic missiles over Japanese territory, including twice with the Hwasong-12. On both occasions, as planned, the dummy reentry vehicles splashed down in the northern Pacific Ocean, clear of Japanese territory. But future successes are not guaranteed; should a future North Korean missile fail at the wrong moment in its overflight, its trajectory may come to resemble an attack on Japan. Even with a dummy payload, an incident like that could spark a serious crisis in Northeast Asia. North Korea's missile tests, which violate its obligations under UN Security Council resolutions, come with no formal warning or notice, leaving regional neighbors and the United States to interpret Pyongyang's intentions for themselves once the engines are ignited.

Hwasong-12: Guam Sighted

It only took two weeks for the testing campaign to recover from the Chongsin-dong disaster. On May 14, 2017, the Hwasong-12 flew successfully for the first time, soaring to the greatest heights ever achieved by a North Korean ballistic missile at the time (2,111.5 kilometers) and spending most of its thirty-minute journey outside of the Earth's atmosphere. North Korea had once again lofted this powerful missile to ensure that it would not overfly Japanese territory. It landed off the Peter the Great Gulf in the Sea of Japan, within Russia's exclusive economic waters and a little more than 200 kilometers out from Vladivostok, the largest city in the Russian Far East. Moscow joined a UN Security Council statement condemning the launch, but did not publically protest this 'visitation' from North Korea, drawing a contrast with Japan's repeated indignation at the launches that had been landing in Japanese economic waters since 2016.

Even better for Kim Jong Un, the United States and South Korea acknowledged that North Korea had demonstrated a new intermediate-range ballistic missile. One analyst observed shortly after the test that it "represents a level of performance never before seen from a North Korean missile."[12] High-resolution images released after the launch made apparent that the "March 18 Revolution" engine was sitting under the Hwasong-12, propelling it to those great heights. Putting two and two together, several analysts came to the unsettling conclusion that the Hwasong-12 would represent an ideal building block for a true intercontinental-range ballistic missile. Indeed, there would be very little stopping North Korea from doing this. Kim was known already to possess heavy launch vehicles capable of carrying ICBMs (see Chapter Eight) and North Korean engineers had been acquainting themselves with the rocket science necessary for more than a decade. The writing was on the wall.

On August 28, 2017, a longstanding Japanese fear came true: with further testing of the Hwasong-12. North Korean nuclear-capable ballistic missiles were not just landing in Japanese waters, but overflying Japanese territory. Under Prime Minister Shinzo Abe, certain parts of Japan had started implementing emergency drills. Schoolchildren would rehearse what to do in the case of a North Korean ballistic missile attack. While Japanese territory had been overflown twice before—in 1998 and 2009—neither of those launchers were explicitly designed to carry nuclear payloads. The Hwasong-12 was a different matter: North Korea had made no secret of the fact that it was meant to carry a "large-sized, heavy nuclear warhead." After the August launch, Pyongyang released images of precisely such a warhead: the 'Peanut,' its most powerful ever. The reality of the North Korean threat sank in like never before in Japan.

It was not only Japan that was in for a shock. On September 14, 2017, another launch, again overflying Japan, saw the Hwasong-12 fly to an astonishing 3,700 kilometers. The significance of that day was unmistakable: for the first time ever, a North Korean ballistic missile had demonstrated an actual flight range capable of striking the U.S. territory of Guam. Sweeping away the ambiguous performance of the abortive Hwasong-10, Kim Jong Un had now shown unequivocally that he had a missile in his arsenal capable of carrying a nuclear payload to U.S. territory and military targets. The Guam-killer, that essential piece of North Korea's nuclear forces, had been introduced.

What's more, Kim might be prepared to use it. In August, following Trump's threats of "fire and fury," he had visited his Strategic Rocket Force commander, General Kim Rak Gyom, who showed him detailed plans to surround Guam with an "enveloping strike" of four Hwasong-12s. The moment was disconcerting for American observers. Kim had a political objective: for the United States to cease bomber flights out of its air base there in the direction of North Korea. When General Kim announced that the supreme leader would be considering these plans, he declared Trump "a guy bereft of reason" who could only understand "absolute force." Kim was fleshing out the credibility of his nuclear forces and now toying with the idea of using the Hwasong-12 for what Thomas Schelling might have termed compellence: telling your adversary that you will impose costs until they comply with your demands.

Kim did not authorize the launch, leading to headlines that he had "backed down" from his plan—even though this was never North Korea's intention. After the two Hwasong-12 overflights of Japan, which had crystallized the credibility of the missile's flight range, Trump stood before world leaders at the UN General Assembly and threatened to "totally destroy" North Korea. The Trump administration, with greater seriousness than before, once again had begun contemplating a possible limited strike on North Korea. Kim's deterrent against the United States was really coming together, but the rapid pace of progress and the nature of U.S. leadership could have led to a catastrophe.

Going Long

Now that he had intermediate-range ballistic missiles that could carry a nuclear warhead to the nearest U.S. territory, it was only natural for Kim to set his sights on the next—the ultimate—prize: intercontinental ballistic missiles that could carry a nuclear warhead to the contiguous forty-eight states of the continental United States. As North Korea began serious ICBM development in 2012–15, there were many hurdles and partial failures standing in the way of realizing that dream—but every setback was a lesson learned, and every breakthrough short of the ultimate accomplishment moved Kim Jong Un closer to holding the U.S. homeland at risk.

It goes without saying that nuclear-tipped ICBMs are not an easy technology to develop, deploy, and operate. Setting aside the already complex task of miniaturizing a nuclear weapon to fit it, there are a few unique physical challenges in flying from one side of the globe to the other. ICBMs must carry a significant payload, but they must also gain great altitude to reach their far-off destination—so they carry a great amount of fuel, too. Unsurprisingly, this makes them incredibly cumbersome, even prior to launch. Road-mobile launch vehicles must be able to bear this weight through transport, erection and launch (to this day, the United States avoids this problem for its advanced Minuteman-III ICBMs by deploying them exclusively in silos instead).

On top of this, North Korea's known ICBM designs all use highly volatile liquid fuel—not an ideal choice for road-mobile missiles, and one unique to North Korea, but sensible for short-term deterrence requirements, given Pyongyang's far greater experience with liquid-propellant rocket engines. That brings us to the last problem on the ground: finding a reliable engine capable of powering such a missile. For the ICBM, though, the troubles that set it apart from smaller, shorter-range missiles really begin outside the atmosphere. ICBMs, as a matter of principle, are multi-stage missiles. The simplest way to conceptualize this is to imagine two or three smaller rockets stacked on top of each other. The bottom—or first—stage will have the greatest thrust capacity, since its task is to lift itself and everything atop it through the Earth's dense atmosphere. Upper stages will be smaller, and their engines will often be different, in many cases optimized to burn their fuel in the zero-oxygen, zero-drag environment of space. These multiple development requirements are challenging.

In the United States, even without a nuanced understanding of North Korea's intended nuclear force structure or strategy, it had been assumed for decades that an ICBM would be an obvious developmental milestone. That is partly why the first North Korean test flight to overfly Japan in 1998, a Taepodong-1 satellite launch, spooked American observers and particularly the Japanese, who watched with shock as a made-in-North-Korea rocket failed and crashed west of their territory, despite having been launched on a trajectory to overfly the main Japanese island of Honshu. That 1998 space launcher would have made a rather poor ICBM in practice, but at the time, it was the clearest manifestation of North Korea's intent to pursue an intercontinental-range strike capability. American officials knew then that the best they could hope for was to delay North Korea's development of an ICBM. The incentives for Kim Jong Il to pursue such a weapon were simply too great.

Though North Korea agreed to a long-range missile test moratorium at Berlin in 1999, Kim Jong Il's resolve hardened after the 2002 crisis that led to the collapse of the Agreed Framework. In 2003, as Kim watched the United States storm and invade Iraq, the way forward appeared clear: develop nuclear weapons and ICBMs at all costs. His son Kim Jong Un's greatest achievement would be the realization of that dream—and the journey started with the Hwasong-13.

April 15, 2012, was a big day for North Korea. It marked the centennial of Kim Il Sung's birth (and, perhaps inauspiciously, the sinking of RMS *Titanic*). Kim Jong Un had formally held the reins of power in Pyongyang for hardly five months since his father's death and the manner in which his grandfather's birth centenary was commemorated would mean everything for him and his new regime. The elder Kim, after all, was revered as the founder of North Korea and the closest thing to a deity in the country. As of 1997, Kim Il Sung's birth in 1912 had also come to mark the year one of North Korea's very own *juche* calendar, making 2012 *juche* 101—a particularly auspicious milestone. To celebrate, as in previous years on Kim Il Sung's birthday, there was a major military parade through Kim Il Sung Square in central Pyongyang.

Toward the end of the parade, North Korea revealed the great crescendo: something it had never before shown publicly. Six large eight-axle heavy trucks, painted in a jungle camouflage, were carrying what appeared to be six ballistic missiles larger than anything North Korea had ever displayed, and looking suspiciously like ICBMs. The dozens of journalists who had been invited to Pyongyang to observe the event were surprised by this propaganda bonanza, intended to strike fear into the hearts of the Americans. The April display came in the same month as the collapse of the so-called 'Leap Day Deal' agreed with the Obama administration on February 29, following a North Korean satellite launch. This parade was meant to demonstrate the resolve and ability of the new, young leader, Kim Jong Un, to ensure that North Korea's national defense remained robust. The Hwasong-13 had arrived.

In a matter of days, analysts began questioning what they had just seen in Kim Il Sung Square. Two German rocket engineers put out a widely covered analysis suggesting that the Hwasong-13 was nothing but an elaborate, ultimately unconvincing mock-up with several design inconsistencies—part of a "nice dog and pony show."[13] While the display may have been suggestive of North Korea's programmatic interest in an ICBM capability someday, the Hwasong-13 was not it, they suggested; this missile would never fly. The engineers were largely right—the Hwasong-13 never saw flight-testing and would gradually fade from prominence in North Korea as Kim's program moved on to bigger and better things. But it did spark animated debate about the prospects of a North Korean ICBM capability, in the United States and elsewhere.

The Hwasong-13 mock-ups may not have convinced those analysts, but they did mislead popular opinion in another way: they inadvertently persuaded Americans that North Korea was a tin pot dictatorship engaging in cheap propaganda tricks, with a stunted ability to actually threaten the United States. American late night show host Conan O'Brien, referencing popular coverage of the Germans' dismissive analysis, presented satirical "exclusive" footage of a North Korean military parade that was nothing but a dinky sedan, with a missile nosecone affixed to the front and a few fins on the back. The Hwasong-13 became another joke in a long running series of North Korean embarrassments. But not everyone was laughing—and those who did would not be laughing for long. After the Hwasong-13 made another appearance at a July 2013 parade—this time to commemorate the sixtieth anniversary of the Korean War armistice—the U.S. National Air and Space Intelligence Center released a report reiterating that, even though the Hwasong-13 had not been flight-tested, the missile "[showed] the determination of North Korea to achieve long-range ballistic missile and space launch capabilities." As late as 2015, the commander of the North American Aerospace Defense Command and U.S. Northern Command confirmed that the U.S. assessed the Hwasong-13 as "operational today." This was not in fact the case,[14] but it was telling that the U.S. was practicing its ballistic missile defense scenarios against a target missile like the Hwasong-13. The possibility of a North Korean nuclear missile striking the homeland could no longer be ignored.

On October 10, 2015, North Korea held a military parade in Pyongyang to commemorate the seventieth anniversary of the founding of the Workers' Party of Korea. Once again, Kim watched and clapped as several weapons systems rolled through Kim Il Sung Square. As in 2012, the parade reached a crescendo with the reveal of an apparent ICBM—four new mock-ups on the back of the same heavy-goods truck used before. This was the Hwasong-13 mod 2, and it told an unnerving story about North Korean intentions for the ICBM program. Its reentry vehicle was blunter than the first Hwasong-13: instead of designing sleeker, more modern reentry vehicles that would benefit from greater speed or accuracy as they hurtled toward the Earth, a blunter design, based on U.S. and Soviet vehicles used for long-range missiles in the 1950s and 1960s, would require less sophistication to manufacture and test.[15] Was Kim Jong Un in a hurry to complete his deterrent?

Another important and alarming revelation at the parades of the Hwasong-13 was the provenance of these large trucks carrying the mocked-up missiles. Quickly, eagle-eyed open source analysts more or less ascertained that they had come from China.[16] In 2013, the UN Panel of Experts on North Korea concluded that Pyongyang had imported the vehicles with falsified end-user certification: the Chinese manufacturer had delivered the trucks expecting that they would be used for forestry, apparently missing their obvious dual-use nature for a country that had long coveted a heavy launch platform for large, road-mobile missiles. In 2017, the Chinese company, Wuhan Sanjiang Import & Export Co, was sanctioned by the U.S. Treasury Department.

These trucks, designed for heavy duty forestry applications, were not cheap. North Korea had gone to the trouble of procuring them, modifying them to resemble integrated ICBM launch vehicles, and using them in a parade—all this was an early warning sign that the mocked-up Hwasong-13 probably was not their final purpose. The investment underscored the seriousness and urgency of Kim Jong Un's interest in developing a militarily useful ICBM capability. Most concerningly of all, the truck model actually appeared *oversized* for the Hwasong-13 at the time. The vehicle could have accommodated a much larger missile—and it would not be long until it did.

8

GOING INTERCONTINENTAL

I appreciate candor in diplomacy, but this was, perhaps, overdoing it!

William J. Perry, former U.S. secretary of defense, on being told
by a North Korean general that Pyongyang would use "nuclear
weapons to destroy your cities—not excluding Palo Alto!"

By the mid-2010s, it was clear that the North Korean ICBM was coming, and soon. This should not have been a surprise to anybody looking at Kim Jong Un's motivations for completing this ultimate stage of his nuclear deterrent. No other nuclear power faces the unique targeting challenge of North Korea, whose borders sit adjacent to a technologically superior adversary and whose territory nonetheless remains vulnerable to a far-off hostile superpower with supreme military power, capable of striking it with conventional and nuclear weapons alike with little warning. For decades, the barrels of KPA artillery units have been aimed at Seoul, a metropolitan area of some twenty-five million, and successfully keeping at bay a full-scale resumption of the Korean War, and by 2016 Kim

Jong Un had his standardized nuclear bomb, but he remained acutely aware that his small nuclear arsenal was vulnerable to overwhelming preemptive non-nuclear strikes by the United States. In the North Korean strategic imagination, it did not matter how much death and destruction it could sow against its U.S.-allied neighbors; so long as the United States itself remained untouchable, the DPRK was vulnerable.

By early 2017, South Korea and Japan could suffer enormous damage in the event of war from North Korean artillery units, short-range nuclear missiles and medium-range submarine-launched nuclear missiles. The U.S. territory of Guam was taken care of with the Hwasong-12, which was first tested successfully that May. But for the deterrent to be complete, Kim would have to develop missiles that could be hurled halfway around the world. What mattered—the ultimate prize—was the ability to hold the United States' homeland at risk with nuclear weapons. Only then—once North Korea could demonstrate the ability to threaten the U.S. homeland with nuclear weapons, to everyone from the president to the average American citizen—only then would it become *unthinkable* for the White House to consider even a limited use of military force against North Korean soil. Better yet, Pyongyang could begin to stress the sinews of the U.S.—South Korea and U.S.—Japan alliances, by raising doubts that the United States would truly risk one of its own cities to save those in Northeast Asia.

These objectives meant that the intercontinental-range ballistic missile (ICBM) would become the crown jewel of the country's strategic forces. States design strategic weaponry with target sets in mind and for North Korea to reach any meaningful targets in contiguous forty-eight United States, a true ICBM would be necessary. There is not a precise, universal definition of an ICBM, but the United States and the Soviet Union agreed on a commonly accepted minimum range in their arms control talks: 5,500 kilometers. For North Korea, however, the tyranny of geography meant a more punishing definition of a truly deterrent ICBM: 6,400 kilometers, according to the state newspaper *Rodong Sinmun* in 2017.[1] That range was roughly the distance from North Korea to Anchorage, the largest city in Alaska—the U.S. state closest to North Korean territory. But this range objective was a *minimum* guideline; under no circumstances would the North Koreans stop before they could range Washington, D.C. at least. Only then would the United States take the hint and accept a new *modus vivendi* with a nuclear North Korea.

Hwasong-14: The First Milestone

July 4 is best known as the United States' Independence Day, but it also holds special significance for North Korean missile launches in the twenty-first century. In 2006, in the evening hours of Independence Day celebrations in the United States—the morning of July 5 in North Korea—Kim Jong Il had decided to make good on an earlier North Korean threat to do away with the 1999 moratorium agreed with the U.S., conducting a series of missile tests. Eighteen years later, Kim Jong Un kept his father's old tricks in mind for July 4, 2017, when it was his turn to launch a missile as Independence Day fireworks lit the skies on the U.S. East Coast. The new Hwasong-14 was launched with the "March 18 Revolution" engine first developed for the intermediate-range Hwasong-12—the 'Guam-killer.' News reports quickly began to cite South Korean, Japanese, and U.S. data on the missile's trajectory, and that is when it became apparent that North Korea might just have crossed an important technological threshold.

The missile flew to a modest range of 933 kilometers, but unease swiftly set in after reports picked up on another data point: the missile had flown for *thirty-seven minutes*. Given that flighttime, there was no way this was something short-range. The discrepancy between the two figures made clear that the North Koreans must have lofted a massive missile to shorten its range. After several hours, newspapers in South Korea and Japan reported that the missile had flown to an apogee—or maximum altitude—of 2,802 kilometers. To place that altitude in context, the International Space Station normally orbits at a little over 400 kilometers. Putting together the three pieces of data, the reality of what had just transpired hit us in the face: North Korea had just successfully flight-tested its first-ever ICBM, crossing a longstanding benchmark and making good on a task that Kim had set out at the beginning of the year.

Nearly a year and a half on from the last sighting of the "unlucky" Hwasong-13, Kim Jong Un's 2017 New Year's Day address had not been subtle: he remarked that over the previous year North Korea had "entered the final stage of preparation for the test launch of [an] intercontinental ballistic missile." All signs pointed to the threshold being crossed in 2017 and, on July 4, it had finally happened. Later that same night, Korean Central Television held a special broadcast, all but underlining the historic significance of the day's momentous achievement. Ri Chun Hee, KCTV's former premier news anchor, came out of retirement to make the announcement. Minutes later, the Hwasong-14, North Korea's first successfully flight-tested ICBM, was revealed to the world. As we saw with the Hwasong-13, overseas observers of North Korea's weapons programs had grown used to Pyongyang showing off ICBM designs, no matter how impractical they might have appeared. But the missile Ri introduced that night was the real deal.

Kim Jong Un's March 18 Revolution engine had finally had its first proper outing. Given that the later-released video footage showed Kim leisurely viewing missile preparation and receiving briefings, the ground crews were not operating with speed and efficiency as a top priority. In one short segment, Kim could be seen smoking a cigarette, mere feet away from the ICBM, which would presumably soon be fueled with highly volatile rocket propellant. Unless Kim is particularly relaxed about matters of life and death, this suggested that the Hwasong-14 was possibly designed to be fueled after erection, rather than being fueled horizontally before roll-out, as with the Hwasong-12—but who around him would have told the supreme leader to put out his beloved cigarettes?[2]

The U.S. intelligence community, at least, was not taken completely by surprise: it had been closely scrutinizing activity at North Korean missile manufacturing facilities. On June 2, one month before the test, U.S. spy satellites had seen unusual activity at the Sanumdong missile factory—a large VIP delegation, comprising twelve sedans, had arrived at the main assembly hall, where North Korea was known to have stored its older, untested Hwasong-13s and even assembled parts of its previous space launchers.[3] The visit—coupled with new, large shipments around the area—was taken seriously as a sign that something was coming: possibly something big. But the initial working assumptions were that North Korea was either developing a new space launch vehicle, or perhaps more Hwasong-12 launchers. The truth, it would turn out, was more sinister.

The warning signs kept on coming. The United States had devoted considerable assets to tracking transshipment of missile components from Sanumdong to other parts of the country where Kim had conducted recent testing. On June 22, Kim traveled to the trusty static engine test stand at Sohae; around the same time, U.S. signals intelligence intercepted apparent telemetry checks by North Korean missile scientists, simulating what appeared to be a lofted ICBM test. The North Koreans had set up a previously unused paved area near the high-importance Panghyon Aircraft Factory, apparently for Kim to observe an

ICBM launch. CIA analysts had suspected the upcoming July 4 as a possible date, given Kim Jong Il's precedent. On the morning of the test itself, a highly advanced U.S. spy satellite passing over North Korea observed the fueling and preparation of the Hwasong-14 out in the open.[4] All in all, U.S. intelligence was well prepared for the first test of a North Korean ICBM—but that did not make its success any less shocking.

In a matter of weeks, U.S. intelligence analysts arrived at a conclusion that a second North Korean ICBM launch was likely. After July 4, U.S. spy satellites were closely monitoring any movements by the Hwasong-14 launch vehicle, and had spotted it in Kusong by mid-month. U.S. analysts expected a test around July 27—the day the Korean War armistice was signed in 1953, celebrated as "Victory Day" in North Korea—"for the optics."[5] In the lead-up to this second launch, the UN Security Council remained logjammed over how to respond. One of the main inhibitors was Russia's insistence that the July 4 missile was not an ICBM at all, but only a medium-range missile. This position may not have been obstructionism at all, but borne of a poor sensor array in Russia's Far East. The Russian intelligence assessments of the missile's flight time, range and apogee roughly suggested that Moscow's terrestrial radars had success-fully tracked the first stage of the Hwasong-14's flight, but then lost the missile.[6] The Russian government had a long history of misjudging North Korean missile and satellite launch activities, pointing to a pattern.[7]

Complicating matters, however, official Russian statements appeared to contradict themselves, raising the possibility that Moscow was delaying proceedings at the Security Council delib-erately. A July 8 letter from Russia's Permanent Mission at the UN to the UN secretary-general stated that the launch had been tracked by an early-warning radar station in Irkutsk, southeast-ern Siberia, while Foreign Minister Sergei Lavrov told reporters later in the month that Russia's data was from radars "just on the border with North Korea"—nowhere near Irkutsk.[8] Later, in August, the North Koreans fired back with an editorial titled "Is Russia Sightless or Is It Mimicking the Blind," lashing out at Moscow's refusal to recognize the Hwasong-14 as an ICBM. The North Koreans perceived this as "big power" arrogance—noting that even the United States, the so-called "empire of evil," had conceded them their historic achievement.[9] The Russian statements on the nature of the test succeeded at delaying unified Security Council action as North Korea prepared its second test of the Hwasong-14.

By July 26, once again, U.S. intelligence had more or less identified the chosen test site: the Mupyong-ni Arms Factory.[10] This was where North Korea had conducted serious modifications to the Chinese heavy logging vehicle that had carried the never-tested Hwasong-13, adapting the truck to carry ICBMs instead of lumber. This time, the launch was scheduled for after dark—the North Koreans appeared eager to convey the idea that they were ready to use their ICBMs, day or night. The missile had been modified since July 4, suggesting an ongoing development process; but this second test also had the partial hallmarks of an operational test. The Hwasong-14 flew for 45 minutes, even longer than on July 4. It also reached the highest-ever point any North Korean missile had reached at roughly 3,700 kilometers and covered a range of 1,000 kilometers, splashing down in the Sea of Japan.

That night, tired Japanese drivers on the northern island of Hokkaido, commuting home after a long day's work, saw a remarkable sight in the sky at around twenty-eight minutes past midnight. A bright object streaked down through the night sky, eventually disappearing. Japanese television news broadcast footage of what was likely the missile's spent second stage, burning up as it reentered the atmosphere.[11] Kim Jong Un would only get useful data on the reentry vehicle with a test under more realistic conditions, when maximum range rather than maximum altitude would be the goal, but the CIA's preliminary assessment in August was that North Korea's ICBM reentry vehicles would likely perform adequately if flown on a normal trajectory to continental U.S. targets.[12] This was supported by data "gathered from ground, sea, and air-based sensors" and analyzed by the U.S. National Air and Space Intelligence Center.[13] In other words, there was no reason to doubt that Kim Jong Un now had a minimally functional and credible ICBM system on his hands. The UN Security Council finally agreed on action against North Korea, unanimously voting for further economic sanctions.

Despite the decades of evidence that North Korea was pursuing ICBMs, many described the Hwasong-14 as a "game-changer." The two successful tests in July 2017 apparently crossed an important red line for the United States. One day after Kim Jong Un's New Year's Day address that year, U.S. President Donald J. Trump had tweeted: "North Korea just stated that it is in the final stages of developing a nuclear weapon capable of reaching parts of the U.S. It won't happen!"[14] Two successful ICBM tests later, that left the United States in a difficult position. In South Korea and Japan, hushed conversations began in earnest about the implications of the new North Korean capability for the robustness of their respective alliances with the United States. U.S. Secretary of State Rex Tillerson declared Hwasong-14's July 4 debut a "new escalation of the threat to the United States, our allies and partners, the region, and the world."[15]

The North Koreans, meanwhile, were exuberant, calling the July 4 test a "gift" for the United States. But Kim also underscored a very subtle opening in the KCNA statement announcing the first successful ICBM tests. He "stressed that the DPRK would neither put its nukes and ballistic rockets on the table of negotiations in any case nor flinch even an inch from the road of bolstering the nuclear force chosen by itself *unless the U.S. hostile policy and nuclear threat to the DPRK are definitely terminated.*"[16] *If* and *unless* tend to be the most important words in many North Korean releases. North Korea was clearly signaling that the ill-defined U.S. "hostile policy"—the basket of measures containing everything from the U.S. nuclear triad to troop presence in South Korea and Japan—was the necessary concession for Pyongyang putting its nuclear arsenal on the negotiating table. This was not a comprehensive rejection of bargaining; rather, it was a first invitation to arms control, from one nuclear power to another. This theme would become more prominent later in 2017, as North Korean capabilities grew further. Before the year was over, the 'Guam-Killer' Hwasong-12 saw two more pivotal tests. But the real surprise—the *pièce de résistance* for Kim Jong Un—came in November.

Hwasong-15: The Biggest of Them All

The differences in missile design between the first and second tests of the Hwasong-14, just a few weeks apart from one another, showed how seriously Kim's missile scientists were experimenting with possible improvements to the first North Korean ICBM, unsatisfied with what they had observed at first testing despite the enormity of that milestone. Four months later, on November 29, this progress came to fruition, as North Korea carried out the first-ever launch of its largest and most powerful ballistic missile to date, the Hwasong-15.

On August 29 and September 14, 2017, North Korea had launched two Hwasong-12 IRBMs respectively, overflying Japanese territory each time, but this November launch broke a nearly three-month-long lull in ballistic missile testing activity. For 2017, this was a lengthy break: between February and September, North Korea had tested missiles on a near-biweekly basis. The launch also came unusually late in the calendar year. It seemed that Kim Jong Un did not enjoy traveling to remote locations to observe missile launches in the less hospitable months. Under his rule, such testing campaigns have generally wrapped up for the year by September. The November launch was a notable exception, and so the missile tested was bound to be exceptional too. Just as the world had finished digesting the implications of the two previous tests, the November launch quickly refocused attention on the country's rapid advances in ICBM technology.

As with the Hwasong-14 in July, this debut of the Hwasong-15 was not entirely unexpected. For one thing, North Korea watchers knew that Pyongyang was sitting on the untested, parade-ready Hwasong-13 designs. In the early autumn, rumors of a new ICBM had emerged in the South Korean press. In early October, a Russian parliamentary delegation visited Pyongyang and received an intriguing briefing revealing that North Korea was indeed developing another ICBM that could range the United States. "They even gave us mathematical calculations that they believe prove that their missile can hit the west coast of the United States," Duma member Anton Morozov told Russian state media upon his return from Pyongyang. "And in general, their mood is rather belligerent." Morozov's comment on the capability of ranging the west coast of the United States suggested a degree of humility on the part of the North Koreans; the Hwasong-14 had already been assessed by the U.S. intelligence community to be capable of ranging not only the west coast of the country, but possibly even as far as the Midwest with a reasonably heavy nuclear payload. The Hwasong-15, however, was about to take North Korea's capabilities to another level entirely.

In early November, Kim Jong Un paid a visit to the so-called March 16 Factory, known for production of "large-scale truck[s]," in the South Pyongan Province town of Pyongsong—a hotbed for military vehicle manufacturing. One week later, in the late evening of November 28, a KPA Strategic Force missile crew there began preparing for the first-ever launch of the Hwasong-15. This choice of location for the Hwasong-15's debut test flight was significant. As far as anyone knew, North Korea was still using the six Chinese heavy logging trucks it had imported in 2011 as its ICBM launchers, but great strides had been made in 2017 towards developing indigenous launch vehicles for ballistic missiles, including the intermediate-range Pukguksong-2 and the short-range Hwasong-6 precision variant, or KN18. North Korea might soon cross yet another important threshold: indigenous production of heavy launch vehicles for large ICBMs. Kim's tour of the facility underlined major advances, including serious modifications to the Chinese-origin launch vehicle: the new Hwasong-15 was so large—60-some feet in length—that North Korean engineers had to give the truck a monstrous ninth axle, lengthening it considerably. It also looked like an entire building had been constructed either for modifications to the vehicle or for the Hwasong-15's big night out.

The Hwasong-15 was another liquid-fueled missile and, from a simple glance, it was clear that this was the largest ballistic missile ever designed by the DPRK. It was not the largest piece of kit North Korea had ever launched; that distinction went to its Unha space launch vehicles. But those had not been designed for nuclear payload delivery—and certainly not for road mobility. The Hwasong-15's size was, no doubt, an important feature for Kim, who aspired to hurl the thermonuclear 'Peanut' he had tested in September to every corner of the United States—including the U.S. president's self-proclaimed 'Winter White House,' the Mar-a-Lago estate in West Palm Beach, Florida. Even on the least charitable assumptions about North Korea's capabilities, a successful test of this behemoth would prove amply Kim's ability to deliver even the clunkiest thermonuclear weapon to American shores.

As the night carried on, U.S. spy satellites observed launch preparations over multiple orbital passes for more than ninety minutes.[17] (Later, the U.S. Defense Intelligence Agency would assess that the missile had a sixty-minute wartime readiness time).[18] Kim was briefed on the chosen trajectory for the test flight, as with previous launches. The North Korean leader took a personal interest in these matters and always made sure to be filmed and photographed inspecting every stage of preparation—from the missile's loading onto the launch vehicle, to its fueling, and its eventual pre-launch erection out in a field near the new annex building. Anticipation was high: if the Hwasong-15 worked, it would mark a seminal moment in the country's history and eclipse its younger brother, the Hwasong-14, just months after the smaller missile had been successfully tested for the first time. Finally, at 2:47 a.m. local time on November 29, the Hwasong-15 was off, on the customary highly lofted trajectory. As the first reports of a missile launch became public that evening in Japan, however, there was immediate concern that this would be yet another overflight of its territory, as with the IRBM tests from both land and sea—most recently, with the August and September test flights of the Hwasong-12. Tokyo had reason to believe that Pyongyang was entering a new phase of belligerence wherein ballistic missile overflights of Japanese territory would become normal.

That evening, crew and passengers aboard a Cathay Pacific intercontinental flight from San Francisco to Hong Kong reportedly saw either a spent upper stage or its reentry vehicle coming down.[19] "Be advised, we witnessed the DPRK missile blow up and fall apart near our current location," a crew message said after the flight. This incident generated concerns over aviation safety above the Sea of Japan, given Kim Jong Un's rapid testing regime during 2017. Even though the probability of a collision between two objects in three-dimensional space is small, airlines have to factor this into their risk assessments. A missile test failure, for instance, could result in a large debris onslaught that might damage aircraft during descent.

The Hwasong-15 flew for fifty-three minutes and forty-nine seconds, an unusually long flight time even for an ICBM, and the missile reached an astonishing apogee at nearly 4,500 kilometers above the earth's surface. On the surface, it ranged 950 kilometers. In video released by the North Koreans, extra space could be seen in the payload fairing, which could one day accommodate technology to help the missile evade U.S. missile defenses, or multiple warheads. The missile generated a massive 80 tons of thrust at ignition, double the first-stage thrust seen in the Hwasong-14 just a few months earlier. North Korea had chosen its largest-ever missile to try out for the first time a relatively complex steering mechanism, with a long history in Soviet, Russian and U.S. rockets (both ballistic missiles and space launchers). How North Korea had suddenly mastered gimbaled thrust vectoring remains a mystery; the Hwasong-15 demonstration was so remarkable that some overseas experts regarded it as clear evidence of significant foreign research and development assistance. November 2017 was the first and only time North Korea is known to have test-flown a ballistic missile using this technology—and it worked.

U.S. officials were surprised, both by this technical achievement and by the very existence of the Hwasong-15. While they had anticipated a missile launch from Pyongsong, U.S. intelligence agencies had suggested another intermediate Hwasong-12 or intercontinental Hwasong-14 launch; not this astonishing feat. On February 28, 2018, the North Koreans would inaugurate a monument to the "great November 29 Victory" at the Hwasong-15's launch sites, engraved with the launch date, the names of all the scientists and engineers who had been involved with the missile's realization,[20] and a poem, emphasizing the importance of "nuclear possession" and referencing the July 4 and March 18 "revolutions" of the same year: the first tests of an ICBM and its engine respectively.[21] Against expectations, Kim very suddenly had his prize—so what next for his deterrent?

After the Hwasong-15: Launch and Reentry

Even after the successful November test, U.S. military intelligence assessed the rate of production of these new ICBMs as slow. In late 2017, the U.S. Defense Intelligence Agency estimated that, in all likelihood, serial production would take until 2020. In March 2019, as the United States and South Korea prepared for joint military exercises, one of the planning assumptions for war scenarios was that North Korea would have an inventory of just two Hwasong-15s—this despite the United States acknowledging that six launchers were available for the missile, and despite Kim's 2018 New Year's Day address calling for the mass production of ballistic missiles.[22]

North Korea's three ICBM tests of 2017 allowed Kim Jong Un to openly declare on the first day of 2018—to North Koreans and the world—that his "deterrent" was complete. Within North Korean borders, this was presented as a historic accomplishment—the final realization of a decades-long project for regime security and economic growth. But, as Kim's New Year's Day directive indicated, the completion of the deterrent, while true in qualitative terms, was not close in quantitative terms. Since the two July 2017 tests of the Hwasong-14, Kim had begun to see signs that parts of the U.S. policymaking apparatus were taking his ICBM threat seriously. North Korean *credibility* was taking hold. But this in itself was going to require further efforts: one disadvantage of people believing you have a credible nuclear force is that they might try to do something about it, and the Americans were definitely starting to believe.

In September 2017, after the summer's successful tests of the first ICBM, General Joseph Dunford, the top U.S. military officer, told a Senate hearing that "We should assume today that North Korea has that capability and has the will to use that capability."[23] That same month, Kim claimed to have successfully tested the Peanut thermonuclear weapon; General John Hyten, the chief of U.S. Strategic Command, said that it would be irresponsible for U.S. military planners not to take this seriously.[24] In October, CIA Director Mike Pompeo—who would become the next secretary of state—suggested that "We ought to behave as if they are on the cusp of achieving [ICBMs]." All these signals built Kim's confidence that the terror that underlies successful deterrence had been instilled in the minds of the Americans.

One characteristic of ICBMs in particular has made them one of the world's deadliest weapons: their atmospheric reentry speed is so great that terminal missile defenses on the target territory are left as sitting ducks. Even shorter-range missiles like the Scuds can offer a nasty challenge to most ballistic missile defense systems, but of course the payload of an ICBM magnifies the threat, and the North has touted these advantages in its propaganda. In March 2017, shortly after the United States and South Korea confirmed the deployment of THAAD, a state-controlled North Korean news site highlighted that Pyongyang's missiles "are very fast ... [South Korea's defense systems] cannot but be hit by such rockets as they can never detect the sign of launch."[25]

Nevertheless, there were—and are—skeptics of North Korea's capabilities. Many experts have argued that the twice-tested Hwasong-14 and the once-tested Hwasong-15 can hardly be regarded as credible systems for any sort of nuclear-delivery mission. While this may be true by the engineering and industrial standards of sophisticated, mature missile powers like the United States and Russia, where flight-tests occur by the dozens before operational deployment of a new system, North Korean standards are different. For Kim Jong Un, once the qualitative capability has been *mostly* demonstrated, forcing his opponent to begin planning for the worst, he is content to call the day a success. The U.S. Department of Defense has a term for this: initial threat availability.[26] During his September 2017 visit to New York, North Korean Foreign Minister Ri Yong Ho warned any doubters to be careful what they wished for, threatening an atmospheric nuclear test detonation off a ballistic missile.[27] This would likely have failed, but it would have been malpractice for American planners to operate under that assumption. Kim may have only stopped testing when he did because of U.S. officials' public statements on the perceived significance of 2017's events. Those statements allowed him to calculate that he had sufficient leverage to approach the negotiation table.

Nevertheless, through 2018 and 2019, work remained underway in North Korea on advancing the national strategic nuclear deterrent, and much still lies ahead. Kim might now be confident of ensuring his survival against all odds, but he has to make sure, by strengthening the size and sophistication of his ICBM arsenal, that forcible nuclear disarmament will not be on the cards either. Though not a consensus view, parts of the U.S. intelligence community as well as the UN Panel of Experts on North Korea remain convinced that North Korea will press ahead to develop a solid-fuel ICBM, for the advantages of responsiveness and survivability that the liquid-fueled Hwasong-14 and Hwasong-15 lack.[28] In 2019, Kim had started showing off a range of new solid-fuel missile capabilities, suggesting rapid progress. The liquid-fueled Hwasong-14 and Hwasong-15 were sufficient for Kim's deterrence needs in 2017, but still represent inelegant systems. No country has ever deployed fully road-mobile liquid-propellant ICBMs, given the operational and logistical difficulties; North Korea may be relying on these missiles as a stopgap until it finally masters solid fuel technology.

For the purposes of operationalizing something close to a credible minimum nuclear deterrent against the United States, though, the existing two missiles will do in quality terms. Quantity seems to be the priority—North Korea is on the home stretch in terms of missiles, item three on the all-important deterrent checklist. In all likelihood, then, Kim Jong Un will now turn toward the next technology to be crossed off the list: mastering launch and reentry for his brand-new intercontinental ballistic missiles.

ICBM Launchers: A Bottleneck?

Kim Jong Un's 2018 New Year's Day diktat for mass production of "nuclear warheads and ballistic missiles" was not a surprising order to give at this point in his nuclear program. It was time to turn from innovation to multiplication. Throughout 2018, the world saw North Korea's nuclear weapons and ballistic missiles take on a far lower profile than in the preceding years. The testing campaign of 2016–17 had given the world headlines almost every other week, but at the Foundation Day parade on September 9, 2018, only conventional weaponry was on show, with no touting of nuclear-capable systems during Kim's diplomatic charm offensive. But, even as the low-key parade was rolling through Kim Il Sung Square, behind the scenes, there were reports that Kim's mass production directive was being followed to the letter.

U.S. Secretary of State Mike Pompeo, testifying to the Senate Foreign Relations Committee just weeks after June's Singapore summit between Kim and Trump, could not deny that North Korea was still enriching uranium for use in additional nuclear warheads. Later in the summer, *The Washington Post*, citing U.S. intelligence assessments, noted that North Korea was manufacturing additional Hwasong-15 ICBMs at the well-known

Sanum-dong Research Center. Even as diplomacy proceeded, it was clear that North Korea was determinedly working toward a preconceived notion of an ideal nuclear force structure. The outside world did not know exactly what that structure was, but there were some important hints that launch and reentry would be key features.

If North Korea was serious about using its weapons for what Kim described in his New Year's Day address as "a powerful and reliable war deterrent," he would need more missiles—but also the means to launch them. One important constraint on further development of North Korea's nuclear arsenal after 2017 was its reliance on externally sourced launch vehicles for ICBMs, namely the extensively adapted Chinese logging trucks used for the Hwasong-13, -14 and -15. Based on nearly all available evidence to date, North Korea appears to have received only six of these trucks from China. As of 2018 at least five of the six have been modified for use with the larger Hwasong-15. The precise numbers matter, because more launch vehicles mean less reloading in a war, and a more significant threat overall. Both North Korea and the United States plan to go first in any conflict on the Korean Peninsula, and U.S. preemption scenarios, in particular, plan to swiftly destroy Kim Jong Un's ICBM force—so Kim will want as many launchers as possible, and six will not be enough.

In reality, North Korea may not even count on reloading its ICBM launchers in wartime at all, expecting their destruction either before launch, or after a single launch. Still, as North Korea manufactures additional Hwasong-15s, it would make sense also to end dependence on foreign-imported vehicles to transport and launch them. The investment in the six logging trucks has been substantial to date, but Kim surely intends to unshackle himself. These kinds of launch vehicles are difficult to manufacture, and especially with the high reliability and endurance necessary for their use in a nuclear force. (A forestry truck breaking down may mean lost revenue; road-mobile ballistic missiles breaking down can be the difference between a grudging shot at survival and certain defeat for the North Korean regime.) However, the emphasis given to the March 16 Factory in the launch of the Hwasong-15 suggests that North Korea may be inching closer to an indigenous ICBM launch vehicle. In August 2018, a medium-confidence assessment from the U.S. Defense Intelligence Agency underscored that new Hwasong-15 launch vehicles were being manufactured at the facilities at Pyongsong.[29] By the end of 2019, North Korean construction crews had largely completed a major expansion of the facilities; satellite imagery suggested that the facility's capacity for outputting vehicles could have grown considerably.[30]

Other modes of basing may appeal to Kim as well. Rail-mobility for ballistic missile launchers could have a future in North Korea, given existing railroad networks and tunnels. Silos are likely a nonstarter given that, once detected, they are sitting ducks to a disabling precision strike using conventional weaponry—but, with some investment, North Korea may one day be able to implement the sort of scheme deployed by China for the DF-5, its largest ICBM. To better conceal its limited stock of this missile, China built multiple decoy siloes, each designed externally to appear identical to the real thing in satellite imagery. There is some evidence from North Korea's use of extensive tunnel networks and underground facilities that such an approach would be well within reach should this path be pursued.

In the meantime, as we saw with the land-based Pukguksong-2, North Korea has also been exploring off-roading capabilities for its launch vehicles since early 2017, with tracks replacing wheels in a new range of all-North Korean vehicles. While the launcher for the medium-range Pukguksong-2 is still far too small for a missile like the Hwasong-15, and while Kim has largely favored these sorts of vehicles for his solid-fueled missiles, a large liquid-fueled ICBM may one day appear on such a track-bearing launcher too, which would be a huge advancement. In short, Kim Jong Un may be standing at a crossroads for future development of his ICBM launchers, but he's not short of paths to take.

Space Launchers: War and Peace?

One type of launch vehicle for which indigenous development has long been underway is the space launcher, as North Korea's space program has evolved alongside its nuclear arsenal. These have always been presented to the outside world as innocent satellite launchers for civilian scientific purposes, but it is not much of a leap between the design goals for a satellite and those for an ICBM. Both, once launched, travel to great heights, in excess of 1,000 kilometers outside the earth's atmosphere. The only difference is what happens once this altitude is reached: as author Douglas Adams observed in *The Hitchhiker's Guide to the Galaxy* (1979), the secret to flight "lies in learning how to throw yourself at the ground and miss." A satellite in low-earth orbit successfully misses the earth until it decays over time and does not any more; but the whole purpose of an ICBM payload is to come back down again. The question of getting "up there" in the first place, however, is the same for both uses. The world's first ever satellite—the Soviet Sputnik-1—was launched from a modified R-7 ICBM launcher.

Given these similarities, it is unsurprising that U.S. intelligence first began to seriously contemplate a North Korean nuclear threat to the homeland in the wake of a leap forward in space launch technology. In 1998, Kim Jong Il, in power for four years, oversaw the first and last launch of the Taepodong-1, a space launch vehicle; as we saw in Chapter One, this would ultimately lead to the Berlin Agreement with the United States. On

August 31, 1998, North Korean state media announced the country's first successful insertion of a satellite payload into an unspecified orbit. Pyongyang claimed that the purpose of the satellite (the Kwangmyongsong-1) was to broadcast into the cosmos two beloved revolutionary anthems: "the Song of General Kim Il Sung, and the Song of General Kim Jong Il." Yet U.S. intelligence could see where all of this might lead. The following year, 1999, saw analysts predict that the United States would "most likely" face an intercontinental-range ballistic missile threat from North Korea by 2014.

The U.S. National Intelligence Council's (NIC) unclassified summary of a 1999 National Intelligence Estimate placed North Korea alongside Russia and China as the only other country that would "most likely" pose such a threat. (Threats from Russia and China, of course, really did exist at the time of the estimate.) Alongside these countries, the NIC assessed that Iran "probably" and Iraq "possibly" would pose a similar threat: "We judge that North Korea, Iran, and Iraq would view their ICBMs more as strategic weapons of deterrence and coercive diplomacy than as weapons of war."[31] Several months later, North Korea announced that it would build on its success with a launch of the Kwangmyongsong-2 satellite (though that launch ultimately would not take place for another eight years).

By 2003, the United States had made up its mind about the Taepodong-1: it would be a lousy ICBM and so North Korea was probably not going to deploy it as one. Although the launcher was still referred to as an ICBM from time to time, in news articles, blogs or even occasionally in official documents, that was not a helpful way to view it. But the U.S. Defense Intelligence Agency also clarified its belief that the Taepodong-1's importance was not only as a major propaganda coup; it was also a proof-of-concept and test bed for complex missile technologies. George Tenet, then director of the CIA, testified to the Senate Armed

Services Committee in 1999 that an improved Taepodong-1 could "deliver a very small payload to ... parts of the United States," and the not-yet-publicized Taepodong-2 could "deliver significantly larger payloads to mainland Alaska and the Hawaiian Islands and [at least] smaller payloads to other parts of the United States."[32]

The Taepodong-1 was an unacknowledged failure, but North Korea's burgeoning space program became a prominent source of national pride in the 2000s and 2010s. On July 4, 2006, Kim Jong Il oversaw a failed test launch of the larger Taepodong-2, ending the Berlin Agreement moratorium. The satellite failed forty-two seconds into flight, and no imagery was released, but North Korea's ambitions as a civilian space-faring country were furthered—and engineers gathered data on engines and stage-separation that would prove useful in ballistic missiles. As so often occurs with North Korean testing, the timing of the launch was symbolic, coinciding with the U.S. launch of the space shuttle Discovery. In 2009, Kim Jong Il made his second and last satellite launch vehicle attempt, carrying the long-promised successor satellite on a new launcher, the Unha-2. Again the launch failed, with the payload lost to the sea, but that year the U.S. National Air and Space Intelligence Center repeated the warnings of 1998–99: that North Korea could use satellite test launches to work toward larger, better space launchers and—yes—ballistic missiles.[33]

Under Kim Jong Un, the North Korean space program would find itself transformed. Kim came to favor a launch site on the western coast, Sohae, leaving behind the northeastern Tonghae site that his father had used. On April 13, 2012—a few days before Kim Il Sung's centenary birthday—it was time to try out the Unha-3 launch vehicle, with a third-iteration satellite to match. This may have been part of Kim Jong Un's attempt to establish himself, coming just four months after his father's death, or—more likely, given that short timeframe—it may have been the fulfillment of one of Kim Jong Il's last decisions. Certainly, the North Koreans had made a huge deal of the peaceful civilian use of space shortly before his death: on November 29, 2011, KCNA published a white paper titled "Space Is Common Wealth" that lashed out at the United States for scrutinizing North Korea's space activities.[34]

Despite these protestations, the United States clearly continued to worry that Kim Jong Un's seemingly peaceful satellite program was destined to evolve into an ICBM program. Even though the Unha-3 launch failed around one minute into flight, the event succeeded in scuttling the agreement concluded just weeks earlier: the Leap Day Deal, which had promised a freeze on North Korean long-range missile testing, among other things. The two sides had not agreed to a single text, and as with the collapse of the Agreed Framework twenty years earlier, the United States judged the Unha-3 launch to have violated the spirit, if not the letter, of the deal (the North Koreans evidently did not consider it a "long-range missile").

As Kim Jong Un's resolve persisted, the omens of future ICBM launches were not going anywhere. A fourth satellite launch in December 2012 successfully inserted the payload into a polar orbit, a fact that the United States confirmed; as of 2019, the satellite remained in low-earth orbit. South Korean debris recovery on this occasion found a potpourri of foreign components, even as most of the airframe itself was manufactured indigenously, including from the United States, United Kingdom, China, the former Soviet Union, and even Switzerland.[35] On February 7, 2016, Kim Jong Un oversaw a further successful satellite launch. This launch was particularly provocative as it took place just one month after Pyongyang claimed to have tested a hydrogen bomb, the Kim-4 test. There was public concern about the size of the satellite, which was assessed to have been twice as large as anything Pyongyang had attempted to previously launch—suggesting great strides in its launch technologies.[36]

In 2013, Kim Jong Un had set up a new National Aerospace Development Administration (NADA) to pursue peaceful space activities "on a legal basis," according to North Korean state media; this was done through the 12th Supreme People's Assembly, a meeting of North Korea's analog to a national parliament, another sign that genuine focus was being placed on the civilian space program. Similarly, the famously "non-nuclear" military parade of September 2018 still included a float making prominent reference to the space program. In September 2015, a CNN reporter was given access to Kim Jong Un's glitzy new General Satellite Control and Command Center: "It looks like the Starship Enterprise from the outside."[37] For the Kim regime, the space program had become an emblem of national pride and self-reliant modernity. Efforts were also made to keep it above board. Unlike ballistic missile tests, space launches in the Kim Jong Un era were accompanied by notices to the International Maritime Organization, providing a launch window and coordinates for debris splashdown zones.

All the same, Kim's space program was still seen internationally as a fig leaf for the regime to begin experimenting with long-range ballistic missile technology. The UN viewed the space launches as a violation of Security Council resolutions banning North Korea from testing any ballistic missile technologies.[38] The Taepodong-1's core technology—and eventually that of its successors through 2016—ultimately represented a technological dead end for the flight-tested ICBMs lying ahead in 2017, and there are known serious disadvantages to using space launchers as a "poor man's ICBM", such as their vulnerability while sitting on a launch pad. But the inherent fungibility between a space launcher and an ICBM remains. Even so, when North Korea did eventually build an ICBM, it did not rely on the most fundamental technologies underlying its space launchers.

Given his emphasis on science and technology as the corner-stones of national self-reliance and economic growth, so long as Kim Jong Un reigns in North Korea, the space program will continue and NADA will receive particular attention. While Pyongyang took steps during the 2018 diplomatic surge to dismantle facilities at the Sohae launch site, these were partial and reversible, and the very fact that Sohae was on the table as a concession in denuclearization talks amounted to an admission that there was a nuclear force component to the space launch program, despite decades of insistence to the contrary. Ultimately, even a complete and permanent dismantlement of Sohae would not prevent North Korea from continuing with its space program: Pyongyang also has the option open to pursue a road-mobile space launcher. This would be unusual, but not unprecedented; China and Israel have both launched light satellites in this mode. Alternatively, it could refurbish and reopen the east coast launch facilities at Tonghae/Musudan-ri, which have gone unused since 2009.

The dismantlement at Sohae in 2018 was eventually paused after the collapse of diplomacy between U.S. President Trump and Kim and indicators had been in place that the young leader had big plans for his space program. On December 21, 2017, shortly after the launch of the Hwasong-15 and Kim's celebration that his nuclear deterrent was "complete," a group of Workers' Party officials, including Kim, drove out from Pyongyang to the Sanum-dong Research Center, a missile factory and known space program site. Kim had already visited once before in 2016, prior to the launch of the Unha-3 that February; North Korean footage showed Kim inspecting the Unha-3 at the site and playfully patting the satellite launcher's nose. Shortly after this December 2017 visit, U.S. spy satellites detected evidence near the facility of a new type of North Korean satellite launch vehicle.[39]

This built on hints dropped by NADA representatives the previous month, who had told a visiting Russian expert in

November that they had grand plans to launch two new satellites. While the first was within the capabilities already demonstrated by North Korea, the second was much more interesting: "This is a communication satellite which works on a geostationary Earth orbit and weighs over 1000 kg."[40] If a serious objective, that would require something much more powerful than the Unha launchers. At the time of the Russian expert's visit, North Korea's test of the massive Hwasong-15 had yet to take place. When that missile appeared later in the month, it became clear that its 80-ton-force first-stage booster would provide a completely different and viable foundation for a new generation of space launch vehicles. In the end, the ICBMs beat the space launchers to the finish line—but Kim Jong Un may now show the world just how, in the age of the Hwasong-15, North Korean space launch aspirations can be pushed to new heights—literally.

The Reentry Question

It must sometimes seem to Kim Jong Un that his work is never done. Even now that North Korea has successfully demonstrated a behemoth ICBM, and even after launch is eventually fully indigenized, there will still be a further hurdle to clear: what goes up must come down. Pyongyang still has not cracked the reentry vehicle problem, and it was this that allowed skeptics in the United States and elsewhere to remain complacent even despite the historic Hwasong-15 test of 2017. For long-range ballistic missiles—particularly those that exit the atmosphere and reenter it to complete flight—reentry is among the most complex physical challenges for designers. The Hwasong-14 and Hwasong-15 demonstrated to the whole world that North Korea had figured out—and even finessed—the art of sending a large missile up, but it was less clear if it had figured out how to bring the pointy end back down to a sufficiently low altitude to deliver its nuclear payload. Without crossing that final threshold, North Korea could publish awe-inspiring launch footage, and U.S. officials might start to sit up and take notice, but Kim could still potentially fail to convince the United States that the "nuclear threat" from its forces was real. This would get in the way of the "balance of power" Pyongyang seeks.

The physical challenge of ballistic reentry is mostly simple to wrap one's head around and has long been understood by scientists and engineers in more developed countries with longstanding missile programs. Simply put, a given projectile—be it a missile's reentry vehicle, a space shuttle, or a reentry capsule with an astronaut inside—is drawn toward earth by gravity alone, while facing immense aerodynamic drag once it leaves the vacuum of space and passes through the earth's atmosphere. Humans breathe air without difficulty, but for dense, solid objects traveling at great speed, air resistance is not a trivial force. The immense energy of a physical object undergoing ballistic atmospheric reentry compresses the air in front of it, resulting in structural stress and massive heat generation, easily in excess of 1,500° Celsius. Some objects—like small meteors—succumb entirely to this heat, causing them to burn up in the atmosphere. That is why only the largest meteors—or mammoth asteroids—are capable of actually colliding with the earth's surface.

In other words, it is far easier to send things into space—whether nuclear missiles or humans—than to safely return them. With astronauts, the experience of reentry can be improved by using non-ballistic reentry (where the trajectory is diverted from a ballistic one), but this is not desirable for most ballistic missiles. North Korea must overcome both the technical and the engineering challenges of designing a reentry vehicle that could survive the stresses of intercontinental-range flight, and—more importantly—credibly convey to the United States that it should not second guess the performance of its reentry vehicles. For years, American bravado has permitted defense planners to sleep easy at night, knowing that North Korea's nuclear payloads would have a high probability of burning up in the atmosphere above American cities. John Schilling, an aerospace engineer who has long tracked North Korea's development of space launcher and ballistic missile technology, noted in October 2015 that "North Korea has never demonstrated the ability to build a reentry vehicle that can survive at even half the speed an ICBM would require." He added: "If and when they do, what is presently a theoretical threat will become very real and alarming."[41]

Reentry, therefore, would be a natural area for Kim Jong Un to focus on, now that his ICBMs themselves have been tested successfully. As far back as 2016, weeks after its fourth nuclear test, the regime gave a highly important public demonstration of its seriousness about mastering reentry technology. On March 15, during the annual U.S.—South Korea Key Resolve/Foal Eagle joint military exercises, KCNA covered a visit by Kim Jong Un to the high-profile Chamjin Missile Factory. You might recall its engine test stand from Chapter Five, where it was described how the factory was used to test engines for indigenous short-range missiles including the Hwasong-5 and Hwasong-6. In March 2016, this very same stand was used to validate North Korea's progress toward a survivable reentry vehicle that could make it to the U.S. homeland. Kim was there to view an "environmental simulation" of ballistic missile reentry. In the KCNA's published photographs, Kim can be seen grinning as he examines a well-charred nose cone recently blasted from a short-range missile engine under high heat stress.

It is impossible to ascertain in the open source whether this test was enough to declare the job done in terms of developing missile-ready, heat-resistant materials for successful reentry. But Kim certainly appeared content to say so, according to KCNA:

We have proudly acquired the reentry technology, possessed by a few countries styling themselves military powers, by dint of self-reliance and self-development, thus making great progress in the ballistic rocket technology that helps increase the independence of the country's defense capability and munitions industry and remarkably enhance the invincible might of the powerful revolutionary Paektusan army.

The South Koreans were immediately doubtful of Kim's claims. "What North Korea announced today is North Korea's unilateral argument. According to our military's judgement, North Korea hasn't secured missile re-entry ability yet,"[42] a Ministry of Defense spokesman said. In the United States, the test was also slammed by some commentators as a stunt—surely blasting a mocked-up reentry vehicle nose cone with the heat from a Scud engine could not replicate the physical stresses endured during real atmospheric reentry? Yet the simulation was not a total circus act for Kim Jong Un's benefit. During the 1970s, the United States had conducted similar simulation exercises in its development of new types of warhead materials; with adequate sensor equipment, static burn simulation tests on a warhead could provide useful data "representative of actual ICBM flight conditions."[43] The similar design of the March 14, 2016 reentry test strongly suggests that North Korea knew about this U.S. testing, and expected the U.S. intelligence community at least to take the hint.

Public pronouncements on the unconvincing nature of the reentry test were meant to reassure the South Korean and American populations, but, in North Korea, it was sure to annoy. After all, the purpose behind the simulation had been to signal the growing credibility of its nuclear force development. This dismissal and disbelief from Kim's adversaries is dangerous—the KCNA report hinted at what might become necessary to convey the reality of the nuclear threat: "a nuclear warhead explosion test and a test-fire of several types of ballistic rockets capable of carrying nuclear warheads will be conducted in a short time to further increase the reliability of nuclear attack capability."

In other words, there is no reason to believe Kim will leave things there in terms of realizing and proving his reentry capabilities.[44] North Korea may be working toward additional means of testing reentry vehicles without flight-testing, including possibly at a new space environment testing center in Pyongyang itself.[45] While this facility would not allow much in the way of testing a vehicle's ability to withstand reentry, it would give North Korean engineers a better understanding of how to engineer nuclear warheads to travel outside of the earth's atmosphere, dealing with electromagnetism and other environmental factors. What's more, there are outstanding reentry challenges beyond the materials science: even after a warhead has survived its return to the atmosphere above the U.S., there are the final challenges of accuracy and precision.

For a ballistic missile to be useful, it needs to have a reasonably high probability of delivering its payload to a sufficiently small defined area. Given the massive distances involved, the guidance, accuracy, and precision requirements for any ballistic missile system are amplified when the range is intercontinental. These concerns could be overcome by working toward larger nuclear yields (all else being equal, if you throw something bigger, it is more likely to hit your target), but this solution is inelegant. As Kim Jong Un continues work on the accuracy problem, we can expect to see *at least* one realistic test-flight (preferably several by the standards of most ordinary missile development programs). This will require maximizing a long-range missile's range, rather than highly lofting it to avoid a crashdown on foreign soil. As of mid-2020, North Korea had not yet done this with an ICBM, but, as we know, launches of the intermediate-range Hwasong-12 have exhibited such a trajectory, overflying Japan. If Kim really wants to settle doubts as to his reentry capabilities, he will surely take this step in the future with an intercontinental missile.

The reentry question remained unresolved through 2019, but what still works to Kim's favor is the basic probabilistic reasoning at the center of assessing nuclear risks. Nuclear weapons, by their sheer destructiveness, give policymakers pause even when the probability of their use or successful detonation is very low. As of late 2017, the U.S. Defense Intelligence Agency had defined the probability rate of the intermediate Hwasong-12 as a moderately high 50 per cent.[46] So if four Hwasong-12s were to be launched at Guam, U.S. defense planners had a working assumption that two would successfully detonate on target. For the less-tested Hwasong-14 and Hwasong-15, the number was a lower 25 per cent.[47] Meanwhile, for North Korea's liquid-fueled short-range and medium-range missiles, including the Nodong or the Hwasong-6, the assessed probability of success was greater than 50 per cent.[48]

These probabilities would be unacceptably low by U.S. standards for launch, but North Korea may be less particular—and they are still high stakes with which to gamble massive loss of life and environmental destruction. Furthermore, this assessment was caveated with the warning that the success probabilities for the ICBMs could rapidly rise should North Korea resume testing—particularly testing on more realistic trajectories. Sowing that doubt in the mind of an American leader is sufficient for North Korea. Until the day its reentry vehicles are proven, fear of even one North Korean nuclear warhead striking a U.S. city should serve Kim's deterrent just fine. But given the low reliability of these missiles even after their testing in 2017, holding Kim Jong Un to a moratorium on testing has immense value. Unfortunately, frustrated with the U.S.'s inflexibility in negotiations and a lack of reciprocal concessions, Kim announced an end to his voluntary moratorium in December 2019, stating that his country had "no grounds to be unilaterally bound any longer by the commitment."[49]

The more North Korea tests, the more it can refine and validate its capabilities. Additionally, there is one final item on the five-point deterrent checklist that Kim must still perfect: even once all the technological components of nuclear launch and detonation are fully, successfully in place, his whole nuclear deterrence strategy can fall apart if he does not deal effectively with the questions of command and control.

9

FEAR, COMMAND, CONTROL

To practice nuclear deterrence, North Korea has to deter undesirable action against itself, and its adversaries must believe that its nuclear weapons are credibly fielded, deployed, and usable. We have seen the astounding leaps forward in physical capability under Kim Jong Un, but before reflecting on where this has left the world post-2017, we need to think about the glue that holds a nuclear force together: command and control. Command and control, or C2, is not about whether you can successfully test nuclear bombs and launch ballistic missiles in peacetime; it is about how and whether your leadership might be able to ensure that these systems are on standby for use in an actual crisis. Accordingly, one of the most significant demands on the North Korean regime in the early years of the twenty-first century, and an ongoing challenge for the future, has been the design of a sufficiently robust C2 architecture.

Given the general opacity of the North Korean state, and the fundamental nature of nuclear command as an organizational and technical enterprise, little public-domain information exists about how exactly North Korea has gone about this. Even so, there are several universal challenges related to nuclear C2 that we know Kim Jong Un has had to contend with. In the early Cold War, these demands were theorized to be more or less mechanical. So long as their responsibilities were well organized, humans in the C2 chain—from the authority with the power to order nuclear weapons release, all the way down to the individual military unit charged with their launch—were expected to behave rationally and swiftly, like a well-oiled machine. But amid multiple crises, it became quickly clear that, as a former U.S. ICBM launch control officer has put it, "nuclear organizations do not behave like ... highly abstract models of rational decision."[1] This will almost certainly be particularly true in North Korea, where command and control challenges will be acute.

New nuclear weapons states feel the inadequacies of command and control most sharply, as the experiences of India and Pakistan during their 1999 and 2001–02 crises demonstrated. Even with the information gaps surrounding North Korea's C2 choices, the available evidence on the country's nuclear strategy can help us make sense of the range of choices available to Kim. His strategic objectives in fielding nuclear weapons will determine his choices regarding their command and control. This chapter considers the likely options open to Kim for C2 as he perfects his nuclear deterrent, as well as the risks of serious miscalculations in a crisis, from Kim downwards, given the authoritarian peculiarities of his regime.[2]

Use Authority: Who Can Launch Nuclear Weapons?

One of the most fundamental questions that any state seeking to mobilize its nuclear forces must answer is: who can authorize a launch, and under what circumstances—and what checks and balances might exist on this authorization? Subsidiary to this question are other, more technical considerations. For instance, who can decide to assemble nuclear weapons, mate them to their missiles, and move them out into the battlefield? Who has nominal and legal authority over these decisions, and who oversees their physical implementation? How experienced are the military and technical units overseeing the handling and management of nuclear weapons?

In a centralized, monolithic, and authoritarian state like North Korea, with highly assertive civilian control of the military, the only authorities that can issue a valid order for use of nuclear weapons are: the country's supreme leader; the chairman of the State Affairs Council; or the supreme commander of the Korean People's Army. All of these people are Kim Jong Un and only Kim Jong Un. Kim himself definitively clarified this aspect of nuclear command in April 2013 with the "Law on Consolidating Position of Nuclear Weapons State," which declared that the country's "nuclear weapons can be used only by a final order of the Supreme Commander of the Korean People's Army."[3]

In the Kim Jong Un era, this civilian control of the nuclear button has been hinted with Kim's elevation of scientists and engineers over the armed forces, and nuclear weapons propaganda has gone to particular lengths to emphasize this. For instance, during Kim's two famed inspections of mocked-up nuclear devices, the 'Disco Ball' and the 'Peanut,' KCNA's photographs were staged to underline the supreme leadership's control over these weapons, with Kim featuring centrally. The 'Peanut' inspection images did not even feature any uniformed military officers. The 2018 New Year's Day address further underscored the point: as he announced completion of the deterrent, Kim remarked that "the nuclear button is on my office desk all the time." The remark soon drew a boast from President Trump that, unlike Kim's, "my Button works!"[4] But Kim was probably taking a bit of poetic license to convey that he and only he possessed the physical means to issue a valid authorization of nuclear use. While it is still unclear exactly how Kim can physically set in motion a nuclear launch, he almost certainly does not possess a cartoonish single "button" on his desk; no nuclear weapons state works this way.

The limitations of such a button are obvious—especially for a country facing the unique threat perception of North Korea. For instance, U.S. National Security Advisor Zbigniew Brzezinski once received a 3 a.m. phone call announcing the approach of announcing the approach of up to 250 enemy missiles.[5] Though Brzezinski's call was a false alarm and he lacked the authority to launch nuclear weapons, the example serves to demonstrate the role that flexibility and speed play in nuclear decision-making. Were North Korea's nuclear weapons only usable when Kim is in close proximity to his "office desk," their deterrent value would be considerably limited. The United States could just strike when Kim was fast asleep. In reality, as far as the physical aspects of control are concerned, a range of stakeholders within North Korea play a role, possibly from the Reconnaissance General Bureau to the KPA Supreme Guard Command to the Nuclear Weapons Institute.[6]

Since we know that North Korea is explicit on the point that Kim—and only Kim—can authorize nuclear use, inseparably enjoining him and his nuclear forces is crucial for his deterrent goals. This must be as true when Kim is located in Pyongyang as when he is in a far-flung corner of the country, or beyond— hence the inadequacy of a single "nuclear button." The United States and Russia have solved this particular problem with the nuclear "football" and the *chemodanchik* or *cheget* respectively. A military officer is assigned to trail the civilian leader with launch authority, offering up the relevant tool should the moment come. In the United States, every president since Dwight D. Eisenhower has had the nuclear arsenal within a few paces of his person during all official duties.

The football, it turned out, not only would allow a launch to occur within minutes if necessary, but also had another important symbolic role to play, one that bears particular relevance in the North Korean case: it underlined civilian control of nuclear weapons. This was part of the reason why, in 1994, U.S. President Bill Clinton turned down a proposal by Boris Yeltsin, his Russian counterpart, to do away with their respective briefcases of the apocalypse. "What if we were to give up having to have our finger next to the button all the time?" Yeltsin suggested during a phone call. "They [the military] always know where to find us, so perhaps we could agree that it is not necessary for us to carry the *chemodanchik*." Clinton decided to mull things over: "Well, I'll have to think about this—all we carry, of course, are the codes and the secure phone." When Yeltsin raised the issue again in 1997 ("Let us say we get rid of the nuclear footballs?"), Clinton soon gave a decisive answer: "When I took this job, I understood the symbolic importance that the football has in terms of civilian control over the military's decisions." "It has nothing to do with you," he assured Yeltsin.

The Russian premier was disappointed. At the time, the burden Yeltsin and Clinton bore was unique and he knew that. On the 1994 call, he had told the U.S. president: "You and I are the only leaders who have to do this."[7] Now, that may no longer be the case. U.S. and South Korean intelligence agencies have carefully scrutinized this issue and it appears that Kim does have something of a rudimentary football-*ish* capability that connects him to his nuclear forces.

In 2017, U.S. intelligence analysts tasked with tracking Kim Jong Un's activities and whereabouts in North Korea began noticing a new type of signature associated with his movements and known sites linked to the Supreme Guard Command, the elite corps charged with Kim's security.[8] Specifically, the signal appeared to be to do with a new kind of radio transmitter, which one U.S. analyst described as likely being North Korea's "nuclear football" command device. These kinds of TETRA radios might be appealing as a method of mobile nuclear C2, even if rudimentary compared to the systems in use by advanced nuclear weapons states. Kim's ability to command his nuclear forces could travel with him, impervious to American or South Korean attempts to disrupt the telecommunications network in a crisis. TETRA would also be highly scalable and networkable across North Korea's relatively compact territory. One North Korean firm is known to have sold advanced radio communications equipment, using front companies to operate out of Malaysia, Singapore, and Hong Kong. However, the U.S. intelligence community has not fully assessed how North Korea has networked its C2 infrastructure outside of its known hardened command sites.

For instance, it is unclear if North Korea had operationalized a rudimentary form of nuclear C2 through other means before these radio units appeared. Pyongyang's nuclear arrival coincided with the proliferation of wireless telecommunications technology worldwide. Cellphones have an interesting enough history in North Korea. Kim Jong Il once grew paranoid that a cellphone had been used as a trigger in what he called an assassination attempt: the Ryongchon catastrophe. On April 22, 2004, a massive explosion left the northern North Korean rail station at Ryongchon in flames, just hours after Kim's distinctive train had passed through.[9] Cellphones were temporarily banned in North Korea and as many as 10,000 phones seized by state authorities.[10] Cellphone adoption has since resumed and skyrocketed in the country.

So we know who can order a nuclear strike, and we have some ideas about how he might be able to do so. This leaves the question of the conditions in place for such a strike to be considered legitimate. A clause in the 2013 law enshrining North Korea's nuclear status codified a strategically useful "negative security assurance" that Pyongyang will not use its nuclear weapons to threaten, blackmail, or coerce nonnuclear states, with an important caveat:

> The DPRK shall neither use nukes against the non-nuclear states nor threaten them with those weapons unless *they join a hostile nuclear weapons state* in its invasion and attack on the DPRK. [emphasis added]

North Korea is no nonproliferation paragon, but enshrining in law this definition of the valid use of nuclear weapons—which makes South Korea and Japan fair game for nuclear attack—should give both countries an incentive to reconsider their alliance with the United States. If the alliance is successfully undermined, then the reassurances within this legal provision also serve to deter North Korea's neighbors from developing nuclear weapons of their own. In reality, however, this restriction is not viewed seriously within the nongovernmental strategic communities in Seoul and Tokyo. For one thing, the law does not clarify any means to prevent the supreme leader from issuing a nuclear strike order when these conditions are not met. Officially, both countries concern themselves with North Korean nuclear weapons use against their territories.

Predelegation, Devolution, and 'Doomsday Machines'

Tokyo and Seoul are not the only ones to have considered the circumstances in which there might be a North Korean nuclear strike: Kim Jong Un himself has certainly done so. Like any other leader with the bomb, Kim's nuclear decision-making must contend with a dilemma famously articulated by American political scientist Peter Feaver in 1992: "leaders want a high assurance that [nuclear] weapons will always work when directed and a similar assurance the weapons will never be used in the absence of authorized direction."[11] This always-never dilemma is one of the central questions in designing nuclear command

and control. For North Korea, solving this C2 conundrum is critical to its ability to actually implement its nuclear strategy, which centers around preserving the regime and Kim Jong Un atop it. Unauthorized or even accidental nuclear weapons use by those who physically handle the country's bombs and missiles would be disastrous, especially if interpreted by the United States, South Korea, and Japan as sufficient *casus belli* for an all-out conflict. A C2 failure is a strategy failure, and Kim's nuclear deterrent is only as robust as his C2 systems.

One of the first problems for Kim will have been that of predelegation: the question of whether nuclear use authority can be sent down the military chain of command in the build-up to a crisis, if not in peacetime. Predelegation is risky, but can seriously augment deterrence. For instance, all known evidence suggests this is not the case, but if Kim issued standing peacetime orders for the country's Strategic Rocket Forces to release nuclear weapons at the sign of an oncoming invasion, then that might encourage the United States, South Korea, and Japan to exercise the utmost restraint in their regional activities. On the other hand, however, this might also constitute a recipe for a disaster.

If a civilian aircraft's transponder malfunctions in flight, North Korean air defense radars might interpret a passenger plane as a nuclear-armed American strategic bomber; and if authorization has already been predelegated, that could set off a chain of events leading to Kim Jong Un's demise, with the leader only informed after irreversible preparations of a rapid-response solid-fueled ballistic missile—a Pukguksong-2 perhaps—had already begun.[12] North Korea's archaic early warning systems, based on aging Soviet radars, make its predelegation problem particularly acute.[13] Political scientist Paul Bracken's classic Cold War work *The Command and Control of Nuclear Forces* (1983) includes a concise and instructive chart showing the brutal decision-making stakes for early warning personnel weighing up whether or not to report a single sighted aircraft as an enemy attack.[14] A variant is reproduced below:

U.S. move:	American bomber incoming!	No American attack underway.
North Korean interpretation:		
Yes, it's an attack!	DEAD HERO	HARD LABOR, AT BEST
No, it's something else.	DEAD BUM	–

These parameters present a serious dilemma for the well-disciplined North Korean operator determined to carry out their duty, and they are dependent upon several variables: an operator might be predisposed toward failing safe (non-intervention without explicit authorization, in case it is a false alarm) or failing deadly (preplanning a retaliatory strike in case it is real) based on their own definition of their task; bureaucratic incentives might skew decision-making; any launch might still require either the active assent of Kim Jong Un, given the risks of responding to a false alarm; and ideology—including positive ideology in the form of fealty to the leader and state—might intervene. In China's October 1966 nuclear test, a 12-kiloton nuclear weapon, atop a medium-range ballistic missile, was launched some 800 kilometers over China's own territory. The test's purpose was nominally scientific, but the immensely risky decision was made by Nie Rong-zhen, a marshal of the People's Liberation Army, who thought the act was necessary in the context of the Cultural Revolution![15]

In light of these considerations, North Korea's reasons for not implementing any known form of predelegation become clearer. Besides, under Kim Jong Un, the tendency has been for the military to come under *more* assertive civilian command, not less. The 2013 law codifying North Korea's nuclear status equally enshrined Kim's position as the sole commander of those forces, and this makes sense when we think about the strategy behind the deterrent: to preserve Kim Jong Un atop the regime. North Korea has had every reason to assure the outside world that its nuclear weapons would *not* be predelegated to specific military units or even to General Kim Rak Gyom, commander of the KPA Strategic Rocket Force; despite his loyalty, giving him the nuclear button would make him an unacceptable locus of control beyond Kim Jong Un himself. Political scientist Vipin Narang, whose theory of strategic postures we saw in Chapter Three, has argued that even countries like North Korea, with a strategy of asymmetric escalation and early first use, might not predelegate launch authority except under the direst circumstances.[16]

If not predelegation, then how about devolution? This is the question of what happens when the legitimate power vested with nuclear use authority is away or killed. This need not be a life or death situation: with Kim Jong Un's turn to overseas travel from 2018, questions remain about how nuclear use authority might be transferred while the supreme leadership is thousands of kilometers outside North Korea's borders; Kim would almost certainly lack the capabilities to order a valid nuclear launch in these conditions, so who inherits his "nuclear button" when he's away—if anyone? In the U.S. context, the football handles launch commands from anywhere on earth. In the case of the president's death, devolution procedures are formalized in the order of presidential succession, whereby the vice president, the speaker of the House of Representatives, the president *pro tempore* of the Senate, and so forth are bequeathed commander-in-chief authority—including to authenticate or issue nuclear launch orders. A chain of command like this is not universal among nuclear states; for instance, the United Kingdom has no fixed line of succession in case the prime minister is incapacitated.[17]

North Korean thinking on devolution procedures is not well known, but scholars have speculated that Pyongyang may follow a logic similar to Washington's, with command over the country's nuclear weapons falling immediately to the regime's *de facto* number two. Alternatively, should the *paektusan* bloodline prevail over party hierarchy, Kim's sister, Yo Jong, or brother, Jong Chol, might immediately inherit authority.[18] Yo Jong, in particular, has been reported to have attended significant guidance events alongside Kim Jong Un, including the unveiling of the 'Disco Ball' fission bomb. She was photographed at both an August 2019 test launch of a large-caliber rocket artillery system and a September 2019 test, indicating that her proximity to military affairs has been growing. In the September case, KCNA's report on the test listed her name second only to the KPA chief of staff, ahead of other prominent military personnel in attendance. In 2020, her star rose further as she was appointed to a key Worker's Party politburo position. As Kim Jong Un's children grow, devolved command might fall to his chosen eventual successor.

Questions of devolution are inherently linked to overall nuclear strategy. For instance, who inherits the button in the event of Kim's sudden wartime death is a concern for North Korean planners who need to concern themselves with planning retaliatory strikes to deter such an event from occurring in the first place. Death by natural causes is no doubt a concern for Kim Jong Un, who has never appeared to be in the best of health, but it is a secondary concern to the core problem of lethal regime change through American military might. Given the objectives we know are driving Kim's nuclear strategy (survival through deterrence), his adversaries must seriously consider that the country's command and control procedures could be designed to *fail deadly*: to guarantee a complete and overwhelming nuclear release after a major deterrence failure. In the North Korean case, the condition for a major deterrence failure would be the untimely death of the supreme leader at the hand of hostile foreign forces.

A "fail-deadly" scenario should not be written off as fantastical or based on some caricature of North Korea as a uniquely paranoid regime. As recently as the late 1960s, the United States had in place a similar plan known as 'Project Furtherance'.[19] Documents declassified in 2012 articulated the contours of this plan, which put in place procedures to initiate a "full nuclear response" against *both* the Soviet Union and China should the president be killed, incapacitated, or otherwise unreachable as a result of—or during the course of—an attack against the United States. We might even assume that North Korean strategists involved in designing the Kim regime's nuclear command and control systems are aware of this bit of history.

Of course, for a fail deadly mechanism to work, the world has to know about it. As Dr. Strangelove remarks to the Soviet ambassador in the eponymous film, "The whole point of a Doomsday Machine is lost if you keep it secret!" The fundamental incentives that brought the United States to implement Project Furtherance do exist in today's North Korea, but there is no indication that any sort of Doomsday Machine has been developed by Pyongyang. However, if relations between the United States and North Korea revert back into crisis and acrimony once more, there may be such an announcement. At that sobering point, we can suppose that Kim will have developed a specific C2 infrastructure to go with the policy.

Kim's Nukes at Sea: A Special Headache

One aspect of Kim's nuclear forces particularly highlights the ongoing risks of a North Korean nuclear deterrent without complete C2: the at-sea deterrent. To recap what we learnt in Chapter Six, Kim's nuclear submarine force is modest and not thought to be operational, but is undergoing active development, and North Korea has a very good reason to take its nuclear weapons to sea: to have a survivable nuclear force as a credible threat for a retaliatory second strike, even if all land-based systems have been destroyed. North Korea's relatively compact geography and persistent U.S. reconnaissance heighten the risk to its land-based nuclear forces, and we can see these anxieties in the regime's extensive use of underground facilities to conceal and harden ballistic missiles and their support equipment. In other words, we can expect to hear more from Kim Jong Un's *Gorae* and modified *Romeo* ballistic missile submarines, and the Pukguksong-1 and new Pukguksong-3 submarine-launched ballistic missiles. However, command and control for sea-based nuclear forces, in both peacetime and crisis, represents a particularly challenging iteration of the always-never C2 dilemma.

One important reason for this is that, in order to be useful, at-sea forces have to be fully assembled and ready when put out to sea. Even states that favor fail-safe arrangements have to make significant compromises on this strategy at sea due to the physical location on the submarine of 'locked and loaded' weapons. Though the Korean People's Navy has extensive, decades-long experience with conventional submarine operations, Kim may be concerned that it simply does not have the crew or organizational experience required to run a safe and robust nuclear deterrent patrol. Crew and personnel reliability are a critical component of C2, particularly in a crisis, when there are acute psychological pressures on a submarine crew that may not even have a way of communicating with authorities on shore. In the tumult of a crisis, and under the physical constraints of a submarine, the crew may be prone to erratic decision-making, which could lead to unauthorized or accidental nuclear release.

Other sea-faring nuclear states have developed command principles to reduce these risks. For instance, so-called two-man or even three-man rules incorporate on-ship procedures, whereby multiple commanding officers must assent to the release of a nuclear weapon. But the physical obstacles between the crew and a nuclear release are considerably smaller at sea than on land, since the nuclear warhead and SLBM are already mated. For the KPN commanding officer on board the *Gorae*, during what his superiors have told him is the start of a possible war with the Americans, worried about his boat being intercepted by enemy anti-submarine capabilities and unable to contact anyone on shore, the incentives to use or lose his nuclear weapons are terrifyingly high.

In designing sea-based nuclear C2, states choose between two basic models: a bastion, or a continuous at-sea deterrent. The latter is the gold standard for a truly survivable and fearsome sea-based nuclear force, but extremely technically demanding and costly to sustain. The United States and the United Kingdom today maintain continuous at-sea deterrents—for Britain, its four *Vanguard*-class ballistic missile submarines comprise the entirety of its nuclear deterrent. This sort of a model requires excellent onshore communications infrastructure to ensure that nuclear submarines can remain tethered to the national leadership, and utmost personnel reliability and discipline to ensure that the decision to release nuclear weapons is not made in haste, even if that communication line is lost. North Korea is nowhere close to this and unlikely to get close anytime soon.

Other nuclear powers with an undersea deterrent generally employ the bastion model. As the name implies, under this system submarines are kept at or near their home port, in the nuclear state's territorial waters, and are only flushed out with their weapons in a crisis. The core weakness of the bastion model is that, in an enemy first-strike scenario, having one's submarines in a known and relatively compact area is a huge vulnerability. This latter observation certainly describes North Korea's predicament: it operates a lone ballistic missile submarine—with at least one more under construction—and its adversaries enjoy overwhelming advantage in nuclear weaponry, anti-submarine warfare, and precision conventional weaponry.

Even with multiple submarines, then, North Korea will not be content to have some of its most survivable nuclear weapons sit at port if the indicators of a possible crisis have begun to set in (for example, the earlier scenario involving a possible U.S. bomber entering its airspace). At the first signs of trouble, the incentives will be overwhelming for Kim Jong Un to flush his submarine-launched nuclear weapons out to sea. Currently, the North Korean port of Sinpo is well known for its role in supporting the country's undersea deterrent. As a result, the submarine would likely be sunk as it left port in a preemptive enemy strike. Knowing this, Kim's standing orders to the Korean People's Navy would err on the side of caution, prompting the *Gorae* and its successors to leave their berths as soon as possible—increasing the risk of an over-hasty or accidental launch.

Such risks can be reduced by incorporating a go signal into at-sea C2: requiring a coded control device to be activated before launch of on-board nuclear weapons. This has been the case, for example, with the U.S. and UK Trident D5 SLBM. However, such an external validation requirement is probably not part of North Korea's SLBMs. There are good reasons for this: if Kim constructed onshore communications arrays for the specific purpose of long-range, over-the-horizon communication with its nuclear submarines, the United States and its allies would likely destroy these as part of their initial strike. Not requiring external validation would keep his undersea deterrent, once deployed in a crisis, credible.

Given the dilemmas described above, and recalling that any accidental or unauthorized nuclear launch is as good as death for Kim Jong Un, there are no particularly good or easy choices for Kim. The decisions that he may perceive to best augment deterrence also come with the greatest risks. Kim's final choices about sea-based C2 remain unknown, but there is little doubt that North Korea is fundamentally serious about pursuing this most survivable of options for its overall nuclear deterrent. In something close to 'peacetime,' the *Gorae* and its successors may not be a concern. However, in a crisis, the C2 concerns about North Korea's sea-based nuclear weapons delve into the terrifying.

Offensive Cyberweaponry and North Korean C2 Decision-Making

Another element of C2 that Kim must consider, now that his nuclear arsenal is 'complete,' is how to combat the possibility of hostile cyber interference in his command and control systems. In September 2017, U.S. Cyber Command (CYBERCOM) targeted the networks used by the North Korean Reconnaissance General Bureau.[20] The operation used rudimentary technology to exact a distributed denial of service attack: enough to serve as a shot across Pyongyang's bow, sending a message, but to avoid compromising any vulnerabilities in North Korea's networks that CYBERCOM may have identified and be hanging on to for use in a real crisis (a 'zero day' exploit). This operation was the result of a directive from President Trump that "involved actions across a broad spectrum of government agencies" to pressure North Korea.[21] It took place between September 22 and 30, according to a U.S. official with knowledge of CYBERCOM's activities.[22]

U.S. offensive cyber capabilities are some of the country's most closely guarded secrets, designed to serve as an 'ace up the sleeve' in a crisis scenario. Cyberweapons cannot do everything, but they can do a lot. If U.S. hackers could disable a North Korean missile launcher, that would be as good as a so-called counterforce capability, on a par with missile defense systems like THAAD: disabling Kim's weapons before they could arrive at their targets. In reality, North Korea's launchers, missiles, and guidance technologies are unlikely to be digitally networked in a way that would expose them to U.S. cyberpenetration before launch or in flight—but the United States has nevertheless pursued so-called 'left-of-launch' means of dealing with North Korea's rapidly developing missiles, and from 2017 these leaked in the press. In March that year, the *New York Times* revealed that a "new antimissile" approach had been developed, with the core idea being to "strike an enemy missile before liftoff or during the first seconds of flight."[23] The details remained shrouded in secrecy, but the overall impression spreading was that the United States had developed the means to remotely destroy North Korea's missiles.

In November, the same *New York Times* reporters followed up, revealing "a range of cyber and electronic-interference operations" begun in 2014 under the Obama administration to slow the development of the medium-range Hwasong-10, "with mixed results."[24] That began to get closer to the truth: U.S. operations had largely targeted the industrial processes and machinery involved in construction of Hwasong-10 components. While this could hinder North Korea's missile development, it was not the magical 'left-of-launch' capability that had originally been described, whereby an operator in Fort Meade, Maryland, might push a button to destroy a North Korean missile seconds into flight—or on the launch pad. Ultimately, the United States was never sure of the precise effect that its industrial interference efforts had had on the North Korean missile program. For instance, while the Hwasong-10 in particular suffered a very high failure rate, leading to the cessation of its flight testing after 2016, North Korea's spectacular record of successes in 2017, culminating with the Hwasong-15 ICBM, suggested that the U.S. sabotage effort had largely failed.

These cyber operations have implications for nuclear C2; they show the United States' ability and willingness to use novel means to interfere in North Korea's organizational systems. After all, if component production for a non-operational missile can be remotely compromised, how can Kim be sure that his C3—command, control, and *communications*—might not be similarly targeted in a crisis or early in a war? For Americans, the idea of developing capabilities to disable or hobble Kim's missile production might sound like a no-brainer—an easy win for American security in peacetime—but this endeavor could easily backfire. If these offensive cyber capabilities prompt Kim to make more dangerous choices about C2, they might increase the possibility of a North Korean nuclear release.

Between the 'left-of-launch' approach and the 2017 CYBER-COM operation, the use of offensive, secretive, and undisclosed cyber capabilities has become a part of the U.S. pressure toolkit against North Korea. A May 2017 Department of Defense document explained why, describing the techniques as "non-kinetic," falling short of the United Nations charter definition of a "use of force."[25] This classified document was not designed for public consumption, but once leaked it confirmed that the U.S. government reserved the right to use cyberwarfare against its adversaries as it saw fit. For U.S. nuclear adversaries, including North Korea, this is old wine in a new bottle, just one of several U.S. non-nuclear options for destroying Kim's weapons in a crisis. But what does distinguish these capabilities is the lack of warning associated with their impending use. As we saw in Chapter Three, North Korea's nuclear strategy hinges on its ability to monitor a U.S. military buildup near its territory that might indicate an imminent invasion. By definition, cyberweapons do not come with these kinds of indicators.

The most promising way for the United States to use these capabilities in peacetime would be to take Kim at his word on the "mass production" of missiles and nuclear weapons since New Year's Day 2018, and work to penetrate North Korean facilities, baking small imperfections into serially produced weapons. But these capabilities—and U.S. intentions in using them—send North Korea a dangerous message about possible U.S. behavior in a crisis. In wartime, it is well known that a major American objective would be to deprive Kim Jong Un early on of the means to use his nuclear weapons, by any means necessary. This is a difficult task in the realm of physical combat: despite today's advanced means of surveillance and reconnaissance, there is no guarantee that even advanced American stealth fighters—all but invisible to North Korean air defense crews—would be able to find and destroy every nuclear-armed North Korean missile before any could be launched in retaliation. For Kim's nuclear strategy to succeed—for an invasion and regime change to be called off—it would be enough for even a small portion of his nuclear warheads to successfully hit their targets in South Korea, Japan, or the U.S. homeland.

The value of cyberwarfare in a U.S.—North Korean conflict is therefore obvious. Depending on North Korea's command and control infrastructure—whether it is based on radio, cellular, fiber optic, or, perhaps, soon even satellite communications—severing Kim from his nuclear C2 may be the surest way to prevent a North Korean launch. Even if this is not Washington's intention, and if the September 2017 CYBERCOM intrusion was nothing more than psychological warfare, the consequences for North Korean C2 are serious. If Washington can reliably ensure that Kim does not have access to his nuclear weapons in a crisis, then his deterrence is no more. U.S. insistence on threatening Pyongyang with cyber attacks could push Kim toward a dangerous C2 choice: predelegation of nuclear weapons, which would make their use in a crisis more—not less—likely. In the worst case, we could see the emergence of a fail-deadly "Doomsday device," the C2 equivalent of a dead man's trigger: a peacetime order from Kim that his untimely demise, or even rumors of it in the fog of war, must result in the release of any and all nuclear weapons still available to the Korean People's Army.

Negative Controls, Safety, and Surety

Even in the absence of predelegation policies, Kim needs to have in place "negative controls"—the apparatus serving the 'never' side of the always—never dilemma. Regimented procedures and technical choices can both help secure nuclear weapons and prevent their unauthorized use or accidental detonation. Robust negative controls contribute to the broader enterprise of nuclear surety: ensuring both that nukes are not misused and that those meant to operate, maintain, and secure them are not harmed in the course of their duties.

North Korea cannot rely on personnel discipline and reliability alone here. The KPA's Strategic Rocket Force is thought to consist of well-disciplined personnel, chosen for a range of values including ideological fealty to the state and Kim himself. What is unknowable is whether a subset of these personnel charged with operating ballistic missiles engage in risky behavior. This problem is not unique to North Korea, but inherent to nuclear risk. Certainly, military professionalism alone has proven to be no barrier to dangerous behavior elsewhere. For instance, in 2014, more than two dozen U.S. Air Force missileers were charged with drug use and cheating on competency-check exams.[26] The KPA's application of military justice may be capricious enough, and punishment in North Korea arduous enough, to deter this kind of behavior, but it cannot be counted out.

In North Korea, procedural and personnel-based negative control may prove a lesser concern than the possibly lackluster implementation of technical negative controls, such as a use inhibition device: a contraption physically designed to impede human users from arming a nuclear weapon without valid authorization. In North Korea, nuclear warheads are not mated in peacetime with their ballistic missiles, and this requisite step for launch is a form of check and verification.[27] Design components can be incorporated into existing weapons that would require the end-user to

input an externally supplied code that authenticates valid authorization and permits mating with a missile. Pakistan, which has a
similar nuclear strategy to North Korea's, has spent much of its
energies since the early 2000s developing such negative controls,
partly due to the possibility of armed nonstate actors penetrating
Islamabad's nuclear weapons complex.[28] But exactly how far North
Korea has got in the physical design of safety standards and
mechanisms—and of its weapons more broadly—is a serious dark
spot in existing U.S. intelligence assessments.

We do know one thing that indicates Kim has begun to think
about this aspect of C2. As of late 2017, the U.S. assessment is
that North Korea operates a single storage site for its manufactured warheads and their fissile cores: an underground facility
known to the United States as Yongdoktong, northeast of the
city of Kusong.[29] That decision alone suggests a high degree of
concern about negative controls. Given the geographic breadth of
North Korea's ballistic missile operation areas, and without any
truly secure second-strike capability, a single storage site for all
warheads leaves North Korea vulnerable against a U.S. bolt-
from-the-blue strike, whereby American stealth fighters could
destroy the site before the KPA Strategic Force could access any
nuclear weapons. What's more, storing warheads throughout the
land, close to their missiles, would provide a critical operational
advantage: with minutes being precious at the start of a conflict—especially one that North Korea expects its enemies to
initiate—warhead units must be mated to ballistic missile units
as quickly as possible.

So why would Kim keep the bombs contained together and
separate from their missiles? To impose a further safeguard
against the possibility of their use without authorization. In navi-
gating the always—never dilemma, Kim has evidently erred on
the side of never allowing his "treasured sword" to be used without his command. This may change as the country manufactures

more warheads and becomes more confident in the overall robustness of its C2. Beyond Yongdoktong, there are other compelling candidate facilities for warhead storage—such as the Hagap underground facility in Chagang province, and a facility known as Wollo-ri[30] near Pyongyang, thought to be associated with warhead manufacturing primarily—if Kim later chooses to disperse his warheads for better responsiveness in a crisis.

A final question mark—with no known high-confidence assessment within the U.S. intelligence community—surrounds whether or not North Korea has incorporated coded control devices. Unlike use inhibition devices, where the code must come in real time from an external authority, coded control is a form of predelegated authority. One functional means of coded control that would be easy for North Korea to implement would be a three combination lock on a coded control panel, with the code to each lock known by one, and only one, member of the crew. The locks could ultimately be bypassed with physical force and a launch still initiated, but the step would slow down (a bit) a crew of mutineers eager to start a nuclear war, for instance. In terms of a technical rather than procedural coded control *device*, warhead units could require an authorization code to enable prearming circuitry within their packages upon delivery to missile units. The United States, for instance, uses what it calls permissive action links, or PALs (But not on board its submarines.).

American PALs, however, are complex devices built to high cryptographic standards and with procedural input from the U.S. National Security Agency.[31] Occasionally, analysts have suggested that the United States, Russia, or China could assist North Korea in developing these capabilities, but any such collaboration would represent a severe violation of Article 1 of the Treaty on the Non-Proliferation of Nuclear Weapons (NPT), whereby the treaty-recognized nuclear weapons states agree not to assist other states in nuclear weapons development. The treaty does not carve out an exception for assistance with technical mechanisms that would make existing nuclear weapons safer.

Another likely technical challenge to effective C2 is not about negative controls, but basic safety and surety: the reliability of warheads, especially now that North Korea is proceeding to mass production of nuclear weapons. Even better-sourced programs have faced such problems. In the early 1960s, as the United States deployed the Polaris A-1 SLBM, it was quickly discovered that early production units of that missile's W47 nuclear warhead did not meet the "one-point safety" standard for U.S. nuclear weapons designs.[32] North Korea's own warhead safety requirements remain unknown, but the country's resource constraints suggest that its nuclear development program would largely prioritize end results over safety. If, in the course of mass warhead production, North Korean scientists were to discover a serious safety fault in their existing designs, they might not have the option of simply shelving a known working design for something else, as the United States was eventually able to do with the W47.

Given the explosive power of nuclear weapons, even a partial unintentional explosive release could be disastrous for Kim, drawing retaliation. But even without a nuclear explosion, the mix of conventional explosives and radiological materials presents risks. During the U.S. Air Force nuclear bomber fire of September 1980 in Grand Forks, North Dakota, the bomber was on alert status—had the wind simply changed direction and set fire to the nuclear weapons on board, we could have been facing a radiological incident "worse than Chernobyl," according to one account.[33] North Korea's use of liquid-fueled missiles would further raise the possibility of such a fire.

Nuclear weapons are not the only concern—risks of unreliable missile technology also abound. For instance, if a poorly tested North Korean ballistic missile were to crash while overflying Chinese territory on a trajectory toward the United States, it might detonate on Chinese soil. We have already seen one example of an engine failure resulting in crash landing in an urban area: the 2017 launch of a North Korean intermediate-range ballistic missile. An unsafe partial nuclear yield release, then, is not unimaginable as the result of such an accident. Kim's negative controls need to both preserve his place atop the chain of command and also prevent technical accidents.

Mastering C2 Isn't Easy

Kim may have declared that his deterrent is complete, but he must ensure that his proverbial "nuclear button" remains both usable, and only usable in the right circumstances. The nuclear enterprise for a state like North Korea is akin to running a large company, but one where the room for employee error is low and the cost of employee underperformance is the probable death of the CEO, the board of directors, and many of those under them. Robust nuclear command, control, and communications will be needed to hold together the country's nuclear strategy. As we saw in Chapter Three, Kim Jong Un needs his nukes, but—like everybody else—his hope is never to use them. For Kim Jong Un, sitting astride a small, relatively poor country, with fewer nuclear weapons than he would like and great scrutiny of his intentions by a powerful adversary, a single nuclear mishap—or unauthorized use—would lead to the end of his regime, undermining everything the deterrent stood for.

The odds of this may not be as small as many would like to think. As political scientist Scott D. Sagan observed in the 1990s, large organizations "function within a severely 'bounded' form of rationality: they have inherent limits on calculation and coordination and use simplifying mechanisms to understand and respond to uncertainty in the external environment."[34] His point was this: organizations fail; they make poor decisions; and nuclear organizations are no exception—particularly those with strong military involvement and traditions. Organizations led by and comprising rational human beings can certainly have a strategy, but they can also produce irrational and dangerous outcomes. At some point, Kim must wonder if the stresses of C2 are worth the benefits of deterrence, but the record offers a resounding "Yes" for North Korea. The country's nuclear intentions have been slow-moving enough, its military is experienced enough, and its leadership is insecure enough to put in place procedures to keep the nuclear enterprise chugging along.

As such, command and control will also be a major area of focus for the United States, Japan, and South Korea as they seek to find C2 vulnerabilities that would prevent North Korea from using its nuclear weapons against them in a crisis or a war. With this in mind, the world should expect North Korea to continue to evolve—and eventually modernize—its C2. Kim's emphasis on science and technology for a robust national defense is not just about building better missiles, and especially not now that that side of the deterrent has crossed the ICBM threshold. If Kim's "nuclear button" is not satisfactory today, it will be tomorrow. Until that moment comes, his deterrent is not truly complete— and we should take that risk seriously, as we look at how the world has chosen, and might yet choose, to deal with a nuclear North Korea.

PART THREE

NUCLEAR COEXISTENCE?

10

THE ARSONIST AND THE FIREFIGHTER

2017 was a landmark year in two ways, opening the current phase of North Korea's nuclear story, and nothing short of a new nuclear age. The first of these pivotal developments we have already seen in Part Two: Kim Jong Un claimed to have "completed" his deterrent, triumphantly celebrating the culmination of a decades-long program as he launched successful test-flights of intercontinental ballistic missiles that could strike the U.S. homeland. This has left him free to ease up on missile testing, and instead focus on the remaining qualitative weaknesses of his deterrent while building up his arsenal in quantitative terms. The other historic event of the year was the inauguration of Donald J. Trump as president of the United States. Put together, 2017 had left the world with an unprecedentedly loose-tongued and impulsive president in the White House, and an unprecedentedly nuclear-capable supreme leader in Pyongyang. This final part of the book will look at the collision and convergence of those two forces since 2017, and at where this new order leaves us in the 2020s, in the face of the North Korean nuclear threat.

During 2017, the United States and North Korea came close to nuclear disaster. Shortly after his election, Trump had met with outgoing U.S. President Barack Obama, who impressed on his successor that North Korea would stand out as his administration's most urgent foreign policy problem. Trump took a special interest in Kim Jong Un early on. As president-elect, his first request for a classified intelligence briefing concerned North Korea's ballistic missile and nuclear capabilities.[1] The launch of the medium-range Pukguksong-2 in February 2017, while Japanese Prime Minister Shinzo Abe was visiting the United States, spurred this interest further. By April, the Trump White House had identified the contours of its North Korea strategy, which was announced less than two weeks after Kim's military parade showcasing a cornucopia of new missile systems. The strategy—"maximum pressure and engagement"—came to define Trump's first year of North Korea policy. As part of the effort, American diplomats, including Trump's first secretary of state, Rex Tillerson, toured the world, seeking sanctions compliance from a range of countries, including China and Russia. What would make tensions spike in 2017, however, was largely the president's unconventional demeanor and tendency to issue bombastic threats that could easily have been interpreted by North Korea as an indicator that the United States was moving closer to a military strike.

In April, Trump issued an erroneous statement that a U.S. naval "armada" was on its way to the waters off the Korean Peninsula.[2] The USS *Carl Vinson* carrier strike group was actually in waters off Indonesia at the time, but a U.S. president openly declaring that an "armada" was bound for North Korea was not something Pyongyang was accustomed to. That same month, the White House literally bussed in the entire U.S. Senate for a classified briefing on North Korea—sparking speculation in the United States of a U.S. strike on Kim's facilities.[3] The fact that Trump's first year in office coincided with the crescendo of Kim's *byungjin* missile testing campaign appeared to be an unfortunate coincidence, but it had real risks—especially once the North Koreans began responding to what they viewed as U.S. saber-rattling.

By August, Kim was openly trying his hand at coercion. As we saw in Chapter Seven, the North Korean side presented detailed plans to strike at the waters near Guam with the newly tested intermediate-range Hwasong-12, spurring Trump to warn North Korea that it would witness American "fire and fury" if it did not cease issuing threats. Later in the year, the United States, for the first time in more than a decade, converged three carrier strike groups in the Pacific Ocean. Finally, throughout 2017, the U.S. deployed both non-nuclear and nuclear-capable strategic bombers to airspace around the Korean Peninsula as part of allied reassurance for Japan and South Korea. The North Koreans, as in the past, viewed these aerial operations as highly threatening.

These signs could easily have been interpreted as an American threat of nuclear first-use, given the president's over-the-top language, which departed from more standard U.S. deterrence rhetoric toward North Korea.[4] In September, Trump stood before the world's gathered leaders at the UN General Assembly and threatened to "totally destroy" North Korea. "The United States has great strength and patience, but if it is forced to defend itself or its allies, we will have no choice," Trump read carefully from his teleprompter. Unlike his off-the-cuff "fire and fury" remark, this was a calibrated demonstration of where official American policy stood at the time. Kim no doubt had also noted that, a month earlier, Trump's national security advisor Lt. Gen. H.R. McMaster had suggested that the North Korean leader was not rational.[5] For Pyongyang, the indicators of a possible U.S. surprise attack were growing—and with it, the dangers of an inadvertent nuclear war.[6] For their part, U.S.

Department of Defense combatant commands were undertaking scenario-planning for a Korea contingency.[7]

"Rocket Man is on a suicide mission for himself and for his regime," Trump had said in his UN speech, further underscoring the idea that the administration had little regard for Kim's intellect or rationality. Within a day, North Korean state media fired back, colorfully calling Trump a "mentally deranged U.S. dotard."[8] Not long afterward, a warning came from the North Korean side that any U.S. bombers straying not just into, but even simply near, its claimed airspace would be shot down with extreme prejudice. Ri Yong Ho, the North Korean foreign minister, said that he regarded Trump's remarks at the UN as tantamount to a declaration of war.[9] Historically, in a bid to avoid North Korean overreaction, the U.S. military had largely given heed to Pyongyang's unilateral claim of a 100 kilometer coastal exclusion zone, even though international law only provides 12 nautical miles of territorial sea and airspace. It was telling that Kim's Foreign Ministry no longer felt sure that this would be the case. As we saw in Chapter Eight, Ri also suggested that the North Koreans might look to conduct an atmospheric nuclear test—an event that would represent an unparalleled provocation from North Korea and constitute the first such event in some thirty-seven years. (China was the last to conduct an atmospheric nuclear test, in 1980.)

At the same time, the North Koreans, having realized halfway through that Trump was no ordinary American president, had begun making attempts to understand what drove him to act and speak as he did. Dennis Rodman, a retired American basketball star who considered himself a friend to Kim Jong Un, traveled to Pyongyang in June 2017 and delivered a copy of *The Art of the Deal* (1987), Trump's best-known book on business deal-making.[10] In early January 2018, North Korean state media positively reviewed Michael Wolff's *Fire and Fury* (2018), an insider account of the Trump administration's unique dysfunctions and personality clashes.[11] By the end of 2017 and into the early days of 2018, credible reports had emerged suggesting that the White House was seriously contemplating a limited strike on North Korea—to give Kim a "bloody nose."[12]

On January 1, 2018, however, Kim Jong Un had set in motion a series of events that would quickly begin a massive easing of the tensions of 2017. In his New Year's Day address, while Kim celebrated the completion of his deterrent and warned the United States that his "nuclear button" was ready for use, he also extended an olive branch to South Korea.[13] Fully aware that he had a willing counterpart in South Korea, where progressive president Moon Jae-in had been inaugurated in May 2017, Kim expressed interest in the North participating in the PyeongChang Winter Olympic Games, slated to begin in South Korea the following month. With that gesture, the crisis of the previous year was on its way to winding down—at least for a while.

PyeongChang to Panmunjom

This olive branch initiated a remarkable period of diplomatic outreach to the world. For the six years after his father's death in December 2011, Kim Jong Un had refused to leave North Korea's borders. On the rare occasions when a foreign head of government or state traveled to North Korea, he had left the formalities to Kim Yong Nam, the ceremonial head of state. This was the case, for instance, in October 2013, when Mongolia's president, Tsakhiagiin Elberdorj, visited the country but did not meet Kim, at least not publicly. Years later, on January 1, 2018, using the occasion of his New Year's Day address to the country, Kim Jong Un extended an olive branch to South Korea—one that he knew South Korea's pro-engagement president, Moon Jae-in, would be eager to take. Speaking to the nation and the world, he acknowledged that the year would mark the seventieth anniversary of North Korea's founding in 1948 and the upcoming Winter Olympics, calling on the two sides to "celebrate these great national events," in order to "improve the frozen inter-Korean relations and glorify this meaningful year as an eventful one noteworthy in the history of the nation."

That was the spark that lit a year of blazing inter-Korean diplomacy. Within thirty-eight days of Kim's address, South Koreans watched spellbound as his sister Kim Yo Jong became the first person of the *paektusan* bloodline to cross the inter-Korean Demilitarized Zone, for talks with South Korean officials. Kim's sister fascinated South Koreans, receiving tremendous news coverage, although her exact activities and commitments to officials in Seoul were ambiguous.[14] In early March, Moon sent a small delegation to Pyongyang in return, including two of his most trusted advisors. The director of the National Intelligence Service Suh Hoon and Moon's National Security Advisor Chung Eui-yong were wined and dined by an eager Kim Jong Un, who apparently conveyed his intent to give up his nuclear weapons—or so Chung reported on their return south, using that perennial term unique to the Korean diplomatic lexicon: denuclearization.[15]

This optimism crystallized quickly within the Moon administration, although it diverged sharply from the view of the U.S. intelligence community, which was not sharing all its intelligence on North Korea with its ally. Shortly after the South Korean delegation visited Pyongyang, preparations began for an inter-Korean summit. Chung would shuttle to Washington, D.C. later that week for meetings with the U.S. president and his top advisors. After a brief stay at the White House, he held a press briefing on the driveway outside. Despite the odd optics—he had no American official by his side—Chung announced that "President Trump appreciated the briefing and said he would meet Kim Jong-un by May to achieve permanent denuclearization."[16]

THE ARSONIST AND THE FIREFIGHTER

In less than two full months, and seemingly with just one visit each way, inter-Korean diplomacy had shifted the narrative from talk of a limited U.S. "bloody nose" strike on North Korea to the prospect of a historic summit between the countries' leaders. Understandably, hopes for these blossoming relations across the Peninsula were high. In March, in honor of the historic closeness between Pyongyang and Beijing, Kim would break his years of isolation and travel to meet Chinese President Xi Jinping. Kim Jong Un made unilateral efforts to create the conditions for what he believed would be a successful diplomatic opening. In April 2018, he unveiled a set of directives announcing an end to ICBM and nuclear device testing, and the dismantlement of the Punggye-ri test site where all six of North Korea's nuclear weapons tests had been conducted between 2006 and 2017.[17] That same month, Kim Jong Un himself met South Korean President Moon Jae-in for a historic leaders' summit, the third in North Korea's history and the first since his father's meeting with Roh Moo-hyun in 2007.

The April inter-Korean meeting was a watershed. South Korea—and the world—watched transfixed as Kim Jong Un walked across the military demarcation line at the Panmunjom Joint Security Area. Moon Jae-in had been posted at the JSA as a young South Korean soldier in 1976, when the U.S.—South Korea alliance nearly went to war with the North after the Korean People's Army soldiers killed two U.S. Army officers over a tree. Now, Moon and Kim embraced, held private talks, and seemingly established a personal rapport. Emotions ran high in South Korea, where, depending on one's political standing, the moment was either the harbinger of peaceful reunification or the start of Seoul's capitulation to a conniving North. At Panmunjom, Moon and Kim signed a joint declaration, the first of three major diplomatic agreements to which the North Korean leader would sign his name in 2018's flurry of diplomacy. The declaration picked up on familiar themes, including the establishment of a "permanent and stable peace regime." That pledge referred to a longstanding aspiration among many South Koreans to replace the "armistice regime" that had reigned over the Peninsula since 1953 with something more permanent—a *de jure* peace treaty ending the Korean War.

The Panmunjom declaration also addressed denuclearization, referring to the goal of making the Korean Peninsula "nuclear-free" and echoing the terminology of the 1994 U.S.—North Korea Agreed Framework. For Moon Jae-in, who saw the Panmunjom summit as the first step on a long road to realizing peace on the Peninsula, ensuring that North Korea committed to denuclearization—however vaguely—would be important, since the inter-Korean diplomacy was serving as a building block for the Trump administration's efforts. For the two Koreas, 2018 continued to be a remarkable year through the summer and into the autumn. In September, South Korean President Moon Jae-in touched down at Pyongyang's Sunan Airport for another summit with Kim Jong Un. This came almost exactly one year after Kim had overseen the launch of a Hwasong-12 from that same airfield: the one that had ended up overflying Japan on its way to demonstrating the capability of ranging Guam. Moon's arrival in the North Korean capital was another reminder of how swiftly tensions in the region had given way to negotiations and talks.

One important accomplishment of the September Pyongyang summit was a Comprehensive Military Agreement between the two Koreas, the groundwork having been laid down over month-to-month military talks at the DMZ. The agreement saw both sides commit "to completely cease all hostile acts ... that are the source of military tension and conflict."[18] It was unparalleled in ambition on the Korean Peninsula, and its implementation largely carried through the final months of 2018 and into 2019. In October 2018, it was confirmed that, for the first time in five years, UN Command forces on the Peninsula had resumed use of a trans-DMZ hotline with the KPA and were speaking twice daily.[19] The Korean Peninsula was no closer to being rid of nuclear weapons, but it was a little bit further from an imminent nuclear crisis. Where in 2017, the only communications that were being exchanged across the DMZ were largely bombastic public threats, by the end of 2018, inter-Korean and UN Command—KPA communications had forged a greater sense of stability. The conversations were mundane, but the restoration of the channel was important, and confirmed the importance of the September summit.[20]

Unfortunately, by late 2019, North Korea was determined to put this inter-Korean agreement under stress. In November, Kim Jong Un oversaw what state media called a "real war-like drill" featuring artillery fire that South Korea later said constituted a violation of the historic agreement.[21] Seoul had held its tongue all through 2019 as North Korea launched multiple ballistic missiles, despite the agreement prohibiting both Koreas from undertaking anything that could be interpreted as a "hostile act" against the other.

Moon was also on a mission at Pyongyang to defibrillate the parallel U.S.—North Korea process, which had gotten bogged down in late-August; Trump, citing a dearth of "sufficient progress" on denuclearization, had canceled Secretary of State Mike Pompeo's planned trip to Pyongyang.[22] Moon's goal in September was to make sure that his inter-Korean efforts had something to show on the denuclearization front—and he succeeded. Among other things, Article 5 of the Pyongyang Declaration announced that "the North will permanently dismantle the Dongchang-ri missile engine test site and launch platform under the observation of experts from relevant countries," and that "The North expressed its willingness to continue to take additional measures, such as the permanent dismantlement of the nuclear facilities in Yeongbyeon, as the United States takes corresponding measures in accordance with the spirit of the [Singapore Declaration]."[23] Moon had managed to get Kim Jong Un's signature onto a document that contained the words Yongbyon and Dongchang-ri (or Sohae). The former was the North's overt nuclear fuel production site, and the latter was its space launch station. This went further than both the spring's Pammunjom Declaration and June's Singapore Declaration following the first Trump—Kim summit. It appeared as if North Korea was now ready to get down to brass tacks and talk real concessions.

There were two snags, however: one concerned the way in which these pledges were conditional on U.S. concessions, and the other concerned the limitations of denuclearization progress if only Yongbyon and Sohae were on the table. Upon his return to Seoul, Moon Jae-in oversold his accomplishment in Pyongyang, telling a press conference that closure of the Yongbyon facility would be "tantamount to saying that activities such as the production of more nuclear materials or nuclear weapons have also been suspended." That was an exaggeration: as we know from Chapter Four, even if Yongbyon were to be disabled, two covert uranium enrichment sites including Kangson would remain operational, along with warhead storage, assembly, and maintenance sites. As we will see, this was an important stumbling block in U.S.—North Korean talks during the same period.

The real problem with the Pyongyang Declaration—which would turn out to be the high point of inter-Korean diplomacy in 2018—lay in the "corresponding measures" that it claimed the United States would undertake in exchange for permanent dismantlement at Yongbyon. The meaning of this phrase was not spelled out in the declaration, but to the North Koreans it meant at least partial sanctions relief. Yet, given how wide-ranging the international sanctions regime against North Korea had become by 2018, Seoul could not grant Pyongyang any tangible economic benefits without transgressing international law. Sanctions relief simply was not South Korea's to promise, and of course in the wake of the Pyongyang summit it did not deliver. North Korean enthusiasm for the inter-Korean process quickly dwindled amid signs that Seoul had largely exhausted what it could offer Pyongyang. Through the end of 2018, U.S. and allied intelligence intercepts from within North Korea offered a less optimistic picture of inter-Korean contacts than what was being reported publicly. After Pyongyang in September, Kim issued nonpublic guidance to top Workers' Party cadres that the summit should not change the fact that South Korea remained a hostile "enemy," bent on absorbing the North.[24] In December 2018, as the Korean People's Army began its annual Winter Training Cycle, a longer, more pointed directive was issued to a greater swathe of the Workers' Party, underscoring that Kim would never give in to the South or the United States.[25]

Over the border, optimists in South Korea had initially remained convinced that a historic trip to Seoul by Kim Jong Un for a further inter-Korean summit would be possible. But frustrated Korean supporters of Moon's rapprochement efforts ultimately came to recognize the reality of the situation, lamenting that not only was the once-promising inter-Korean Kaesong Industrial Park unable to resume operations, but South Korea could not even export metal chopsticks to the North. With little to gain from the South, in late 2018 and 2019 the North strategically zeroed in on the process with the United States, where the key to economic relief might be found. By late 2019, North Korea had largely given up on inter-Korean diplomacy as well as its outreach to the United States; after a round of failed U.S.—North Korea talks in Stockholm, Sweden, in October 2019, it became clear that Kim had lost his patience. North Korea had other plans for its future.

The Road to Singapore

Throughout the inter-Korean process, Washington and Pyongyang had been traveling a parallel road. In May 2018, building on the April Panmunjom summit between Kim and Moon, the United States strove to set up its own summit with the North Koreans. That month, while planning was underway, Kim invited a select group of foreign reporters to witness the destruction of tunnel entrances at the Punggye-ri nuclear test site, with CNN broadcasting footage of spectacular explosions. This gesture by the North Koreans was evocative, but to those with longer memories, it bore an uncanny similarity to the ultimately very impermanent 2008 destruction of the reactor cooling tower at Yongbyon.[26] On the face of it, the closure of the Punggye-ri tunnels offered the world hope that North Korea was about to embark on a major reversal in its nuclear posture. But the opposite was true: Kim stated that he had destroyed the nuclear test site precisely because his deterrent was complete: this was an early omen of where U.S.—North Korean talks would and would not go in 2018–19.[27]

Given that the two men had not long ago exchanged threats on a near weekly basis, mistrust between Kim's and Trump's governments remained high. Within the White House, policymaking toward North Korea remained dysfunctional. While Trump was eager to head to the summit with Kim, U.S. National Security Advisor John Bolton was not of the same view. Bolton, a veteran Republican hawk and no friend of North Korea's, had taken over as national security advisor in April, weeks before the inter-Korean Panmunjom summit. Before multilateral talks in 2003, he had called Kim Jong Il a "tyrannical dictator" in his official capacity, leading North Korea to issue a statement calling him "human scum and a bloodsucker," vowing to "not consider him as an official of the U.S. administration." Now, Bolton was entering the White House having already bluntly dismissed the value of direct diplomacy with the North Koreans on television just weeks before being appointed national security advisor: the purpose of the forthcoming summit should be to "foreshorten the amount of time that we're going to waste in negotiations that will never produce the result we want."[28]

Bolton was right about the "result" he sought being out of reach: the North Koreans were not offering to disarm, the one objective that would have been acceptable for the new U.S. national security advisor. Bolton made this clear in another set of public comments referring to one model that he would like to see applied in North Korea. During his stint in the Bush administration, Bolton had overseen Libyan leader Muammar Gadhafi's disarmament of his nascent nuclear weapons program. "We should insist that if this meeting is going to take place, it will be similar to discussions we had with Libya thirteen or fourteen years ago: how to pack up their nuclear weapons program and take it to Oak Ridge, Tennessee," he said.[29]

This remark uniquely outraged the North Koreans. Kim Kye Gwan, a veteran of negotiations with the United States, issued a clear public statement, warning that "if the U.S. is trying to drive us into a corner to force our unilateral nuclear abandonment, we will no longer be interested in such dialogue and cannot but reconsider our proceeding to the DPRK—U.S. summit."[30] Kim also reminded the United States that in 2018, "[The] world knows too well that our country is neither Libya nor Iraq which have met miserable fate[s]." After six nuclear weapons tests and three ICBM flight tests, "It is absolutely absurd to dare compare the DPRK, a nuclear weapon state, to Libya." North Korea's deterrent, after all, had—from North Korea's point of view—been completed: Kim Jong Un was ready to come to the negotiating table from a position of strength, to explore the terms on which the United States and North Korea would coexist as two nuclear powers.

The Libya comparison at the heart of the Bolton—Kim spat was doubly offensive to North Korea, as was clearly shown when U.S. Vice President Mike Pence suggested that the Kim regime might end up like Gadhafi's if it retained his nuclear capability.[31] In 2011, just eight years after parting ways with his nascent nuclear program, the Libyan dictator had met his grisly end after U.S.-led coalition strikes on the country, allowing anti-government rebels to take matters into their own hands. Instead of ensuring his regime's survival against the U.S. threat, Gadhafi had given up his future nukes and ended up literally sodomized with a bayonet.[32] It was easy to see why the North Koreans took exception at Pence's comments, with a veteran North Korean diplomat calling the vice president "ignorant and stupid."[33] Seemingly taking offense in turn, Trump called off the plans for a summit with Kim Jong Un. U.S.—North Korean diplomacy was not off to the best start.

It took sudden intervention by South Korea's President Moon, who called an impromptu DMZ meeting with Kim and got in touch with the United States, to salvage the summit. In due time, the two sides were ready to meet. It had taken a while to decide on a venue that would be mutually agreeable—Trump would not go to Pyongyang, and his U.S. Secret Service protectors would not have let him even if he had wanted to; Kim was unwilling to travel too far—but eventually a location and date were chosen: June 12, 2018, at the Capella Hotel on Singapore's Sentosa Island. Kim and Trump both flew there, neither knowing what exactly they would find beyond the limited language that had been agreed by their staff. The Singapore summit lasted a few short hours. The two men first met privately, with interpreters. Later, they had a broader working meeting with their advisors. They then signed a historic joint declaration—the first document to bear the name and signature of both a U.S. president and a North Korean supreme leader.

In an instant, the Singapore Declaration had supplanted years of bilateral and multilateral statements as the new baseline in the Kim Jong Un era for diplomatic progress. However, given the mere weeks the two sides had had to prepare the summit, the text broke little new ground. It borrowed largely from the long, twenty-five year history of statements the two countries had agreed to, and fell far short of the gold standard Six-Party Talks joint statement from 2005, which had seen North Korea agree to a broad and sweeping set of concessions on the nuclear program. Of course, this all makes perfect sense, if we understand that Kim had not come to Singapore to surrender his nuclear arsenal. We know from Part One why he could not and would not do that.

The core bargain at the center of the Singapore Declaration—and the broader U.S.—North Korean 'process' that would continue through 2019—was this: "President Trump committed to provide security guarantees to the DPRK, and Chairman Kim Jong Un reaffirmed his firm and unwavering commitment to complete denuclearization of the Korean Peninsula."[34] This reference to "denuclearization" was not given additional detail—certainly nothing approaching the granularity of the September 2005 Six-Party Talks statement discussed in Chapter Two. Instead, the Singapore Declaration's four, broad aspirational clauses set out an agenda to build "a lasting and stable peace regime," for instance through recovery of POW/MIA remains from the Korean War. Much of it had been covered before in previous agreements—going back to the June 13, 1993 U.S.—North Korea joint statement, the first between the two governments, twenty-five years almost to the day before the fateful Singapore encounter.

Trump delivered a press conference, announcing the outcomes of the day—including that he was unilaterally cancelling the upcoming joint U.S.—South Korea military exercises, adopting the preferred North Korean designation for these "war games."

Later, South Korean officials would note that their government had not been consulted. For Trump, who had long seen alliances as a burden and military exercises as wastes of money, the decision was a no-brainer: less a concession to Kim and more a convenient excuse. Seeking to sustain the conditions for diplomacy, the United States cancelled a dozen more major and minor military exercises and exchanges with the South Koreans through the summer of 2019. North Korea, however, made no such concessions. In February 2019, the American commander of U.S. Forces Korea and United Nations Command testified that "a force of over one million" were "engaged in individual and unit-level training throughout the country."[35]

The Singapore summit was the headline event of the year for both leaders, but Kim had also spent 2018 meeting lower level officials from other countries, including Singapore's foreign minister, Vivian Balakrishnan, and Russian Foreign Minister Sergei Lavrov. The turn from Hermit King to global diplomat appeared jarring—and it was. When Kim had arrived in Beijing in March to meet with President Xi Jinping, it was entirely without warning, and North Korea watchers had even speculated that it might not have been Kim at all on board his father's famous train, but perhaps a deputy like his sister. So what had provoked this sudden change? The answer to that question is a vital one for understanding what North Korea wants as it matures as a nuclear weapons state.

Cosmetic 'Denuclearization'

After the Singapore summit, senior U.S. officials insisted that it was the Trump administration's "maximum pressure" campaign that had turned the screws on Kim's regime, forcing him to the negotiating table. But for Kim Jong Un, 2018 was an exercise in image rehabilitation. He had managed to present himself as a statesman on the global stage, even winning a summit with a U.S. president—a longstanding propaganda goal for his father and grandfather. The year's diplomatic outreach seemed to confirm that nuclear weapons—once developed and realized—do confer international status on a country like North Korea. The consequences for the future of proliferation may be dire, but Kim could rest assured that no U.S. president would again call North Korea a "fourth-rate, pipsqueak" of a country, as former U.S. President Richard Nixon once had. So why would he come to the table now, only to give it all up?

The May 2018 demolition of the Punggye-ri nuclear test site was presented to the world as a major gesture of willingness to pursue "denuclearization," but its reversibility demonstrated how careful Kim was being about what steps he was willing to take as the diplomatic process kicked off. On the missile side of things, it was much the same story. The Sohae engine test stand, which had played an important role in the realization of the "March 18 Revolution" engine powering North Korea's newest and most capable missiles at the time, came up in June at Singapore: Kim reportedly gave Trump assurances that he would dismantle the engine test stand. Trump claimed that this was a concession he extracted in negotiation, but subsequent reports made clear that Kim had come prepared with this offer.[36] Trump also confirmed at the post-meeting press conference that it was a purely verbal concession: "We agreed to that after the agreement was signed." Curiously, Trump added that the United States knew where the Sohae site was "because of the heat," touting U.S. surveillance capabilities in public.

The symbolic value of shutting down the site where North Korea perfected such an important technology was not negligible. But, by this same measure, now that it had validated that design, the utility of the test stand diminished considerably. Thus Sohae was an exceptionally appealing concession for Kim to offer Trump:

one that had great value as a gesture, but with limited value for 2018's new focus on mass production of ballistic missiles and nuclear warheads, per Kim's New Year's Day directive. Another huge benefit was that dismantling the test stand would be easily verifiable even by commercial satellites, barring the need to allow international inspectors onto North Korean soil.

In July 2018, a month after Singapore, came the first signs of what was unmistakably dismantlement activity, clearly visible even in low-resolution satellite imagery.[37] Further testing at Sohae would now be impossible without a complex reconstitutive effort that could take anywhere from weeks to months.[38] Yet weeks and months may not seem a long time to a regime that has spent decades building its deterrent, and the concrete foundational structure remained in place. More promising was the dismantlement taking place at the nearby satellite launching facilities in July and August, even before the inter-Korean Pyongyang summit in September had put these facilities on the table. This summer dismantlement could be read as a transparency gesture, allowing for greater satellite surveillance to verify that no space launches were imminent or upcoming.

However, it was not to last. By the time the U.S.—North Korea negotiations ground to a halt in late August, with the cancellation of what would have been Pompeo's fourth trip, by all accounts dismantlement activity at both the engine test stand and the satellite launch facilities had stopped. Even after Pompeo's eventual visit in early October, and even when Trump and Kim met again in Hanoi in February 2019, there was no further effort. It appears that North Korea is holding on to Sohae as a dispensable "denuclearization step" card to be played at the right time so as to exact the maximum possible benefit in negotiations with the United States, and Kim does not judge that time to have come yet. Nothing about activities at Sohae to date would suggest that Kim is serious about giving up his nuclear weapons or ballistic missiles. To the contrary, Sohae perhaps epitomizes the cosmetic approach to denuclearization that ended up replacing the initial heady optimism around U.S.—North Korea diplomacy.

This is not such a surprise, let alone a U-turn, when you look more closely at the Pyongyang Declaration that conceded dismantlement at Sohae in the first place. In the aftermath of that seemingly historic agreement, few observers noted the glaring discrepancy between the respective English translations released by South and North Korea. While the two sides had agreed to an authoritative and unitary Korean-language text, the seemingly small divergences between their English translations offer insight into crucial differences of interpretation. The widely circulated South Korean version—the one most non-Korean-speaking analysts have worked off—noted that Pyongyang would "permanently dismantle" the site. By contrast, North Korea's version agreed to "permanently *shut down*" the site. In Seoul's version, the engine test stand and launch pad are to be physically torn down, precluding their further use for testing activity or space launches. In Pyongyang's interpretation, there is no such commitment. It was also unclear from the declaration's imprecise language what exactly was to be dismantled.

These are precisely the kind of questions on detail that would have benefited from a U.S.—North Korea working-level process, but, throughout 2018 and 2019, whatever talks occurred below Trump and Kim were largely focused on setting up the leaders' next summit—and it would not be long before the leader-level talks also began to unravel.

The Hanoi Hold-Up: Reality Sets Back In

The June Singapore summit had inspired frenzied optimism. Trump's decision to meet with Kim was viewed by foreign policy pundits across the partisan spectrum as a possible Nixon-goes-to-China moment—a bold gamble that might change everything. Even skeptics and critics of the president's saber-rattling in 2017 had offered him credit for the gesture, suggesting that the Singapore summit would be worthwhile insofar as it would allow the United States to test Kim's willingness to disarm. Others made a more obvious and mundane point: that talks, even if they conferred prestige on North Korea, would be preferable to a nuclear war. That was difficult to disagree with. What Singapore ultimately demonstrated, however, was that Trump—ever the willing arsonist for the Korean Peninsula in 2017, threatening "fire and fury"—had now found himself positioned as the firefighter, unable to do anything more than respond to the reality of Kim's strengthened nuclear position.

The day after the Singapore summit, Trump claimed that the meeting itself had, in effect, wiped out any nuclear threat posed by North Korea to the United States. Trump's supporters began talking of a Nobel Peace Prize, drawing comparisons to his predecessor, who had won one his first year in office. In South Korea, liberal-progressive supporters of Moon Jae-in also found themselves drawn to Trump's process. But doldrums quickly took over the process and the Trump—Kim honeymoon phase ended quickly. When U.S. Secretary of State Mike Pompeo traveled to Pyongyang to follow up on the outcomes of the Singapore summit, the talks did not go well. Pompeo was sent home empty-handed and a North Korean statement swiped at him for apparently making "gangster-like" demands of the North Koreans. The implication was that he had made requests tantamount to North Korea's unilateral disarmament.

Pompeo made matters worse by introducing his own spin on the Singapore summit and its aftermath. In public, instead of referring to the outcome of the summit accurately—as Kim having agreed (yet again) to "denuclearization of the *Korean*

Peninsula"—he and State Department spokespeople made repeated references to the "final, fully verified denuclearization of *North Korea*, as agreed to by Chairman Kim in Singapore." This was firmly a Trump administration invention. By the end of the year, the North Koreans would lash out at what they saw as the United States' obstinacy on the matter. For Pyongyang, denuclearization of the Korean Peninsula remained a tango for two; Kim had not signed up for the 'Libya model' in different garb.

On January 1, 2019, Kim Jong Un kept up his tradition of a wide-ranging address to the country. He reiterated the North Korean position that, after the actions he had taken in 2018, it was now Washington's turn to reciprocate with the "corresponding measures" that Seoul had been unable to take any further after the Pyongyang summit. Underscoring North Korea's opposition to the U.S. deployment on or near the Peninsula of "strategic assets"—a North Korean phrase used to mean everything from missile defense like THAAD to nuclear attack submarines and aircraft carriers—Kim noted the steps taken by North Korea (the self-imposed testing moratorium, the tunnel closure at Pyunggye-ri, the partial dismantlement at Sohae) and the pledge made to "neither make and test nuclear weapons any longer nor use and proliferate them." This line sounded new and significant, but it was not. It reiterated directives dating back at least to North Korea's March 2013 declaration of nuclear-state status, in which the Kim Jong Un regime had promised to handle nuclear materials securely, not to proliferate them, and only to use nuclear weapons if it perceived its national security and survival to be threatened. (North Korea had also been promising, on and off, not to proliferate its nukes for years under Kim Jong Il).[39]

A little more than a month after this New Year's address, plans for a second U.S.—North Korea summit were in place. In the lead-up to the meeting, hopes began to soar high for a detailed agreement with the North Korean side. Andrew Kim, the CIA officer who had traveled to Pyongyang to meet with Kim Jong Un in planning for Singapore, shared an anecdote in the lead-up to the second summit. When asked by Pompeo whether he was willing to disarm, the supreme leader had responded, "I'm a father and a husband. And I have children. And I don't want my children to carry the nuclear weapon on their back their whole life."[40] The U.S. side chose to interpret that as an assurance that Kim would disarm, but this was not Kim Jong Un saying that he was ready to unilaterally disarm because nuclear weapons are terrible and costly; the burden he spoke of was the one that comes with exercising nuclear deterrence in Northeast Asia, given the need to sustain the "balance of power" with the United States. This was a reiteration of "denuclearization of the Korean Peninsula" as no more than an aspiration—one unlikely to be achieved in his lifetime.

Despite this lack of change, as the second summit drew closer, American negotiators were still convinced that something great could be accomplished. The date was set for February 2019, and the venue chosen was particularly symbolic: the Vietnamese capital of Hanoi.[41] Washington's relationship with Vietnam was a reminder of just how quickly the United States could convert old Cold War enemies into new friends. By the fortieth anniversary of the end of the Vietnam War, the head of Vietnam's governing party had been hosted in Washington, D.C., and the strategic partnership between the two countries feted.[42] Today, Vietnam is among the most pro-American countries in Southeast Asia. Kim chose to take the train to Hanoi, a journey of nearly three days that hearkened back to Kim Il Sung's trip in 1957 to meet North Vietnamese President Ho Chi Minh, another firebrand of self-reliant Asian communism.[43] The opening moments of the Hanoi summit gave Kim Jong Un another chance to remind the world that he was a far cry from his quiet, introverted father, as he, for the first time, answered a question from a Western reporter. *The Washington Post*'s David Nakamura asked if he was "confident" and "feeling good about a deal."[44] Kim, seated next to Trump, answered: "It's too early to tell. I won't prejudge. From what I feel right now, I do have a feeling that good results will come."

He was wrong. The two-day Hanoi summit did not go well for either the United States or North Korea, and both sides appeared to have been caught off-guard. The U.S. team had been expecting a deal and had come prepared; Kim had been presented with the contours of what was likely a prepared text for a would-be joint statement. On the second day of the summit, when Trump and Kim were accompanied by their staff, the U.S. side gave the North Korean leader an explicit U.S. definition of "denuclearization."[45] This was capacious and part of the beginning of the end of the summit. It was not what Kim had come to Hanoi to hear: that the United States was, in effect, still demanding him to submit to a Libya-style unilateral disarmament process. National Security Advisor John Bolton had taken a special interest in the preparation of this document, likely knowing that it would cause the North Koreans to view the diplomatic process itself as a nonstarter.

The final sticking point for the summit—the moment of apparent collapse—came after the North Koreans presented their proposed *quid pro quo*: in exchange for the lifting of certain sanctions clauses across five UN Security Council resolutions passed in 2016 and 2017, Pyongyang would offer up its nuclear fuel production facilities at Yongbyon. The North Korean foreign minister would later confirm after the failure of the summit that these were the sole facilities on offer. The U.S. side swiftly rejected the proposal, but sought to negotiate, seeking North Korean acquiescence, for instance, to covert sites like Kangson. This went nowhere, and the summit ended after two days. At a press conference after the summit's end, Trump confirmed this narrative: "Basically, they wanted the sanctions lifted in their entirety, and we couldn't do that," because, there was no offer of the "sites that people don't know about that we know about."[46]

Just weeks after the Singapore summit, *The Washington Post* had reported that "U.S. intelligence officials, citing newly obtained evidence, have concluded that North Korea does not intend to fully surrender its nuclear stockpile, and instead is considering ways to conceal the number of weapons it has and secret production facilities."[47] A U.S. official who had seen the assessment told me this was based on actionable intelligence: North Korea had been found to be actively seeking ways to deceive the United States on its intentions for the summits, for instance offering a partially manufactured nuclear warhead inventory for dismantlement.[48] These revelations in fact caused panic at the White House, given their contradiction of the official narrative that the Singapore process was leading to measurable progress in limiting North Korea's nuclear capabilities; the U.S. Director of National Intelligence at the time, Dan Coats, was asked to raise the sensitivity of intelligence reporting around the issue.[49] But the reality was now out in the open.

The reactor at Yongbyon, long seen as the beating heart of North Korea's nuclear complex, had lost its luster by 2019 and was likely near the end of its life anyway—it was not the prize it might once have been. North Korea's nuclear complex was now vast, sprawling across multiple sites, and given Washington's knowledge about Kangson, there was thin patience at the Hanoi summit for North Korea's denials. Days before the inter-Korean Pyongyang summit—whose declaration only mentioned dismantlement at Yongbyon—North Korean state media had poohpoohed the very notion of covert sites, calling it "a fiction, [with the intention of] derailing dialogue."[50] As we know, President Moon had provided further cover for this perspective on his return from Pyongyang by saying that closure of Yongbyon would be "tantamount" to ending all production of nuclear materials in North Korea.

Depriving North Korea of access to fissile material has always been a major objective of the United States, but, given the advances Kim's nuclear program has already made, Washington might find itself forced to accept a freeze agreement, at least for the time being—if North Korea was unwilling to acknowledge the existence of covert sites, pressing for their inclusion in any agreement at Hanoi would have lowered the probability of such an agreement materializing. Kim had been betting on Trump and Moon taking the face-saving win of dismantling key facilities at Yongbyon while agreeing effectively to tolerate the covert complexes. But he was, in effect, asking for 90 per cent of all economic pressure to be lifted, in exchange for approximately 40 to 50 per cent of his fissile material production capacity, and nothing on his ballistic missiles or other weapons of mass destruction.

Kim left Hanoi deeply upset. In the final moments as talks broke down, the North Korean side had walked out.[51] Back at the Mélia Hotel, where Kim was staying on Hanoi's Ly Thuong Kiet Street, the North Korean leader returned and slammed his door shut, refusing to speak to his own staff.[52] Later in the day, the North Koreans reconvened to determine their course of action, leading to a press conference later that evening by Foreign Minister Ri Yong Ho. Ri announced that North Korea was shifting its focus—in the short term, at least—from the issue of sanctions relief to that of security guarantees from the United States. Security guarantees had been part of the Singapore bargain, but the change in priorities from March 2019 did not augur well for the trajectory of talks, nor for the prospects of Kim disarming. Several past rounds of verbal assurances of non-hostile intent had failed to convince the North to abandon its nuclear plans; it was unclear what security guarantees North Korea was looking for, or if they could ever be enough.[53]

After Hanoi, reality sank back in on the Korean Peninsula. The effusive speculation at the end of 2018 about a peace treaty to end the Korean War and a visit by Kim Jong Un to Seoul quickly evaporated as the North Koreans hunkered down. Quickly, it became apparent that Kim Jong Un was calibrating away from his 2018 overtures. In April 2019, Kim launched a weapons-testing campaign, with May seeing the first launch of a ballistic missile since the November 2017 test of the Hwasong-15. Over the course of that summer, the North Koreans tested three new types of short-range missiles: two quasi-ballistic missiles and one multiple launch rocket system. In July, Kim also revealed the new ballistic missile submarine under construction at the Sinpo shipyard—the first demonstration of military hardware explicitly designed to carry and launch nuclear weapons since the February 2018 military parade. In December 2019, testing activity resumed at the large test stand at Sohae. The "denuclearization" mask was slipping off, and Kim was reminding both the Workers' Party and the world that he remained committed to developing a strong, indigenous national defense capability. At a high-level party plenum to close out 2019, the North Korean leader emphasized that the Workers' Party should "reliably maintain the constant readiness for action of the powerful nuclear deterrent capable of containing the US nuclear threat and guaranteeing our long-term security."[54]

Even as he resumed some of his pre-2018 habits, and took fire at both Pompeo and Bolton in public statements, Kim maintained a cordial relationship with Trump himself, wisely avoiding any gestures that might alienate the capricious American president. Trump kept insisting to the American press that his great relationship with Kim made anything possible. He once told a political rally that he and Kim had fallen "in love" after their meeting and that the North Korean leader had written him "beautiful letters."[55] The two leaders continued this correspondence after Hanoi, and during Trump's visit to South Korea in

June 2019, the two leaders held a third impromptu summit at the inter-Korean DMZ. Though they resolved to resume working-level talks at that meeting, no such talks materialized afterwards. Instead, Pyongyang bristled at the announcement of U.S.—South Korea joint military exercises in August, even though these were toned down: for Kim Jong Un, they echoed the major 2017 Ulchi-Freedom Guardian exercise that had simulated everything from attempts to "decapitate" him early in a crisis to operations in a post-nuclear attack Korean Peninsula.

After the summer's intensified testing campaign, official media began resuming more pointed references to nuclear weaponry, picking up rhetorical flourishes that had largely been set aside after the turn toward diplomacy in early 2018. That little had changed in North Korean strategic thinking about nuclear weapons was best summed up by a KCNA release on August 31:

> The powerful defense capabilities and war deterrent the DPRK has secured ... are not for threatening other countries but for averting aggression and war by the imperialists, completely ending military threat and thus preserving peace and stability of the Korean peninsula and creating an environment favorable for building an economic giant.[56]

The same release described the country's "treasured sword" as the "greatest victory ever achieved by the Workers' Party of Korea." In the final days of 2019, Kim recalled the "spirit and mettle" of the country, and the "arduous struggle"—an allusion to the famine of the 1990s—that North Koreans endured to develop a "nuclear war deterrent" with "invariable loyalty to the Party and the revolution."[57] These were not the words of a country about to voluntarily submit to disarmament.

Why Kim Came to the Table

If he had no intention of giving up his nuclear force, what did make Kim turn toward diplomacy in 2018? Whatever economic pressure he had been facing in 2017, this was not the primary motivator. Rather, it had everything to do with his nuclear weapons and ballistic missile programs. When Kim proclaimed the successful completion of his deterrent after the flight test of the Hwasong-15, he arrived at an important milestone. What better time to turn toward diplomacy than with the terror of an ICBM now sown in the mind of Americans? Failure to recognize this was the downfall of both South Korea's and the United States' efforts and assumptions in the frenzied year of diplomacy. The North Koreans did care about economic sanctions, but the intensification of the UN sanctions regime across the Bush, Obama, and finally Trump administrations had clearly had a negligible effect on Pyongyang's pursuit of nuclear capabilities. We know that 2017 was a landmark year in terms of the scale and importance of North Korea's achievements, but it was also a year when sanctions reached unprecedented heights, seemingly without consequence for the rapid pace of nuclear force development. Kim had a plan and he stuck to it; that plan had always included a turn toward diplomacy in order to extract concessions, *without* submitting to disarmament.

In this he was even following in the footsteps of China, which is recognized as a nuclear power by the United States: in a bit of historical coincidence, Chinese leader Mao Zedong had won a meeting with President Nixon a year after his first successful test of an ICBM capable of ranging the U.S. homeland. Nixon's famous visit to China kicked off a seven year process toward normalization of diplomatic relations albeit spurred more by the Sino-Soviet split than by the Chinese ICBM. In 2020, it is easy to look at China and see a superpower-in-waiting. But we should not forget how Mao's China was viewed through the 1950s and 1960s, particularly in the United States: as an isolated, uniquely evil regime controlled by a putatively irrational dictator, much like contemporary American hawks' descriptions of North Korea.

Eventually, the United States found itself resigned to the reality of a nuclear China. By the Singapore summit, even as American policy toward North Korea remained predicated on disarmament, more and more current and former U.S. officials in Washington began privately discussing the consequences of Kim's new capabilities. For many, a similar sense of resignation was beginning to sink in. Seen this way, Kim's opening to the United States despite his inflexibility on disarmament does not seem unreasonable.

Some have also pointed out that China's acquisition of the bomb was followed by the period of economic liberalization under Deng Xiaoping, suggesting that the same could be in store for North Korea. It is true that there had been debates within the Chinese regime about whether national defense should be prioritized at the cost of the economy and living conditions.[58] As for monolithic North Korea, we cannot glean much beyond what defectors can reveal of such internal debates, but the post-2017 shift in national and diplomatic strategy suggests a similar impulse.

However, nuclear weapons were a nonfactor in Deng and the Chinese leadership's decision-making at that time, and even if Kim is thinking along these lines, he's unlikely to experience China's economic success. Though twenty-first-century marketization in North Korea has been inexorable—and even tolerated by the regime—the Workers' Party draws the line at allowing foreign cultural influence to seep in and undermine the 'North Korean model.' In 2019, after the collapse of the Hanoi summit, North Korean state media ran a series of editorials emphasizing socialist ideological discipline; in April that year, Kim Jong Un himself used his first public address since Hanoi to order preparations to "vigorously advance socialist construction by dint of self-supporting national economy."[59] He added that this would "deal a telling blow to the hostile forces who ... [miscalculate] that sanctions can bring the DPRK to its knees."[60]

The Trump administration had staked its messaging on the idea that its 'maximum pressure' campaign and sanctions had forced Kim to the table. This April speech to the party elite was a dose of reality that sanctions relief would not be forthcoming. In his 2018 New Year's Day address, Kim had acknowledged the costs endured in the country for the now-complete "mighty sword," commenting that "our people ... had to tighten their belts for long years." After Hanoi, the prospect of enduring those costs for longer—potentially much longer—had become apparent. Later in April, at the first session of the Supreme People's Assembly, Kim addressed the "problem of food" in North Korea; the analogy of belt-tightening—a literal reference to North Korea's late-1990s 'Arduous March' famine—had not only returned as a rhetorical device, but signs of the costs of nuclear weapons procurement over years were becoming clearer.[61] Yet North Korean nuclear resolve remained unswerving. Whatever economic problems would result from the sanctions regime, North Korea would cope through self-reliance—or so Kim Jong Un had said.

It was not, then, the U.S. "maximum pressure" strategy begun in 2017 that had forced Kim's diplomatic turn, as the Trump administration claimed. The story from the White House was that Kim had come to realize the costs of his nuclear program would become unsustainable if his 2017 trajectory continued unchanged, and that the only way out was to begin diplomacy. There was no clear effort by senior U.S. officials to offer a compelling theory for why precisely a regime that had endured years of economic hardship to develop an indigenous nuclear capability would have suddenly buckled—especially right after demonstrating some of the capabilities that marked the true maturation and 'completion' of its nuclear deterrent. Kim had come to the table not because he had been brought to his knees, but because he felt that his leverage was great after his *byungjin* testing campaigns.

What's more, Kim succeeded in this aim. In the second half of 2017, China and Russia had agreed to unprecedented sanctions against North Korea at the UN Security Council, and evidence had emerged that China, which accounted for 90 per cent of North Korea's overseas trade, was beginning to take their implementation more seriously. That would all change on March 8, 2018, when South Korean National Security Advisor Chung Euiyong announced outside the White House that Trump had accepted Kim's invitation to meet. In October 2018, vice foreign minister-level officials from Russia, China, and North Korea trilaterally endorsed an "adjustment" of the international sanctions against Pyongyang, citing the regime's apparent restraint through that year.[62] In December 2019, Russia and China prepared to introduce a resolution at the United Nations Security Council formally calling for sanctions relief for North Korea—probably in a bid to show Kim that his relative restraint between 2018 and 2019 would pay dividends if he persisted.[63] Within less than a year of the Hwasong-15's first test, the road to sanctions relief still was not apparent, but Russia and China now saw more to be gained from slackening their implementation. For now, it seemed, the Kim regime could breathe easy—even if its people would continue to tighten their belts.

11

A DANGEROUS COEXISTENCE

It is the present-day reality that the U.S., which threatened the DPRK with nukes, is now placed under the latter's nuclear threat.

An editorial published in the *Pyongyang Times* on
November 26, 2016, attributed to Choe Yong Nam.

Kim Jong Un now presides over a nuclear state. He's still young and, while his health may not be pristine, he expects to live a full life and die of natural causes at a ripe old age, like his father and grandfather. The short-term prospects of North Korea offering unilateral nuclear disarmament in a negotiating setting appear vanishingly remote. Even as Kim has submitted to diplomacy around the topic of "denuclearization" with the leaders of South Korea and the United States, internal North Korean propaganda has maintained a heavy focus on the benefits of the national nuclear forces. The North Koreans have built monuments to commemorate the sites of the first successful ICBM launches in 2017, and even the intermediate-range 'Guam-killer.' The "treasured sword" is not for sale—not for sanctions relief, nor for assurances of a different sort of relationship with the United States.

The consequences of a nuclear-armed North Korea over the long term remain indeterminate. Short of any diplomatic successes in capping, reducing, or eventually eliminating Kim's arsenal, the United States, South Korea, and Japan are left relying on deterrence and containment. While the Korean Peninsula has known its share of crises since the end of the war in 1953, full-scale hostilities have not resumed. The offensively oriented Korean People's Army was successfully deterred for decades, and now, with the KPA armed with nuclear weapons, the stakes are higher yet. North Korea remains a young nuclear power and may choose to engage in nuclear bargaining—a strategy with a generally poor record of payoff for nuclear-armed states, but one which may tempt Pyongyang. In Chapter Seven we saw some interest from Kim in bargaining of this sort over the war plans to threaten strikes on Guam unless U.S. bomber flights ceased.

A world with a nuclear-armed North Korea also creates new proliferation incentives in South Korea and Japan, particularly given growing concerns in both Seoul and Tokyo about the robustness of their alliance with the United States, which has long extended its nuclear umbrella to both. In South Korea, Kim Jong Un's rapid nuclear advances have led to growing calls—primarily among conservatives—for a renewed introduction of American tactical nuclear weapons to the Peninsula, or even a NATO-style "nuclear-sharing" arrangement, whereby Republic of Korea Air Force fighters would become certified to deliver American nukes. Meanwhile, constitutional restrictions on Japan's military forces continue to loosen under the remarkably durable prime ministership of Shinzo Abe, and talk of nuclear weapons persists in hushed tones amid concerns that the United States, under Donald Trump, may not be the reliable ally it once was.

These proliferation challenges are not insurmountable, but the "decoupling" risks once well known to early Cold War Europe are now readily apparent in Northeast Asia. Just as France left NATO's integrated military command and developed an independent nuclear deterrent over concerns that Washington would not risk its own cities to defend Western Europe against Soviet nuclear attack, so too today are Seoul and Tokyo more difficult than ever to reassure. With Kim's ability to hold Washington, D.C., New York, and Los Angeles under threat, that challenge will remain for the foreseeable future. Some analysts are less concerned so long as U.S. troops remain on the Korean Peninsula—if a North Korean attack on South Korea results in massive American casualties, there is little chance of Washington sitting out a conflict.[1] That may be true, but the longevity of that troop presence on the Peninsula has come under question during the presidency of Donald Trump, who sees all longstanding American alliances as burdensome.

The world will continue to grapple with the implications of Kim Jong Un and his nuclear forces for decades to come. In 2018, after North Korea and the United States had come close to nuclear war, North Korea sought to negotiate a new coexistence as nuclear equals. It is unclear if Washington has made its peace just yet with the emergence of its third nuclear-armed adversary, on top of Russia and China. But North Korea's nuclear weapons are here to stay, and the United States and its allies had best prepare to manage the consequences. In order to do this, we must start really getting to grips with what it is that Kim Jong Un wants to achieve with his nuclear forces; what kinds of response to them can realistically have an effect; and what we are risking, not just from Pyongyang but for the entire international order, if we fail to formulate that effective response.

What North Korea Wants

We have already looked at Kim Jong Un's broad strategy in Part One, but it is worth recapping the core objectives. The first, last, and longest-standing *raison d'être* of Kim's nuclear program is survival. Without doubt, Kim Jong Un's chief priority is to preserve his and his bloodline's domination over the party-state apparatus against internal and external challenges. His *byungjin* line had identified two ways of doing this. The first is to attain international prestige and reduce isolation by demonstrating a powerful, credible and broad nuclear force. The second is to maintain a self-reliant economy that improves the standard of living and provides the elite with sufficient rents to deter broader unrest. There is a further means to survival that features in Kim's ideology today—the longstanding pursuit of a unified Korean Peninsula—but this goal has, since Kim Il Sung's death, taken on an aspirational status.

When Kim Jong Il's youngest son came to power in 2011, he inherited more than a series of titles. Kim Jong Un was now the steward of every aspect of North Korea's state apparatus and heir to the two national objectives that had motivated even his grandfather as early as the 1950s. In 2012 and 2013, Kim's most proximate concern was securing the *paektusan* bloodline against internal challengers. During those early years of his reign, the young leader ruled as an enigma to the outside world, with a power consolidation process that resulted, by 2016, in a purge of over 300 senior regime figures who had served his father.[2] This project reached its apotheosis in December 2013, with the execution of Jang Song Thaek, Kim Jong Un's uncle and a former vice chairman of the once-powerful National Defense Commission. State media announced Jang's execution after a show trial through a special Korean People's Army court on Friday, December 13: "The accused is a traitor to the nation for all ages who perpetrated anti-party, counter-revolutionary factional acts in a bid to overthrow the leadership of our party and state and the socialist system."

At the time, the purge of 'Uncle Jang' surprised even longstanding observers of the North Korean state; eventually, it was rationalized as part of the young Kim Jong Un's power consolidation project. It also crystallized one feature of Kim Jong Un's approach to foreign affairs through 2018: keeping China at arm's length politically. Under Kim Jong Il, Jang had been among the key regime figures in managing the relationship with Beijing. Analysts of the Kim Jong Un regime disagree to this day about whether these early purges signified a show of strength or deep-seated insecurity, but whatever the truth, the young leader emerged in 2013 with his personal leadership consolidated; with his short-term survival ensured, he looked to the long term, beginning in earnest a foundational transformation of North Korea's national standing on the world stage. This started with the March 31, 2013, announcement of the *byungjin* line—Kim's contribution to the country's unique brand of socialist thought, calling for the simultaneous pursuit of economic prosperity and a powerful nuclear deterrent.

We should ask ourselves why we don't use the word disarmament but denuclearization instead in the context of North Korea's nuclear arsenal, when this was the term used for Iraq and Libya, for instance. The explanation is simple: those states were successfully deprived of their chance to achieve a nuclear deterrent, but Kim Jong Un had done it. It seems we will have to get used to talking about "denuclearization of the Korean Peninsula" almost indefinitely. North Korea, certainly, will continue to profess its interest in this goal, even as it remains hesitant about defining it unambiguously. As recently as 2019, senior North Korean officials told their American counterparts in private negotiations that only Kim Jong Un knew the exact meaning of the word. But we do know the *weight* of its meaning for Kim: in 2005, North Korean negotiators at the Six-Party Talks insisted that denuclearization of the Peninsula was Kim Il Sung's final directive. In 2018, Kim Jong Un told Moon Jae-in's presidential envoys in Pyongyang that it was Kim Jong Il's dying wish. We would do well to antici-pate that Kim Jong Un himself may end up sharing the same deathbed wish as his father and grandfather.

The Great Disappearing Act

On September 9, 2018, North Korea demonstrated the terms on which it would prefer to coexist with the United States as a fellow nuclear-armed state. A major propaganda milestone had swung around: the seventieth anniversary of the country's 1948 founding by Kim Il Sung. Yet at this major military parade, less than a year after declaring its nuclear deterrent complete, Pyongyang's nuclear weapons were nowhere to be seen. This was a serious departure from tradition: throughout this book we have seen the use of such parades to impress on the world the country's growing military sophistication as a missile power. On the hundredth anniversary of Kim Il Sung's birth, for example, North Korea had unveiled mocked-up designs of the Hwasong-13, its first possible ICBM. On February 8, 2018, a parade had shown off the two successful ICBMs, the Hwasong-14 and Hwasong-15. But in September, Kim was playing the statesman, dutifully hosting a hodgepodge of world leaders, parliamentarians, and senior diplomats, and he had signed his name on pledges to work in good faith toward "complete denuclearization" of the Korean Peninsula. Nuclear weapons would not be mentioned.

It is possible that the presence of a senior Chinese envoy had been contingent on Kim refraining from showing off any nuclear-capable systems; Beijing, like every other permanent member of the UN Security Council, supports denuclearization. Chinese President Xi Jinping had even delivered a speech in 2013, two months after North Korea's third nuclear test, stating that no Asian country should be able to destabilize the region for "selfish gain"—a statement that was taken as a rare public criticism of North Korea.[3] In any case, as editor of *The Nonproliferation Review* Joshua Pollack put it at the time, Kim Jong Un had "denuclearized Kim Il Sung Square."[4] During the Six-Party Talks process that began in 2005, North Korea had chosen to conduct its first nuclear bomb test despite the diplomacy under-way. Now, though, the deterrent was complete, and brazen provocation was replaced with the courtesy due from one nuclear power to another.

The September 2018 parade was perhaps our first glimpse of what a world with a nuclear-armed North Korea may start to look like, particularly if diplomacy persists and there is actual move-ment toward a normalized U.S.—North Korea relationship.[5] In a clear break with Kim Jong Un's intensive testing campaign in 2016–17, it seems that a newly confident, nuclear-armed North Korea might not choose to brandish the very "treasured sword" it has just acquired. It seems a polite fiction, or at least an under-standing that there is no need to constantly prove the deterrent, may be the path ahead: as early as the Singapore summit, Trump had helped Pyongyang with this lower-key approach by stating that there was "no longer a nuclear threat" from North Korea.

Disarmament by Force

There is no guarantee, however, that the new nuclear age begun in 2017 will be a quiet one. We saw the nonnegligible risk of nuclear war between the United States and North Korea in that year, and if U.S. policymakers continue to wrongly class Kim Jong Un as an irrational figure, a gentleman's agreement will not make much sense to them as a strategy. Trump's national secu-rity advisor for much of 2017 was General H.R. McMaster, who responded to Kim's review of the plans to strike Guam with a reference to the supreme leader's "unspeakable brutality" against his own people, intended as a warning about the type of man you just cannot level with.[6] Mao and Stalin exhibited similar brutality to the Kim dynasty has, and deterrence appeared to work against them—but if Washington truly believes that a qualitatively infe-rior adversary capable of striking the U.S. homeland is really undeterrable, then the rational move might demand striking immediately and ruthlessly, to disarm the regime at all costs.

That McMaster stopped short of recommending this course of action suggested either that his belief in Kim's undeterrability was insincere, or that he has failed to grasp the severity of what an irrational Kim would mean for U.S. national security. But as 2017 wound to a close, a small group of U.S. officials seriously contemplated the logical end to this thought experiment; it was in this context that leaks appeared in the press of a "bloody nose" limited strike idea, to teach Kim Jong Un a lesson. This might have taken the form of a pinpointed use of missiles against a particular North Korean ballistic missile facility. The Trump administration officially denied that such a strike was being considered; its risks were apparent and, in strategic terms, it may have represented the worst of all worlds: risking the initiation of a nuclear conflict—how was Kim Jong Un to know it was only a lesson and not the start of an invasion?—and, if that disaster was averted, only hardening Kim's resolve to retain his nuclear forces at all costs.

However, the Trump administration had shown a certain predilection for limited strikes. In April 2017, the United States had struck a Syrian air base with low-flying cruise missiles after a chemical weapons attack against civilians by the Syrian regime.[7] The North Koreans took note, with the Ministry of Foreign Affairs in Pyongyang issuing a statement in the days after the strike calling it an "act of aggression" that could "never be tolerated." But if the strikes were meant to send a message to North Korea, then it had not been received: Kim Jong Un "is not frightened at such threat."[8] This is not the only example: as political scientist Van Jackson documented, 2017 contained more than a dozen moments when the North Koreans might have interpreted that action was underway for a sudden, all-out attack to forcibly disarm and topple Kim.[9]

This is not just paranoia. The U.S. military does have unilateral war plans to disarm North Korea, and we have seen the

U.S.—South Korea alliance's extensive planning for operations to rapidly destroy Kim Jong Un's weapons of mass destruction, before they might be used against military targets in theater. These plans are complex and detailed, and based on intelligence assessments of North Korea's capabilities that, while robust, are incomplete at best. The danger inherent in their realization is greater now than ever, because the chances of them working are smaller: Kim Jong Un has spent the 2010s making sure that his nuclear forces are no easy target.

The intensified missile-testing campaign between 2014 and 2017 featured launches from all over North Korea, and in 2017 and 2019, Kim introduced indigenous off-road missile launchers that will take his arsenal off the road and into the caves and drive-through shelters of the country's abundant mountains. To disarm Kim by force, the United States and its allies would need to be able to reliably pinpoint and destroy every missile-deliverable nuclear warhead in North Korea before it might be used. Planners generally assume some leeway on that requirement thanks to missile defenses deployed on the Korean Peninsula, in Japan, and on Guam, as well as in Hawaii, Alaska and the U.S. mainland. In theory, these systems would mop up whatever "residual" force might be missed in the initial preemptive strikes. All of North Korea's nuclear weapons might be destroyed in this manner—under a set of heroic assumptions about pre-war planning and intelligence, and the efficacy of missile defenses.

Barring any sudden miraculous technological breakthroughs, heroic assumptions about missile defense would be unwise for policymakers. Though they are often described colloquially as a "shield," the analogy is far from perfect. The United States, as of 2020, had precisely one program designed to protect the continental homeland from North Korean ICBMs: the Ground-Based Midcourse Defense (GMD) system, comprising large missiles that hurl an exoatmospheric kill vehicle high above the earth's surface, with the intention of finding and destroying incoming ICBM reentry vehicles before they begin accelerating toward their target. This kind of missile defense technology is known as hit-to-kill, and is analogized as "hitting a bullet with a bullet."[10] If that sounds like an immensely difficult engineering challenge, it is. The initial U.S. obsession with ambitious missile defense schemes began in the final years of the Cold War, but today, with $67 billion in total spending, GMD is among the U.S. Department of Defense's most expensive programs ever.[11] It has little to show for that spending, boasting a testing record success a little better than 50 per cent.

The dangers of overestimating your missile defenses were amply demonstrated in 2017 by President Trump, who appeared to be under the impression that GMD was vastly more effective than it is—a potentially deadly assumption that could have led to military action against North Korea.[12] "We have missiles that can knock out a missile in the air 97 per cent of the time, and if you send two of them it's gonna get knocked out," Trump told Fox News host Sean Hannity in an interview.[13] 97 per cent was *far* from the overall system effectiveness of GMD, even with multiple interceptors used against a single incoming warhead.[14] Missile defense would be no technological panacea for North Korea's nuclear threat—at least not with acceptable levels of risk to American cities. If Trump were to believe missile defenses were really that good, it's not difficult to see why he might have been drawn into a 'bloody nose' scheme.

The prospect of forceful disarmament, for these reasons and others, is not likely to come to pass—especially given Kim Jong Un's range of capabilities in North Korea. While the Trump administration might have come dangerously close to flirting with the idea—and perhaps even acting on it unilaterally, without informing Seoul or Tokyo—the risks are simply too great. The North Koreans, ultimately, are right about their deterrent: it will keep the Americans at bay. Even before they had nuclear weapons, the multiple serious crises on the Peninsula in the decades after 1953 never escalated into full-scale hostilities, given mutual concerns about the costs of a war. The same calculation drives Kim Jong Un's deterrence strategy today: faced with a superior enemy, the only option is to convey that the costs of war are absolutely not worth the trouble.

Before the nuclearization of North Korea, allied war planners concerned themselves with the civilian death toll arising from artillery shelling of the Seoul metropolitan area; now, the calculation is far more dire. One 2017 simulation attempted to derive the likely human cost of a *single* North Korean 250 kiloton weapon like the thermonuclear 'Peanut,' if detonated over Seoul or Tokyo.[15] It found that, under most scenarios, fatalities would exceed 750,000 in Seoul and 700,000 in Tokyo; injuries in both cities would surpass 2.4 million. Americans—both civilians living in those cities and U.S. forces based on South Korean and Japanese soil—would be among the dead. These effects largely don't account for the more difficult to predict effects that might arise from firestorms in the aftermath of an attack.

Despite these realities, some Americans have remained blasé about the consequences of such a conflict. Speaking after North Korea's first two ICBM tests in July 2017, Lindsey Graham, the senior Republican senator from South Carolina, remarked: "There is a military option: to destroy North Korea's nuclear program and North Korea itself," Graham said. "If there's going to be a war to stop [Kim Jong Un], it will be over there," Graham continued. "If thousands die, they're going to die over there. They're not going to die over here."[16] In other words, Graham was advocating nuclear first-use, the last resort of the coercive disarmer. But, even if these ideas surface from time to time in the public discourse, they represent an option largely considered beyond the pale by the American policymaking community. U.S. war planning for the Korean Peninsula largely focuses on war-initiation using conventional weapons, with plans for nuclear escalation only to respond to North Korean nuclear use.

That is in line with public messaging by successive U.S. administrations, which have promised North Korea an "effective and overwhelming" response to any use of nuclear weapons against the United States or its allies. In 2013, President Barack Obama, with the South Korean president Park Geun-hye by his side, said the United States would defend South Korea with the "full range of capabilities available, including the deterrence provided by [its] conventional and nuclear forces." That phrase was not an overt nuclear threat, but it did not rule out the use of nuclear weapons. Trump's "fire and fury" threat in August 2017 was similarly interpreted to possibly signify use of nuclear weapons. The Trump administration's 2018 Nuclear Posture Review made it clear: "There is no scenario in which the Kim regime could employ nuclear weapons and survive," that document said.

In other words, a preemptive or preventive U.S. nuclear attack on North Korea was always unlikely. It is true that U.S. targeting plans for North Korea have long identified hardened and buried sites that may require nuclear-use for a high enough probability of a single attack disabling their use. In northern North Korea, U.S. war plans have accounted for the mountainous terrain, where nuclear-capable long-range missile systems may be stored and operated in wartime. While these targets may be vulnerable to conventional weapons, American targeting sees low-yield nuclear weapons as a more reliable way to successfully destroy them.[17] At least one U.S. war plan in place as recently as 2017, known internally as OPLAN (Operational Plan) 8023, relied on the use of twenty nuclear Trident D5 submarine-launched ballistic missiles launched from a single U.S. *Ohio*-class ballistic missile submarine to destroy, with a very high probability of success, all known North Korean weapons of mass destruction facilities.[18] It makes sense to launch such an attack from nearby submarines rather than from homeland ICBMs, which would have to overfly Russian territory, or bombers, which have a long flight time to the Korean Peninsula.

However, the United States has only identified one 'super-hardened' military target in North Korea: the Chonbongdong command and control node, which is calculated to require a 1.68 megaton surface nuclear blast, or a 34-kiloton blast with 9 meters of subsurface penetration. This is the sole North Korean target for which American planners consider that nuclear use would be almost entirely necessary.[19] Otherwise, conventional, precision weaponry would do the trick. What's more, U.S. planners do not envisage any real possibility of OPLAN 8023 ever being used given the apocalyptic death tolls envisaged; even if the United States 'won,' it would have lost in moral terms, having killed millions of people whose only crime was being born within the wrong set of borders. Not only would the use of nuclear weapons against North Korean weapon facilities represent a grossly disproportionate use of force—resulting in massive environmental damage and untold civilian deaths—it would constitute an egregious violation of international humanitarian law.

Still, disturbingly, research has found that insofar as American public opinion is concerned, nuclear first-use against North Korea is far from unthinkable. One study found that even though most Americans thought that Kim Jong Un could be deterred, a disconcertingly high number—33 per cent—saw a preventive nuclear first-strike as justifiable.[20] "There is no significant change in the percentage who would prefer or approve of a U.S. nuclear strike when the number of estimated North Korean fatalities increases from 15,000 to 1.1 million, including 1 million civilians."[21] The study's authors concluded that a "rally round the flag" effect was at play, with American attitudes toward nuclear weapons use spiking with perceived risk in a crisis. The American public also largely views disarmament by force as a rather promising option against North Korea: one third of respondents suggested they expected that, three out of four times, a non-nuclear U.S. strike would "successfully destroy all of North Korea's nuclear weapons." Many of these same respondents also believed that missile defense would destroy any North Korean missiles that were launched.

In reality, both propositions are dangerously off the mark—and will likely remain so for decades. A war—conventional or nuclear—with North Korea must not be fought by choice. Deterrence and containment, while imperfect, provide a more robust basis for sustainable coexistence with a nuclear-armed North Korea.

Maximum Pressure? Or Sanctions Relief?

If not through force, one option would be to sustain the *status quo* against North Korea unless and until Pyongyang can agree to a complete roadmap for denuclearization. This was the basis of the Trump administration's maximum pressure strategy: both unilateral U.S. and UN Security Council sanctions would remain in place as long as North Korea possessed nuclear weapons. While partial sanctions relief could be granted in exchange for smaller denuclearization steps, this would only be possible after Kim Jong Un had agreed to a roadmap whose final destination was disarmament. In essence, before any concessions at all, the North Koreans had to come to the table with the United States and agree on steps A, B, C, and so on all the way to Z, where Z would be "complete denuclearization," as agreed by Kim in the 2018 Panmunjom and Singapore declarations. But, as we know, the U.S. definition of Z at Hanoi was a nonstarter for the North Koreans, since it amounted to unilateral disarmament. Until this deadlock is broken, sanctions and hostility will be here to stay.

U.S. intelligence agencies repeatedly assessed through 2017, 2018, and 2019 that even the newly expanded UN Security

Council resolutions sanctioning North Korea "have induced minimal effects against the North Korean government, elites, and general economy."[22] Some supporters of sanctions as a viable response to a nuclear North Korea argue that the true effects of the sanctions introduced in August, September, and December 2017 would take until 2020 to really pressure the North Korean economy, and counsel that sanctions need time to have their desired effects.[23] For instance, resolution 2397's provision requiring UN member states to expel all North Korean laborers had a deadline of December 22, 2019.[24] However, sanctions seem only to influence certain kinds of North Korean behavior and decision-making—such as the regime's outreach to China and Russia—and have utterly failed so far to break Kim Jong Un's fierce commitment to the nuclear program he sees as fundamental to his survival.

What's more, sanctions have become a game of cat-and-mouse for the North Koreans, with the regime turning to increasingly creative—if onerous—methods of evasion. Since the 2017 imposition of broad-based trade restrictions across entire sectors of the economy, including a cap on crude oil imports, North Korean commercial shipping vessels have been involved in illicit ship-to-ship transfers of petroleum.[25] Windows of opportunity are opened by the imperfect implementation of sanctions by those who have voted for them, particularly China, which accounts for an overwhelming majority of North Korea's trade. As geopolitical competition and the trade war between Beijing and Washington intensify, China will have less incentive to undertake its sanctions obligations fully and seriously. Proponents of sanctions have recommended that Chinese entities involved in abetting North Korean sanctions evasion should suffer U.S. secondary sanctions, but this too may simply be met with greater circumventive efforts by Chinese and North Korean actors alike.

It is time, then, to rethink this failing policy. Of course, there are several sets of sanctions that should not be up for review, including those that have long targeted Pyongyang's ability to procure materials, technologies, and dual-use goods facilitating the production of ballistic missiles and weapons-grade nuclear fuel. Additionally, the UN arms embargo should remain in place; North Korea should not be allowed to proliferate its capabilities on the global market. Elites atop the North Korean system, including top Workers' Party cadres, should remain under asset freezes and travel restrictions; bans on luxury goods should also stay. Finally, unrelated to Kim's weapons of mass destruction, sanctions continue to play an important role in imposing costs on top North Korean officials directly culpable for egregious human rights violations and criminal activity. Together, these sanctions have played an important part in the "maximum pressure" campaign against North Korea—but they do not represent the totality of international leverage on the regime.

Even as many sanctions will remain in place for the long term, policymakers should be prepared to lift others, in exchange for desirable concessions from the North on its nuclear weapons program. Removing unilateral American sanctions will be legally difficult: U.S. laws predicate that Congress would have to certify North Korean progress on both the disarmament and humanitarian fronts to merit sanctions relief—a high bar. This leaves the eleven UN sanctions resolutions passed since 2006 as the most likely venue for any relief provisions for Kim Jong Un. Relief could include targeted exemptions for humanitarian projects and a limited set of inter-Korean economic projects. Separately, should North Korea submit to significant and verifiable limits on its nuclear forces, the international community limited joint ventures with UN oversight and/or the lifting of sectoral trade bans, such as on the North Korean textiles industry. All of these measures could be implemented with so-called 'snap-back' mechanisms, whereby North Korean defection on agreed-upon verification measures would result in an automatic restoration of any sanctions that had been lifted.[26]

Sanctions relief is something North Korea clearly seeks, and that makes it an important source of leverage for the United States, its allies, and the international community. American insistence on disarmament as a rigid and immovable objective might be based on noble objectives—including supporting the international nonproliferation regime—but it does little to lessen the threat that Kim's weapons pose. Given the real nuclear risks on the Korean Peninsula and to the U.S. homeland today—risks that have the potential for limitless growth in the absence of any engagement with the North—policymakers should ensure that the pursuit of "maximum pressure" does not indefinitely obscure potential pathways to concessions that would make the world safer in the immediate term. But what kind of concessions, exactly, should we seek?

Arms Control with Nuclear North Korea

Kim Jong Un has not and is not offering seriously to give up his nuclear arms, and seems only to accept denuclearization as something that will coincide with total global nuclear disarmament. In the meantime, then, how can we reduce the threat from those nuclear weapons today?

If North Korea is no longer a disarmament problem for the United States and the world—or at least, not usefully conceived of as a disarmament problem—then it is an arms control problem. The North Korean nuclear program may have been a problem to be solved through the 1990s, 2000s, and the early 2010s, but by 2020, if not 2017, it has become a problem to be managed. The question is no longer how to disarm North Korea, but "How do we manage the consequences of a nuclear North Korea?" For some at least, we use the leverage of sanctions to constrain Kim, with the goal of preventing unlimited growth and development of the North Korean nuclear arsenal.

Calls to engage in nuclear arms control with North Korea are immediately distasteful to many in the United States and elsewhere. After all, this was what superpowers with some degree of symmetric capability did during the Cold War, not how the United States approaches 'regional' nuclear powers. Despite American concerns about Mao Zedong's bomb in the 1960s, the United States and China never engaged in bilateral nuclear arms control. But China's deterrent quickly found a somewhat comfortable equilibrium and its approach to nuclear deterrence is fundamentally different from North Korea's. As we saw in Part One, Kim's small arsenal, chronic insecurity, offensive strategic outlook, vulnerable geography, and likely inelegant command and control all produce a dangerous mix, whereby his incentives to use nuclear weapons to ensure his survival are great.

Bilateral nuclear arms control in the context of a deeply asymmetric deterrence relationship like the one that exists between the United States and North Korea has simply never been tried. One classic definition of the purposes of arms control is "the avoidance of a war that neither side wants, in minimizing the costs and risks of the arms competition, and in curtailing the scope and violence of war in the event it occurs."[27] More importantly, arms control can contribute to the establishment of strategic stability between the United States and North Korea, ultimately reducing the risk of nuclear weapons use on or around the Korean Peninsula. Strategic stability is another nebulous term from the Cold War nuclear jargon that strikes some as having no place in discussions of the relationship between superpowers and regional powers. Broadly defined, strategic stability is the meeting of two conditions: both sides lack incentives to use nuclear weapons first, and both lack incentives to increase the size of their nuclear forces. True strategic stability might be impossible given the vast resource gulf between the two countries—there will always be a reason for North Korea to grow its arsenal. But Pyongyang and Washington can at least shape each other's choices in ways that contribute to *increasing* stability between them.

The impulse to begin working toward these objectives is best felt in times of crisis. One such time was the second half of 2017, when the world may have come close to a major war between the United States and North Korea—one that almost certainly would have involved use of nuclear weapons on the North Korean side. Kim Jong Un's diplomatic outreach in 2018–19 lessened the urgency of many of these topics—especially given President Trump's enthusiastic reciprocation of these overtures—but no number of superficial leaders' summits can alter the sustained and longstanding mistrust that underlies the relationship between the two countries. Sanctions relief, for instance, is unlikely to find takers in the United States, raising the odds that a frustrated Kim Jong Un may return to qualitatively advancing his nuclear weapons and ballistic missiles through testing. In short, the prospect of a renewed crisis is very real if arms control is not considered.

An arms control approach to North Korea need not cast aside the longer-term goal of total disarmament. Given the threat Pyongyang represents to the nonproliferation regime, the long-term objective *must* remain North Korea's return to the Treaty on the Non-Proliferation of Nuclear Weapons (NPT) as a Non-Nuclear Weapons State in good standing. This objective has a vanishingly small probability of ever materializing, but placing it at the cornerstone of a less ambitious, piecemeal arms control approach would buttress an international nonproliferation accord under considerable stress. Critics of arms control proposals note that negotiating such arrangements with Pyongyang is as good as granting it nuclear acceptance. But the entire international order cannot be put on the Kim family's shoulders: many countries attempted to pursue nuclear weapons during the Cold War, most of them unsuccessfully, and other would-be nuclear regimes may not be as willing as Kim Jong Un to bear the price of pursuing an independent deterrent. More importantly, whatever the damage to the nonproliferation regime as a result of the United States shifting tack, the benefits in peace and stability for Northeast Asia and the world could well outweigh it—not least because the two are intertwined.

We have seen that one consequence of unchecked nuclear development in North Korea has been the growing possibility of South Korea and Japan pursuing independent nuclear deterrents. In 2017, at the height of tensions, a Gallup poll found that some 60 per cent of South Koreans supported the notion of an independent nuclear deterrent.[28] In Japan, where anti-nuclear attitudes among the public are more apparent for obvious reasons, policy elites discuss the possibility of nuclearization in hushed voices. U.S. President Donald J. Trump's attitudes toward alliances—in effect, treating them as protection rackets—has rattled the balance. Seoul and Tokyo are not on the cusp of becoming nuclear states themselves, but the challenge posed by a nuclear North Korea will require greater American investment than ever in these alliances. After all, U.S. alliances and extended deterrence with these states are not altruistic; Washington sees extended deterrence as part of its nuclear nonproliferation toolkit as well.

Above all, pursuing arms control is not tantamount to the acceptance or legitimization of North Korea's nuclear status. Either both of those milestones have already been crossed, or they are simply red herrings, distracting from more serious problems. The Singapore summit—the first-ever meeting between a sitting U.S. president and a North Korean leader—came less than one year after Kim Jong Un oversaw the first-ever test of an ICBM. That marked a major moment of mainstreaming for nuclear-armed North Korea; previous U.S. administrations had held out the prospect of a leader-level meeting only in exchange for substantial North Korean concessions. The closest they had ever come was the planned, but ultimately unfulfilled, visit by former U.S. President Bill Clinton during the lifespan of the Agreed Framework. In any case, even if it basks in the status that its nuclear weapons afford, North Korea has issued high-level statements on its indifference to formal acceptance as a nuclear power. At the 2017 UN General Assembly general debate that followed Trump's threat to "totally destroy" North Korea, Foreign Minister Ri Yong Ho stated that "We do not need anyone's recognition of our status as a nuclear weapon state and our capability of nuclear strike."[29] What Kim Jong Un needed to be satisfied with his deterrent was not official or legal acceptance that he was nuclear-capable, but *de facto* acceptance of that reality—and we have seen plenty of indicators in this book that this has already occurred, from congressional testimony by military and intelligence officials to incorporation of North Korean ICBMs into joint U.S.—South Korean military exercises and planning, to Kim's meetings with the leaders of nuclear weapons states such as China's Xi Jinping and Russia's Vladimir Putin.[30]

Further back in history, when North Korea became the first country to test a nuclear weapon in the twenty-first century, if its nuclearization was *really* intolerable, that event might have precipitated a military campaign to rid Kim Jong Il of his weapons. We cannot contemplate the counterfactual where the United States would not have been bogged down in military quagmires in Iraq and Afghanistan, but faced with that reality—that shutting down the nuclear program early on simply was not an option at the time—the world was largely able to *tolerate* North Korea's breakout by way of sanctions. The more serious scenario of *de jure* nuclear acceptance for North Korea—Nuclear Weapon State status within the NPT—is unimaginable, but for Pyongyang, it seems that continued *de facto* acceptance and nuclear coexistence with the United States is enough.

Beyond sanctions relief, there is much else that Kim wants. For instance, North Korean diplomats have repeatedly told their

American counterparts in both official negotiations and unofficial dialogues that they would like something resembling the status that India enjoys, as a nuclear weapons-possessing country outside of the NPT with privileged, *sui generis* access to global nuclear commerce. Even that status would be a bridge too far, and accepting such an arrangement for North Korea would irreparably damage the NPT, whose central bargain is that foregoing weaponization grants "inalienable" rights to civilian nuclear energy technologies, but the expression of this desire is a clear indication that, really, Kim does not want to go to war—he wants to talk. There is an opportunity in front of us.

Adopting an arms control approach toward North Korea would set aside the perfect (total disarmament) for the good (nuclear risk reduction). Proposals to this end have been put forward for some time. One of the earliest and best known was the 'Three Nos' proposed by former Los Alamos National Laboratory director Siegfried Hecker, whereby North Korea would agree to the following:

1. No new weapons;
2. No better weapons;
3. No transfer of nuclear technology or weapons.[31]

Many proposals similarly boil down to a three-step *cap-reduce-eliminate* formula. Make no mistake: such an approach would restructure nearly three decades of U.S. policy toward Pyongyang from the ground up, ultimately acknowledging the failure of more than twenty years of nonproliferation policy. Pyongyang can also be expected to seek concessions in this scenario. For instance, in the Kim Jong Un era, North Korea has complained about U.S. and allied actions on and around the Korean Peninsula, including the visits of nuclear submarines to South Korean ports, U.S. testing of homeland missile defense systems, and joint allied exercises. But these North Korean concerns should not deter American policymakers from considering arms control.

A DANGEROUS COEXISTENCE

Above all, the United States, South Korea, and Japan should consider the mechanisms of restraint that might work to limit North Korea's nuclear arsenal. Up to a point, this process might strangely mirror the 'shopping list' that Kim has been working to complete. The first objective might be to limit the production and supply of nuclear weapons fuel and warheads; from there, the focus might shift to limiting Kim's expansive array of delivery systems for these bombs; then the United States could seize the remaining window in which indigenous launch and reentry technology is still developmental. Bringing North Korea's missile arsenal down to zero will not be possible short of a disarmament-by-force scenario, but ensuring that its growth is restrained has obvious interest, as does ensuring that it remains within the qualitative confines demonstrated by the end of 2017. In other words, a major priority of arms control should be to ensure that the 'What next?' considerations at the end of Chapter Eight are not fulfilled: a move to solid-fueled ICBMs for greater flexibility, indigenization of ICBM launch vehicles for self-reliance, and multiple, sophisticated reentry vehicles to erase all remaining doubt that these missiles can hit their target. Naturally, this will require a testing ban—something that North Korea has agreed to more than once before. Another area to watch, as we saw at the end of Chapter Six, would be ballistic missile submarines: ensuring that the fleet of two does not become a truly robust undersea deterrent force.

Without limits, the North Korean nuclear challenge will grow more complex yet, harming the interests of the United States and its allies and Northeast Asian security. Arms control will neither be easy nor ideal, but it will begin the process of managing the many challenges that have arisen from Kim Jong Un's nuclear successes in 2017.

What if the Pessimists Are Right?

The prospect of arms control may be optimistic, for four reasons. Firstly, opponents point to longstanding ideological themes in Pyongyang's official statement of its political objectives on the Korean Peninsula. For instance, even in the Kim Jong Un era, North Korean propaganda has threatened to seek the unification of the Korean Peninsula—ideally under North Korean leadership. Pessimists may also note the Korean People's Army's strategic culture, steeped in a so-called "ambush mentality" and offensive mindset characterized by the sinking of the ROKS *Cheonan* and the shelling of Yeonpyeong Island in 2010. Kim Jong Un's tenure remains young, and as his nuclear arsenal grows, he may be emboldened. Secondly, there is the nature of the North Korean regime, which remains uniquely cruel and oppressive toward its own people. For some, the prospect of sitting down for arms control or mooting sanctions relief with such a regime should be an unthinkable prospect in itself. Thirdly, beyond the Korean Peninsula, pessimists have well-placed concerns about the world's ability to manage a nuclear-armed North Korea while hamstrung by fears of creating incentives for proliferation elsewhere—particularly since the Trump administration's scuttling of the 2015 Joint Comprehensive Plan of Action with Iran, which may provoke a resumption of the nuclear weapons program halted in the early 2000s.

Finally, in rebuttal to those who say the sanctions approach must be softened because it has not deterred Kim, there are those who argue that this means sanctions relief will not be any better a carrot than their imposition was a stick. We have already seen some examples of Pyongyang's cheerful evasion of sanctions and, making the most of the times, the regime has found particular value in turning to cyberattacks and cryptocurrencies as a way to move fungible financial assets outside of the U.S. dollar system. Cybercrime, in particular, has apparent appeal for regimes on the disadvantaged side of asymmetric hostility, given its high-reward, low-risk nature. Even if an attack is successfully attributed to the North Korean regime, as long as the regime benefits financially, it considers the risks worthwhile. Under Kim Jong Un, the Reconnaissance General Bureau (North Korea's external intelligence agency) and its subsidiaries have pulled off everything from sophisticated cyber heists—such as the February 2016 attack on the Bangladeshi central bank—to broad-based ransomware attacks, like the 2017 WannaCry worm attack.[32]

In other words, North Korea has not only hit the headlines in recent years for its nuclear bomb and missile tests: Kim Jong Un has gained a broader reputation as an international menace. The February 2017 assassination of his half-brother at Kuala Lumpur International Airport with the use of a powerful chemical nerve agent may not be a one-off incident; it may instead presage a broader campaign of overseas assassinations of politically sensitive escapees. In the pessimist's view of things, Kim Jong Un may yet choose to test the kinds of mischief his nuclear weapons might now enable him to get away with. For South Korea and Japan, these concerns in part contribute to the intolerability of a nuclear-armed North Korea.

Even while regime survival through existential deterrence remains the core purpose of North Korean nuclear strategy, worries persist in Seoul and Tokyo that Pyongyang may take on an increasingly coercive turn in the 2020s. Kim Jong Un has only been in power for a little more than eight years by the time of writing in 2020, but it took his father until his sixteenth year in power to try something as provocative as the twin Cheonan-Yeonpyeongdo attacks of 2010. Given North Korea's reputation for risk acceptance, these possibilities cannot be ruled out. While North Korea's nuclear weapons help Kim sleep better at night, their effect on Northeast Asian peace and security over the long run remains very much uncertain.

Shifting Geopolitics and a 'New Way'

If that is the case, then why should the world even bother with attempts at containment, given that sanctions relief and arms control will both have political costs and security risks? The answer is simple: we have no choice. If the United States and its allies do not step forward to address head-on the reality of a nuclear North Korea, then somebody else will fill that space; and Washington may not like how that would turn out for the global order. On the first day of 2019, Kim Jong Un issued a stark warning to the United States. While he left the door open for diplomacy, he warned that if the United States "attempts to uni-laterally enforce something upon us"—disarmament—then North Korea would be forced to "find a new way." Kim did not define this "new way," but left it on the table as a cryptic and foreboding signal that diplomacy with the United States was not considered the only path forward.

The diplomatic process that began between Washington and Pyongyang in 2018 coincided with the breakout of a trade war between the United States and China, and the Trump adminis-tration fully leaning into what it called "great power competi-tion" with Beijing. Just as Kim Il Sung took advantage of com-peting Soviet and Chinese patronage after the Sino-Soviet Split in the 1960s, so too might Kim Jong Un fully leverage the ben-efits that come with greater frictions between the United States and China. The 2018 outreach to the United States was an attempt to explore whether North Korea could place itself in the position that China once occupied between the two Cold War superpowers. As Kim's hopes for a new era in U.S. relations were swept away after the Hanoi summit in February 2019, it quickly became clear that Kim was also seeking to court Russia. In April 2019, Kim took his first overseas trip since Hanoi, to the far eastern Russian city of Vladivostok, where he met President Vladimir Putin. As part of a December 2019 intra-party leadership reshuffle, former ambassador to Moscow Kim Hyong Jun was appointed to lead the Workers' Party's International Department, while in February 2020 Sin Hong Chol, a vice foreign minister, was appointed ambassador to Moscow.[33]

In other words, with a fundamentally North Korean sense of self-reliance, Kim appears reluctant to put all his eggs in one basket. His hedging strategy is not just between Moscow and Washington, but between all three major powers with stakes in Northeast Asian security—Russia, the United States, and also China. Under Kim's father and grandfather, Pyongyang's undeniable economic dependency on cross-border trade had been a longstanding vulnerability, and all the more acute after the collapse of the Soviet Union; in the early Kim Jong Un years, relations between Pyongyang and Beijing quickly dipped, with high-level exchanges coming more or less to a standstill by 2015. But a new chapter is opening. We should not forget that Kim began his 2018 diplomacy blaze by calling first on Xi Jinping. Kim returned to meet the Chinese president again both before and after the historic Singapore summit with Trump, and yet again in January 2019, shortly before Hanoi. Finally, in June 2019, Xi became the first Chinese leader in fourteen years to step on North Korean soil. During this trip, one of North Korea's famous, awe-inspiring "mass games" demonstrations was held to recall the sacrifices of the Chinese People's Volunteer Army during the Korean War. Even in 2019, some sixty-six years since the armistice, the two sides were reaffirming their blood ties—that they were still as close as "lips and teeth," as Mao had once said. The optics of these summits—carefully staged and beamed to the outside world exclusively by Chinese and North Korean state media—could indicate an enduring and historical strategic partnership in the age of a nuclear North Korea, even as Pyongyang remains deeply distrustful of Beijing..

For China and Russia, North Korea's possession of nuclear weapons appears to have taken a back seat since 2018 while diplomatic progress has forged ahead in other areas. None of this bodes well for the prospects of North Korean disarmament, nor for U.S. interests in the region; the United States and its allies can either join Moscow and Beijing in accepting and dealing with a nuclear North Korea, or else find themselves on the outside of the new power dynamics possibly taking shape on the Peninsula.

An Uneasy Coexistence

North Korea's success with its own nuclearization has forced the world into an unsavory—if gradual—process of recognizing that coexistence will in all likelihood be the only plausible path going forward. Barring a shock internal event that topples the regime, including the sudden or untimely death of Kim Jong Un from illness, North Korea is not going anywhere any time soon—and neither are its nuclear weapons. This reality has slowly begun to sink in. In January 2019, while presenting the U.S. intelligence community's assessment of global threats before a U.S. Senate panel, former Director of National Intelligence Dan Coats acknowledged that "We currently assess that North Korea will seek to retain its WMD capabilities and is unlikely to completely give up its nuclear weapons and production capabilities because its leaders ultimately view nuclear weapons as critical to regime survival."[34]

The dark side of coexistence is what Kim's nuclear weapons will mean for the millions of innocent people within his borders, especially those born into deprivation and ardor outside of Pyongyang. Human rights and human security will—and must—remain part of the international policy agenda toward North Korea, but the reality is that Kim's nuclear weapons give him sufficient international leverage to continue ruling as a tyrant as he sees fit. North Korean gulags will continue to exist, as they have for decades. Yet coexistence should not frighten Americans,

South Koreans, or Japanese. It is not *legitimation* of North Korea's nuclear status; it is a reckoning with reality. Coexistence is not automatic or easy. It requires a coming to terms with the basic fact that, just as the United States and its allies deterred North Korea for decades before it had nuclear weapons, so too does North Korea deter its adversaries today from pursuing a forcible change to its leadership. Kim's "treasured sword" is here to stay. The world should do all it can to ensure that it remains sheathed.

APPENDIX

COMPLETE LIST OF U.S. INTELLIGENCE COMMUNITY DESIGNATIONS FOR NORTH KOREA (AS OF 2019)[1]

What follows is a complete accounting of known North Korean missile systems—cruise, ballistic, rocket artillery, and even satellite launch vehicles—as classified by the U.S. intelligence community. While U.S. intelligence designators for North Korean missiles commonly appear in the KN-XX format in public reporting, this list omits the hyphen, as per the convention used by the U.S. Defense Special Missile and Astronautics Center (DEFSMAC). A separate permanent designation system is used by the U.S. Weapons & Space Systems Intelligence Committee (for example, KN-SS-X-9).

KN-SS-6—Known in the North Korean context as the Musudan/ RSM-25, this missile is also called the Hwasong-10 and referred to in press reports as the BM-25. A liquid-fuel medium-range ballistic missile derived from the Soviet-designed, liquid-fueled, submarine-launched R-27 Zyb (NATO reporting name: SS-N-6 SERB). Did not receive a temporary KN designator.

KN-SSC-1—A North Korean derivative coastal defense cruise missile based on the Chinese HY-2. NATO reporting name: SEERSUCKER. (This system does not have a KNXX designation.)

KN01—The Kumsong-3, also called the KN-SS-X-3, a North Korean derivative of the Soviet-designed, ground-launched Zvedza Kh-35 cruise missile. NATO reporting name: STORMPETREL.

KN02—The solid-fueled, short-range Toksa ballistic missile, a North Korean derivative of the Soviet-designed OTR-21 Tochka.

KN03—A separate modification of the Nodong medium-range missile, sometimes called Nodong Mod 2 by the U.S. intelligence community.

KN04—North Korea's extended-range variant of the Scud. This missile was originally called the Scud-ER, but later officially Scud 2.

KN05—A publicly unseen variant of North Korea's Kumsong-3/Kh-35 variant fitted on a Korean People's Air Force IL-28. This is North Korea's only air-launched cruise missile to ever see flight-testing. NATO reporting name: STORMPETREL.

KN06—The Bongae-5 and Bongae-6 surface-to-air missile systems, also called the KN-SA-X-1. The two variants use different launchers, but the same canisterized missile system. This is North Korea's attempt to recreate the Soviet-designed S-300PMU system.

KN07—A range extension of the SN01/KN-SSC-2. The U.S. intelligence community assessed that this may have been designed partly for use as a land-attack cruise missile for the Korean People's Navy.

KN08—The Hwasong-13 three-stage, liquid-fueled ICBM.

KN09—North Korea's 300mm multiple-launch rocket launcher,

classified by U.S. intelligence as a close-range ballistic missile for its range and guidance capabilities. Previously known as KN-SS-X-9 during testing and KN-SS-9 after entering service in 2018.

KN10—An early attempt by North Korea to iterate on the Scud-C/Hwasong-6 for greater terminal maneuverability.

KN11—The Pukguksong-1, a solid-fuel, intermediate-range SLBM. Video footage of the first launch of this missile in 2015 appeared to have been doctored to suggest use of liquid fuel.

KN12—A GPS-correcting 122mm multiple launch rocket launcher.

KN13—An indigenous modernization project involving the Soviet-sourced SA-2 Guideline/S-75 Desna surface-to-air missile system and infrared homing capabilities.

KN14—A second modification of the Hwasong-13 intermediate-range ballistic missile, also called the Hwasong-13 mod 2.

KN15—The Pukguksong-2 solid-fuel medium-range ballistic missile—a land-based version of the KN11/Pukguksong-1 SLBM, with an indigenously designed integrated transporter-erector-launcher with all-terrain treads. The U.S. intelligence community also calls this system the KN-SS-X-11.

KN16—A GPS-correcting 240 mm multiple rocket launch system.

KN17—The Hwasong-12 intermediate-range ballistic missile. This missile uses modified Hwasong-10 transporter-erector-launchers.

KN18—An upgraded Scud-C/Hwasong-6 with guidance improvements and control surfaces affixed to the reentry vehicle to improve terminal maneuverability. The missile, when seen publicly, was carried by an indigenously designed integrated transporter-erector-launcher with all-terrain treads.

KN19—The coastal defense variant of the Kumsong-3/KN01 featuring an indigenously designed integrated transporter-erector-launcher with all-terrain treads. The missiles feature a new multi-modal seeker and considerably improved maneuverability and guidance.

KN20—The Hwasong-14 two-stage, liquid-fueled ICBM.

KN21—An upgraded Scud-B/Hwasong-5 with guidance improvements and control surfaces affixed to the warhead to improve terminal maneuverability.

KN22—The Hwasong-15 two-stage, liquid-fueled ICBM.

KN23—The short-range quasi-ballistic missile first paraded in February 2018 and tested in May 2019 that resembles the Russian 9K723/*Iskander*-M. The North Korean designation for this missile is unknown.

KN24—A short-range ballistic missile system first tested in August 2019 that bears a resemblance to the U.S. MGM-140 ATACMS system. The North Korean designation for this missile is unknown.

KN25—A new 600mm "large-caliber" multiple-launch rocket system shown for the first time in July 2019. The North Korean designation for this missile is unknown.

KN26—The Pukguksong-3 solid-fuel submarine-launched ballistic missile.

ND01—The original North Korea-designed Nodong medium-range ballistic missile. The U.S. intelligence community also calls this missile the KN-SS-2. (The KN-SS-1 is the Russian Scud-C.)

SN01—An iterative upgrade of the KN-SSC-1 with a turbojet, also called the KN-SSC-2. This system was exported to Iran, which iterated on the North Korean design and used it as the Ra'ad anti-ship cruise missile.

TD01—The Taepodong-1 satellite launch vehicle, also classified as a technology demonstrator for ICBMs. Also called the Paektusan-1 and the KN-SS-X-3.

TD02—North Korea's Unha-2 and Unha-3 satellite launch vehicles, also classified as technology demonstrators for ICBMs. The Unha-3 additionally gained the U.S. designator KN-SL-1. The TD02 underwent reclassification after 2009. Prior to this, the first Unha-2 also had the designator KN-SS-7.

NOTES

INTRODUCTION

1. Thomas Schelling, "An Astonishing 60 Years: The legacy of Hiroshima," Nobel Lecture, December 8, 2005, accessed November 5, 2019, https://www.ncbi.nlm.nih.gov/pmc/articles/PMC1458836/.
2. Peter Heinlein, "Trump Threatens 'Total Destruction' of North Korea in First UN Speech," *Voice of America*, accessed August 10, 2019, https://www.voanews.com/usa/trump-threatens-total-destruction-north-korea-first-un-speech.
3. Ankit Panda, "False Alarms of the Apocalypse," *The Atlantic*, January 13, 2018, https://www.theatlantic.com/international/archive/2018/01/what-the-hell-happened-in-hawaii/550514/.
4. In December 1952, Kim Il Sung had overseen the establishment of the country's first Atomic Energy Research Institute.
6. Based on open source data tabulation by the Center for Nonproliferation Studies' North Korean Missile Test Tracker. Available at https://www.nti.org/analysis/articles/cns-north-korea-missile-test-database/.

1. A NEW EMPEROR

1. Anna Fifield, *The Great Successor: The Divinely Perfect Destiny of Brilliant Comrade Kim Jong Un* (New York: PublicAffairs, 2019), 63–64.
2. Howard W. French, "Japan Deports Man Said to Be North Korean Leader's Son," *The New York Times*, May 4, 2001, https://www.nytimes.com/2001/05/04/world/japan-deports-man-said-to-be-north-korean-leader-s-son.html.

3. Ralph Hassig and Kongdan Oh, *The Hidden People of North Korea: Everyday Life in the Hermit Kingdom* (Lanham: Rowman & Littlefield, 2015), 35.

4. Kim Hakjoon, *Dynasty: The Hereditary Succession Politics of North Korea* (Stanford, California: Shorenstein Asia-Pacific Research Center, 2015), 176–77.

5. John Delury, "Reform Sprouts in North Korea?," *YaleGlobal Online*, July 26, 2012, https://yaleglobal.yale.edu/content/reform-sprouts-north-korea.

6. Reuters, "Kim Jong-Nam Had Antidote to Nerve Agent That Killed Him in Bag," *The Guardian*, December 1, 2017, https://www.theguardian.com/world/2017/dec/01/kim-jong-nam-north-korea-antidote-nerve-agent-killed-bag.

7. Fifield, *The Great Successor*, 203.

8. Sheena Chestnut Greitens, "A North Korean Corleone," *The New York Times*, March 3, 2012, https://www.nytimes.com/2012/03/04/opinion/sunday/a-north-korean-corleone.html.

9. Adam Cathcart, Robert Winstanley-Chesters, and Christopher K. Green, *Change and Continuity in North Korean Politics* (Oxon: Taylor & Francis, 2016), 3.

10. "New Strategic Line, Instrumental to Building Thriving Nation," *KCNA*, April 6, 2013, https://kcnawatch.co/newstream/1451895862-464363664/new-strategic-line-instrumental-to-building-thriving-nation/.

11. "DPRK Report on the Third Plenary Meeting of the Seventh Central Committee," *NCNK*, April 25, 2018, https://www.ncnk.org/resources/publications/dprk_report_third_plenary_meeting_of_seventh_central_committee_of_wpk.pdf.

12. "The Korean Peninsula: 'Nuclear Weapons State' North Korea Aiming to Become an Economic Power, ROK Seeking Active Deterrence Capability," in *East Asia Strategic Review* (Tokyo: National Institute for Defense Studies, 2013), 146, http://www.nids.mod.go.jp/english/publication/east-asian/pdf/2013/east-asian_e2013_04.pdf.

13. "8th Conference of Munitions Industry Opens in Presence of Kim Jong Un," *KCNA Watch* (blog), December 12, 2017, https://kcnawatch.org/newstream/.

14. Alexandre Y. Mansourov, "Kim Jong Un's Nuclear Doctrine and Strategy: What Everyone Needs to Know," Nautilus Institute for Security and Sustainability, December 16, 2014, https://nautilus.org/napsnet/napsnet-

special-reports/kim-jong-uns-nuclear-doctrine-and-strategy-what-every-one-needs-to-know/.

15. Valentina Zarya, "Kim Jong Un's Moranbong Band Travels to China," *Fortune*, accessed September 3, 2019, https://fortune.com/2015/12/11/north-korea-girl-band/.

16. "Successful Test-Fire of Newly Developed Super-Large Multiple Rocket Launcher Held under Guidance of Supreme Leader Kim Jong Un," *Rodong Sinmun*, August 25, 2019, http://rodong.rep.kp/en/index.php?strPageID=SF01_02_01&newsID=2019–08–25–0003.

17. Jeffrey Lewis, "'Your Mission Is to Keep All This From Collapsing Into Nuclear Hellfire,'" *Foreign Policy* (blog), accessed September 3, 2019, https://foreignpolicy.com/2018/09/18/your-mission-is-to-keep-all-this-from-collapsing-into-nuclear-hellfire/.

18. Anita Kunz, "New Toys," *New Yorker*, January 18, 2016, https://www.newyorker.com/magazine/2016/01/18.

19. Center for Nonproliferation Studies' North Korean Missile Test Tracker.

20. Paul D. Shinkman, "Top U.S. Officer: Kim Jong Un Irrational, Unpredictable," *US News & World Report*, January 23, 2014, https://www.usnews.com/news/articles/2014/01/23/top-us-officer-kim-jong-un-irrational-unpredictable.

21. "'This Week' Transcript 8/13/17: Lt. Gen. H. R. McMaster, Anthony Scaramucci," *ABC News*, August 13, 2017, https://abcnews.go.com/Politics/week-transcript-13-17-lt-gen-mcmaster-anthony/story?id=49177024.

22. "Michael Kirby: 'Holocaust-Type Phenomenon,'" April 26, 2014, https://www.aljazeera.com/programmes/talktojazeera/2014/04/michael-kirby-holocaust-type-phenomenon-2014425124333281170.html.

23. Brian R. Myers, "North Korea's Unification Drive—B.R. Myers," *Sthele Press* (blog), December 20, 2017, https://sthelepress.com/index.php/2017/12/21/north-koreas-unification-drive/.

24. Kenneth N. Waltz, *Theory of International Politics*, first edition (Long Grove, Ill: Waveland Press, 2010), 107.

25. Waltz, 107.

26. Sergey Radchenko, "'We Do Not Want to Overthrow Him': Beijing, Moscow, and Kim Il Sung, 1956," Wilson Center, August 6, 2017, https://www.wilsoncenter.org/blog-post/we-do-not-want-to-overthrow-him-bei-jing-moscow-and-kim-il-sung-1956.

27. Van Jackson, *On the Brink: Trump, Kim, and the Threat of Nuclear War* (New York: Cambridge University Press, 2018), 20.

28. Bruce Bueno de Mesquita et al., *The Logic of Political Survival*, revised edition (Cambridge, Mass.: The MIT Press, 2004).

29. "US Has to Contemplate DPRK's Nuclear Deterrent," *Pyongyang Times* (blog), April 14, 2016, https://kcnawatch.org/newstream/.

2. HISTORY'S TRIALS

1. Robert Jervis, *The Meaning of the Nuclear Revolution: Statecraft and the Prospect of Armageddon*, First Edition (Ithaca: Cornell University Press, 1990).

2. Bernard Brodie, *The Absolute Weapon: Atomic Power and World Order* (Freeport, N.Y: Ayer Co Pub, 1946).

3. "'The Cairo Declaration,' November 26, 1943, History and Public Policy Program Digital Archive, Foreign Relations of the United States, Diplomatic Papers, The Conferences at Cairo and Tehran, 1943" (Washington, D.C.: United States Government Printing Office, 1961, 1943), https://digitalarchive.wilsoncenter.org/document/122101.pdf.

4. Dean Rusk, *As I Saw It*, ed. Daniel S. Papp, first edition (New York: W W Norton & Co Inc, 1990).

5. Rusk, *As I Saw It*.

6. "Soviet Officer Reveals Secrets of Mangyongdae," *DailyNK* (blog), January 2, 2014, https://www.dailynk.com/english/soviet-officer-reveals-secrets-of/.

7. "Soviet Officer Reveals Secrets of Mangyongdae."

8. Ibid. DailyNK (blog).

9. Curtis E. LeMay et al., eds., *Strategic Air Warfare: An Interview with Generals Curtis E. LeMay, Leon W. Johnson, David A. Burchinal, and Jack J. Catton*, USAF Warrior Studies (Washington, D.C: Office of Air Force History, U.S. Air Force: For sale by the Supt. of Docs., U.S. G.P.O, 1988), 88.

10. Motoko Rich et al., "How South Korea Left the North Behind," *The New York Times*, February 6, 2018, https://www.nytimes.com/interactive/2018/02/06/world/asia/korea-history.html.

11. Bureau of Public Affairs Department Of State, The Office of Electronic Information, "Agreement on Reconciliation, Nonagression and Exchanges

And Cooperation Between the South and the North," accessed July 6, 2019, https://2001–2009.state.gov/t/ac/rls/or/2004/31012.htm.

12. William Burr, "The United States and South Korea's Nuclear Weapons Program, 1974–1976," Wilson Center, March 14, 2017, https://www.wilsoncenter.org/article/the-united-states-and-south-koreas-nuclear-weapons-program-1974–1976.

13. Jeffrey Arthur Larsen and Kurt J. Klingenberger, "Controlling Non-Strategic Nuclear Weapons: Obstacles and Opportunities," May 31, 2001, https://www.hsdl.org/?abstract&did=.

14. Jonathan D. Pollack, *No Exit: North Korea, Nuclear Weapons, and International Security* (International Institute for Strategic Studies, 2011), 108.

15. Sheryl Wudunn, "North Korean Site Has A-Bomb Hints," *The New York Times*, May 17, 1992, https://www.nytimes.com/1992/05/17/world/north-korean-site-has-a-bomb-hints.html.

16. Joshua H. Pollack, "What Sort of Deal Does North Korea Expect?," *ArmsControlWonk*, July 18, 2019, https://www.armscontrolwonk.com/archive/1207784/what-sort-of-deal-does-north-korea-expect/.

17. Pollack, *No Exit*, 109.

18. Wit, Poneman, and Gallucci, *Going Critical*, 34.

19. David Fischer, "The DPRK's Violation of Its NPT Safeguards Agreement with the IAEA—Excerpt from 'History of the International Atomic Energy Agency,'" IAEA, 1997, https://www.iaea.org/sites/default/files/dprk.pdf.

20. Pollack, *No Exit*, 109.

21. "Aspin Uncertain Whether North Korea Has Nuclear Weapons," *UPI*, accessed July 6, 2019, https://www.upi.com/Archives/1993/03/14/Aspin-uncertain-whether-North-Korea-has-nuclear-weapons/5261732085200/.

22. The State Department's Bureau of Intelligence and Research did not concur. Michael Gordon and Stephen Engelberg, "Intelligence Study Says North Korea Has Nuclear Bomb," *The New York Times*, December 26, 1993, https://www.nytimes.com/1993/12/26/world/asia/intelligence-study-says-north-korea-has-nuclear-bomb.html.

23. Gordon and Engelberg, "Intelligence Study Says North Korea Has Nuclear Bomb."

24. David E. Sanger, "Carter Visit to North Korea: Whose Trip Was It Really?,"

The New York Times, June 18, 1994, https://www.nytimes.com/1994/06/18/world/carter-visit-to-north-korea-whose-trip-was-it-really.html.

25. For a fuller account of Perry's time in Pyongyang, see his memoirs: http://www.wjperryproject.org/notes-from-the-brink/the-north-korean-policy-review-what-happened-in-1999.

26. North Korea had (unsuccessfully) demanded $1 billion in direct cash compensation for not proliferating its weapons and related technology.

27. Pollack, 138–9.

28. John J. Lumpkin, "The Strike That Nearly Ended the War before It Started," *The Associated Press*, April 13, 2003, https://www.kitsapsun.com/services/cobrand/header/.

29. Pollack, *No Exit*, 141.

30. Ibid.

31. Glenn Kessler, "N. Korea Says It Has Nuclear Arms," *The Washington Post*, April 25, 2003, https://www.washingtonpost.com/archive/politics/2003/04/25/n-korea-says-it-has-nuclear-arms/43bc7e65–2c2a-407e-bf71–64e9e52ac3c9/.

32. "North Korea Nuclear Milestones—1962–2017," *Wisconsin Project on Nuclear Arms Control* (blog), September 29, 2017, https://www.wisconsinproject.org/north-korea-nuclear-milestones/.

33. Kim Kye Gwan, "Spokesman of the DPRK Ministry of Foreign Affairs," June 8, 2003.

34. "Spokesman of the DPRK Ministry of Foreign Affairs."

35. Chuck Hagel et al., "North Korea: Status Report on Nuclear Program, Humanitarian Issues, and Economic Reforms—A Staff Trip Report to the Committee on Foreign Relations United States Senate," *Committee Print of the 108th Congress 2d Session*, February 2004, 32, 3, 15.

36. "N. Korea: Demolition Caused Cloud," *CNN*, September 13, 2004, http://www.cnn.com/2004/WORLD/asiapcf/09/13/nkorea.blast/.

37. "N. Korea: Demolition Caused Cloud."

38. Barbara Demick, "A Cloud That May Be 'Just a Cloud,'" *Los Angeles Times*, September 18, 2004, https://www.latimes.com/archives/la-xpm-2004-sep-18-fg-mushroom18-story.html.

39. "N. Korea: Demolition Caused Cloud."

40. "North Korea Says It Has Nuclear Weapons and Rejects Talks," *The New York Times*, February 10, 2005, https://www.nytimes.com/2005/02/10/

international/asia/north-korea-says-it-has-nuclear-weapons-and-rejects-talks.html.

41. Glenn Kessler, "Signs Stir Concern North Korea Might Test Nuclear Bomb," *The Washington Post*, April 23, 2005, http://www.washington-post.com/wp-dyn/articles/A10477–2005Apr22.html.

42. "Contacts Between Heads of DPRK and U.S. Delegations to Sixth-Party Talks Made," *KCNA* (blog), accessed May 2, 2019, https://kcnawatch.org/newstream/1452005399–93400071/contacts-between-heads-of-dprk-and-u-s-delegations-to-sixth-party-talks-made/.

43. Sun-won Park, "A Proposal for a 'Bosworth Process' With North Korea: Denuclearization and Beyond," *Center for Northeast Asia Policy Studies, The Brookings Institution*, October 2009, 18.

44. "Treasury Targets North Korean Entities for Supporting WMD Proliferation," U.S. Department of the Treasury, accessed May 2, 2019, https://www.treasury.gov/press-center/press-releases/Pages/js2984.aspx.

45. "KCNA Urges U.S. to Compensate for Losses Caused by Scrapping AF," *KCNA*, December 19, 2005, https://kcnawatch.org/newstream/14520 05448-253797686/kcna-urges-u-s-to-compensate-for-losses-caused-by-scrapping-af/.

46. "$1.5 Billion Later, KEDO Pulls the Plug on North Korea Nuclear Construction," *Korea JoongAng Daily*, June 1, 2006, http://koreajoongang-daily.joins.com/news/article/article.aspx?aid=2732443.

47. "SECURITY COUNCIL CONDEMNS DEMOCRATIC PEOPLE'S REPUBLIC OF KOREA'S MISSILE LAUNCHES, UNANIMOUSLY ADOPTING RESOLUTION 1695 (2006)," United Nations, July 15, 2006, https://www.un.org/press/en/2006/sc8778.doc.htm.

48. Sue Pleming, "North Korea Hands over Plutonium Documents," *Reuters*, May 8, 2008, https://www.reuters.com/article/us-korea-north-documents-idUSN0833667920080508.

49. Choe Sang-Hun, "North Korea Destroys Tower at Nuclear Site," *The New York Times*, June 28, 2008, https://www.nytimes.com/2008/06/28/world/asia/28korea.html.

50. Leon V. Sigal, "For North Korea, Verifying Requires Reconciling: The Lesson from A Troubled Past—Part II | 38 North: Informed Analysis of North Korea," *38 North*, December 28, 2018, https://www.38north.org/2018/12/lsigal122818/.

51. Choe Sang-Hun, "Korean Navies Skirmish in Disputed Waters," *The New York Times*, November 10, 2009, https://www.nytimes.com/2009/11/11/world/asia/11korea.html.

52. "KPA General Staff Blasts S. Korean Defense Minister's Outbursts," *KCNA Watch* (blog), January 24, 2010, https://kcnawatch.org/newstream/.

53. Jackson, *On the Brink*, 60–64.

54. Silvia Aloisi, "Over 6 Million People Need Food Aid in North Korea: U.N.," *Reuters*, March 25, 2011, https://www.reuters.com/article/us-korea-north-food-idUSTRE72O54N20110325.

55. "U.S.-DPRK Bilateral Discussions," U.S. Department of State, February 29, 2012, https://2009-2017.state.gov/r/pa/prs/ps/2012/02/184869.htm.

56. "DPRK Foreign Ministry Spokesman on Issue of DPRK-U.S. Talks," *KCNA Watch* (blog), February 29, 2012, https://kcnawatch.org/newstream/.

57. "U.S. Urged to Honestly Apologize to Mankind for Its Evil Doing before Groundlessly Pulling up Others," *KCNA Watch* (blog), December 21, 2014, https://kcnawatch.org/newstream/.

58. "DPRK FM Spokesman Slams U.S. for 'New Sanctions,'" *KCNA Watch* (blog), January 4, 2015, https://kcnawatch.org/newstream/.

599. Jackson, *On the Brink*, 82.

60. Gerald F. Seib, Jay Solomon, and Carol E. Lee, "Barack Obama Warns Donald Trump on North Korea Threat," *The Wall Street Journal*, November 22, 2016, https://www.wsj.com/articles/trump-faces-north-korean-challenge-1479855286.

3. DETERRENCE

1. "President John F. Kennedy's Speech Announcing the Quarantine Against Cuba, October 22, 1962," accessed June 29, 2019, https://www.mtholyoke.edu/acad/intrel/kencuba.htm.

2. Frederick Kempe, "The Worst Day of JFK's Life," *Reuters Blogs* (blog), May 27, 2011, http://blogs.reuters.com/berlin1961/2011/05/27/the-worst-day-of-jfks-life/.

3. Albert Wohlstetter, "The Delicate Balance of Terror," Rand Corporation, 1958, https://www.rand.org/pubs/papers/P1472.html.

4. Paul Bracken, *The Second Nuclear Age: Strategy, Danger, and the New Power Politics*, first edition (St. Martin's Griffin, 2013).

5. "India had carried out what was claimed to be a "Peaceful Nuclear Explosion" in 1974, but the device in that case was not weaponized."

6. Vipin Narang, *Nuclear Strategy in the Modern Era: Regional Powers and International Conflict* (Princeton: Princeton University Press, 2014).

7. India's 2003 nuclear doctrine also announced a policy of No First Use, but New Delhi maintains the right to use nuclear weapons after a biological or chemical weapon attack.

8. "Nuclear Strategies of Emerging Nuclear Powers: North Korea and Iran," *The Washington Quarterly* 38:1, 75–76, accessed July 27, 2019, https://www.tandfonline.com/doi/abs/10.1080/0163660X.2015.1038175?journalCode=rwaq20.

9. Seong-hyon Lee, "China-N. Korea Defense Treaty," *Korea Times*, July 26, 2016, http://www.koreatimes.co.kr/www/opinion/2019/07/197_210355.html.

10. See Todd S. Sechser and Matthew Fuhrmann, *Nuclear Weapons and Coercive Diplomacy*, Reprint edition (Cambridge: Cambridge University Press, 2017).

11. Glenn Herald Snyder, *Deterrence and Defense: Toward a Theory of National Security* (Princeton: Princeton University Press, 1961). For Pakistan's relevance to North Korea's case, see Ankit Panda and Vipin Narang, "Nuclear Stability, Conventional Instability: North Korea and the Lessons from Pakistan," *War on the Rocks*, November 20, 2017, https://warontherocks.com/2017/11/nuclear-stability-conventional-instability-north-korea-lessons-pakistan/.

102 Anna Fifield, "North Korean Hackers Stole U.S. and South Korean Wartime Plans, Seoul Lawmaker Says," *The Washington Post*, October 10, 2017, https://www.washingtonpost.com/world/asia_pacific/north-korean-hackers-stole-us-and-south-korean-wartime-plans-seoul-lawmaker-says/2017/10/10/036fb82c-adc6-11e7-99c6-46bdf7f6f8ba_story.html.

13. Joel S. Wit, Daniel B. Poneman, and Robert L. Gallucci, *Going Critical: The First North Korean Nuclear Crisis* (Washington, D.C.: Brookings Institution Press, 2004), 35.

14. D.L. Brewer III, "Sealift—Operation Iraqi Freedom—Clearing the Hurdles," SEALIFT, June 2004, https://www.msc.navy.mil/sealift/2004/June/perspective.htm. Also referenced in Jeffrey Lewis, *The 2020 Commission Report on the North Korean Nuclear Attacks Against the United States: A Speculative Novel* (Boston: Mariner Books, 2018).

15. "Foreign Relations of the United States, 1952–1954, Korea, Volume XV, Part 1—Office of the Historian: 'Memorandum of the Substance of Discussion at a Department of State Joint Chiefs of Staff Meeting,'" U.S. Department of State, March 27, 1953, https://history.state.gov/historicaldocuments/frus1952–54v15p1/d419. For U.S. considerations of nuclear use in the Korean War, see Richard K. Betts, *Nuclear Blackmail and Nuclear Balance* (Brookings Institution Press, 2010), 39.

16. "Kim Jong Un Guides Drill for Ballistic Rocket Fire," *Rodong Sinmun* (blog), July 20, 2016, https://kcnawatch.org/newstream/.

17. Jeffrey Lewis, "The Map of Death," *Foreign Policy* (blog), April 3, 2013, https://foreignpolicy.com/2013/04/03/the-map-of-death/.

18. Mansourov, "Kim Jong Un's Nuclear Doctrine and Strategy."

19. Ankit Panda, "The US Didn't Send That Carrier Group to the Korean Peninsula, But Did North Korea Know That?," *The Diplomat*, April 19, 2017, https://thediplomat.com/2017/04/the-us-didnt-send-that-carrier-group-to-the-korean-peninsula-but-did-north-korea-know-that/.

20. Author interview data. In 2018, according to a U.S. government source, Japan was tracking approximately 200 suspected North Korean agents on its soil.

21. Vipin Narang, "A New Framework for Thinking about Regional NC3?," Nautilus Institute for Security and Sustainability, September 19, 2019, 3, https://nautilus.org/napsnet/napsnet-special-reports/a-new-framework-for-thinking-about-regional-nc3/.

4. BUILDING THE BOMB

1. The largest conventional explosive is the GBU-43/B Massive Ordnance Air Blast; the smallest nuclear explosive yield comes from a dialed setting on the B61 gravity bomb.

2. Spencer R. Weart, "Scientists with a Secret," *Physics Today* 29:2 (1976), 23–30, http://www.chymist.com/Scientists%20with%20a%20secret.pdf. Alex Wellerstein and Katja Grace, "Interview with Alex Wellerstein," (2015), https://docs.google.com/document/d/1efDOdo4UMK6MZOwKMA424baUbi5FGNKpOnhEO4Fbq7Q/edit?usp=sharing.

3. "The Italian navigator has landed in the New World," Los Alamos National Laboratory, http://library.sciencemadness.org/lanl1_a/LANL_50th_Articles/12–11–92.html.

4. Around 30 fissile material cores had been manufactured for use in actual nuclear weapons, including what was assessed to have been four-to-six high-yield two-stage thermonuclear weapons. Author interview data.

5. Ankit Panda, "US Intelligence: North Korea May Already Be Annually Accruing Enough Fissile Material for 12 Nuclear Weapons," *The Diplomat*, August 9, 2017, https://thediplomat.com/2017/08/us-intelligence-north-korea-may-already-be-annually-accruing-enough-fissile-material-for-12-nuclear-weapons/.

6. Siegfried S. Hecker, "What We Really Know About North Korea's Nuclear Weapons," *Foreign Affairs*, January 2, 2018, https://www.foreignaffairs.com/articles/north-korea/2017–12–04/what-we-really-know-about-north-koreas-nuclear-weapons.

7. David Albright, "North Korean Plutonium Production," *Science & Global Security* 5:1 (December 1, 1994), 65, https://doi.org/10.1080/08929889408426416.

8. Safeguards are technical steps taken by the IAEA under its mandate to ensure that civilian nuclear materials are not diverted toward possible weaponized applications.

9. Albright, 65.

10. Siegfried Hecker, "Visit to the Yongbyon Nuclear Scientific Research Center in North Korea" (Senate Foreign Relations Hearing, January 21, 2004), 5.

11. Randall Mikkelsen, "UPDATE 2-Syrian Reactor Capacity Was 1–2 Weapons/Year-CIA," *Reuters*, April 29, 2008, https://uk.reuters.com/article/korea-north-usa-idUKN2820597020080429.

12. Author interview data.

13. William J. Broad, David E. Sanger, and Raymond Bonner, "A Tale of Nuclear Proliferation: How Pakistani Built His Network," *The New York Times*, February 12, 2004, https://www.nytimes.com/2004/02/12/world/a-tale-of-nuclear-proliferation-how-pakistani-built-his-network.html.

14. Jeremy Bernstein, *Nuclear Iran* (Cambridge: Harvard University Press, 2014), 69.

15. Catherine Collins and Douglas Frantz, "The Long Shadow of A.Q. Khan," *Foreign Affairs*, January 31, 2018, https://www.foreignaffairs.com/articles/north-korea/2018–01–31/long-shadow-aq-khan.

16. Khushwant Singh, "FOREIGN AFFAIRS Pakistan, India and The Bomb," *The New York Times*, July 1, 1979, https://www.nytimes.com/1979/07/01/archives/foreign-affairs-pakistan-india-and-the-bomb.html.

17. Collins and Frantz, "The Long Shadow of A.Q. Khan."

18. Nadeem Malik, "Pakistan: Dr Abdul Qadeer Khan Discusses Nuclear Program in TV Talk Show", *Aaj News Television* (Urdu), August 31, 2009, https://fas.org/nuke/guide/pakistan/aqkhan-083109.pdf.

19. Bob Woodward, "Pakistan Reported Near Atom Arms Production," *The Washington Post*, November 4, 1986, https://www.washingtonpost.com/archive/politics/1986/11/04/pakistan-reported-near-atom-arms-production/acd69089-dff0-424c-ba59-bd3fcac02b76/.

20. Joshua Pollack, "The Secret Treachery of A.Q. Khan," *Playboy*, February 2012, http://carnegieendowment.org/files/the_secret%20treachery%20of%20aq%20khan.pdf.

21. *Reuters*, "Pakistan Denies Bribe from N.Korea for Nuclear Technology," *DAWN.COM*, July 7, 2011, http://www.dawn.com/news/642237.

22. Malik, "Pakistan: Dr Abdul Qadeer Khan Discusses Nuclear Program in TV Talk Show."

23. Alastair Gale, "Study Sees North Korean Advances on Uranium Enrichment," *The Wall Street Journal*, September 23, 2013, https://www.wsj.com/articles/study-sees-north-korean-advances-on-uranium-enrichment-1379959426.

24. Alastair Gale, "Study Sees North Korean Advances on Uranium Enrichment," *Wall Street Journal*, September 23, 2013, sec. Asia, https://www.wsj.com/articles/study-sees-north-korean-advances-on-uranium-enrichment-1379959426.

25. https://nautilus.org/napsnet/napsnet-special-reports/a-return-trip-to-north-koreas-yongbyon-nuclear-complex/.

26. "Seoul, Washington Suspect More N.Korean Uranium Sites," *Chosun Ilbo* accessed February 16, 2019, http://english.chosun.com/site/data/html_dir/2010/12/14/2010121400242.html.

27. Internally, the North Koreans refer to the enrichment site as the 853 Project Office. Ankit Panda, "Exclusive: Revealing Kangson, North Korea's First Covert Uranium Enrichment Site," July 13, 2018, https://thediplomat.com/2018/07/exclusive-revealing-kangson-north-koreas-first-covert-uranium-enrichment-site/.

28. Joby Warrick and Souad Mekhennet, "Summit Collapse Foils Chance to Press North Korea on Suspicious Sites," *The Washington Post*, accessed February 15, 2019, https://www.washingtonpost.com/world/national-secu-

rity/summit-collapse-foils-chance-to-press-north-korea-on-suspicious-sites/2018/05/25/d5a14044–602d-11e8–9ee3–49d6d4814c4c_story.html.

29. Hy-Sang Lee, *North Korea: A Strange Socialist Fortress* (Westport: Greenwood Publishing Group, 2001), 25.

30. Ian Jeffries, *North Korea: A Guide to Economic and Political Developments* (Brighton: Psychology Press, 2006), 66. B.R. Meyers, *The Cleanest Race* (Brooklyn: Melville House, 2011), 41. Michael Harrold, *Comrades and Strangers: Behind the Closed Doors of North Korea* (John Wiley & Sons, 2004), 183.

31. Harrold, 183.

32. Lee, 25.

33. "North Korea Working to Conceal Key Aspects of Its Nuclear Program, U.S. Officials Say," *The Washington Post*, accessed February 12, 2019, https://www.washingtonpost.com/world/national-security/north-korea-working-to-conceal-key-aspects-of-its-nuclear-program-us-officials-say/2018/06/30/deba64fa-7c82–11e8–93cc-6d3beccdd7a3_story.html?utm_term=.7eb6888f091f.

34. Author interview data.

35. Mark Tran and agencies, "North Korea Agrees to Nuclear Deal," *The Guardian*, February 13, 2007, https://www.theguardian.com/world/2007/feb/13/northkorea. Glenn Kessler, "New Doubts On Nuclear Efforts by North Korea," *The Washington Post*, March 1, 2007, http://www.washingtonpost.com/wp-dyn/content/article/2007/02/28/AR2007022801977.html.

36. "Washington Softens Tone on North Korea Uranium-Enrichment."

37. Mike Chinoy, *Meltdown: The Inside Story of the North Korean Nuclear Crisis* (New York: St. Martin's Press, 2010), 330.

38. "Remarks by President Trump in Press Conference," The White House, February 28, 2019, https://www.whitehouse.gov/briefings-statements/remarks-president-trump-press-conference-hanoi-vietnam/.

39. The U.S. assessment as of 2019 was that Kangson had likely served as North Korea's first major gas centrifuge facility, allowing the country's nuclear scientists to experiment with initial gas centrifuge cascades before setting up the facility at Yongbyon knowing that it would one day be shown to foreign scientists. The third covert facility, meanwhile, is thought to have been North Korea's "pilot" uranium enrichment facility—representing its first attempt at setting up the P2 centrifuges starting around 2003.

40. Joseph S. Bermudez, Jr., "Exposing North Korea's secret nuclear infrastructure—Part Two," *Jane's Intelligence Review* 11:8 (1 August 1999).

41. The test was the largest since a Chinese nuclear test in 1992.

42. Sang-Hun Choe, "North Korea Vows to Test a Nuclear Weapon—Asia," *The New York Times*, October 3, 2006, https://www.nytimes.com/2006/10/03/world/asia/03iht-nuke.3012951.html.

43. Choe, "North Korea Vows to Test a Nuclear Weapon."

44. Sang-hun Choe, "North Is Capable of a Nuclear Test, Seoul Official Says," *The New York Times*, August 28, 2006, https://www.nytimes.com/2006/08/28/world/asia/28iht-korea.2619092.html.

45. The U.S. National Geospatial Intelligence Agency uses the coordinates 41° 08' 10" N, 129° 09' 33" E for the locality of Punggye-ri. Choe, "North Is Capable of a Nuclear Test, Seoul Official Says."

46. Richard L. Garwin and Frank N. Von Hippel, "A Technical Analysis: Deconstructing North Korea's October 9 Nuclear Test," *Arms Control Today*, accessed September 23, 2019, https://www.armscontrol.org/act/2006–11/features/technical-analysis-deconstructing-north-korea%E2%80%99s-october-9-nuclear-test. Katharine Sanderson and Jim Giles, "North Korean Blast Seems Small for a Nuke," *Nature*, October 9, 2006, news061009-3, https://doi.org/10.1038/news061009–3. "Statement by the Office of the Director of National Intelligence on the North Korea Nuclear Test" (Office of the Director of National Intelligence), accessed May 8, 2019, https://fas.org/nuke/guide/dprk/odni101606.pdf.

47. "U.S. Intelligence Statement: N. Korea Radioactivity Detected," *CNN*, October 14, 2006, http://www.cnn.com/2006/WORLD/asiapcf/10/14/nkorea.test.sample/index.html.

48. The second North Korean test would come just two days after Roh took his own life.

49. "North Korea Tears up Agreements," *BBC News*, January 30, 2009, http://news.bbc.co.uk/2/hi/asia-pacific/7859671.stm.

50. Author interview data.

51. 유청모, "N. Korea Calls Itself 'nuclear-Armed State' in Revised Constitution," Yonhap News Agency, May 30, 2012, https://en.yna.co.kr/view/AEN20120530005200315.

52. Lolita C. Baldor, "U.S. Said to Delay Missile Test as Korea Tensions Rise," *The Washington Post*, April 6, 2013, https://www.washingtonpost.com/

world/national-security/us-said-to-delay-missile-test-as-korea-tensions-rise/2013/04/06/4a60634e-9f16-11e2-9a79-eb5280c81c63_story.html.

53. Author interview data.

54. Kang Mi Jin, "Cadres Divided on Likelihood of Fifth Nuclear Test," *DailyNK* (blog), May 19, 2016, https://www.dailynk.com/english/cadres-divided-on-likelihood-of-fi/.

55. Jeffrey G. Lewis, "The Clothes Geolocate the Man," Arms Control Wonk, June 8, 2016, https://www.armscontrolwonk.com/archive/1201459/a-tale-of-two-visits/.

56. "(4) Taepodong on Twitter: '@northkoreafront @GeorgeWHerbert @ArmsControlWonk a Better Still from a 720p Video: Https://T.Co/2pBIvpHGPS Https://T.Co/YSZ36gm8EQ' / Twitter," *Twitter*, accessed September 25, 2019, https://twitter.com/stoa1984/status/941021156735254528.

57. Ri Hong Sop and Hong Sung Mu respectively. See Ju-min Park and Soyoung Kim, "North Korea's Nuclear Scientists Take Center Stage with H-Bomb Test," *Reuters*, September 4, 2017, https://www.reuters.com/article/us-northkorea-missiles-scientists-idUSKCN1BF1XE.

58. "Kim Jong Un Gives Guidance to Nuclear Weaponization," *KCNA*, September 3, 2017.

59. Author interview data.

60. Anthony Capaccio, "North Korean ICBM Technology Still Falls Short, Top General Says," *Bloomberg*, August 30, 2017, https://www.bloomberg.com/news/articles/2017–08–30/north-korean-icbm-technology-still-falls-short-top-general-says.

61. Michelle Ye Hee Lee, "North Korea's Latest Nuclear Test Was so Powerful It Reshaped the Mountain above It," *The Washington Post*, September 14, 2017, https%3A%2F%2Fwww.washingtonpost.com%2Fnews%2Fworldviews%2Fwp%2F2017%2F09%2F14%2Forth-koreas-latest-nuclear-test-was-so-powerful-it-reshaped-the-mountain-above-it%2F.

62. David Albright et al., "North Korea's Lithium 6 Production for Nuclear Weapons," Institute for Science and International Security, March 17, 2017, http://isis-online.org/isis-reports/detail/north-koreas-lithium-6-production-for-nuclear-weapons/10.

63. Hugh Chalmers, "Producing Tritium in North Korea," *Trust & Verify*, March 2016, http://www.vertic.org/media/assets/TV/TV152.pdf. Some

Russian nuclear scientists with experience in North Korea disagree (author interview data).

64. "North Balked at U.S.'s Tritium Demand: Sources," *Korea JoongAng Daily*, May 29, 2019, http://koreajoongangdaily.joins.com/news/article/article.aspx?aid=3063621.

65. Martin B. Kalinowski and Lars C. Colschen, "International Control of Tritium to Prevent Horizontal Proliferation and to Foster Nuclear Disarmament," *Science & Global Security* 5:3 (August 1, 1995): 148, https://doi.org/10.1080/08929889508426422.

66. "Kim Jong Un Gives Guidance to Nuclear Weaponization."

67. Author interview data.

68. Ibid.

69. Ibid.

70. "2019 Adherence to and Compliance with Arms Control, Nonproliferation, and Disarmament Agreements and Commitments (Compliance Report)," *United States Department of State* (blog), August 2019, https://www.state.gov/2019-adherence-to-and-compliance-with-arms-control-nonproliferation-and-disarmament-agreements-and-commitments-compliance-report/.

71. Adam Rawnsley, "Satellite Images Show North Korea Scrubbed Nuclear Test Site Before Unilaterally Destroying It," *The Daily Beast*, May 30, 2018, https://www.thedailybeast.com/satellite-images-show-north-korea-scrubbed-nuclear-test-site-before-unilaterally-destroying-it.

72. Choe Sang-Hun and David E. Sanger, "North Korea Agrees to Allow Inspectors Into Nuclear Testing Site, Pompeo Says," *The New York Times*, October 7, 2018, https://www.nytimes.com/2018/10/07/world/asia/pompeo-north-korea-visit.html.

73. "Report of the Fifth Plenary Meeting of the 7th Central Committee of the WPK (Kim Jong Un's 2020 New Year Address)," NCNK, January 2, 2020, https://www.ncnk.org/resources/publications/kju_2020_new_years_plenum_report.pdf/file_view.

5. DETERRENCE CLOSE TO HOME

1. Steven J. Zaloga, *Scud Ballistic Missile and Launch Systems 1955–2005* (London: Bloomsbury Publishing, 2013), 3.

2. Pinkston, *The North Korean Ballistic Missile Program*, 14.

3. Ibid.

4. Young Hwan Ko, "North Korean Missile Proliferation," *Hearing before the Subcommittee on International Security, Proliferation, and Federal Services of the Committee on Governmental Affairs of the U.S. Senate (115th Congress, First Session)*, October 21, 1997, 38.

5. Joseph S. Bermudez, "A History of Ballistic Missile Development in the DPRK" (Center for Nonproliferation Studies, November 1999), http://www.nonproliferation.org/wp-content/uploads/2016/09/op2.pdf.

6. Balazs Szalontai, "The Failure of De-Stalinization in North Korea, 1953–1964: The DPRK in a Comparative Perspective," PhD thesis (Budapest: Central European University, 2003), cited in Sergey Radchenko, "The Soviet Union and the North Korean Seizure of the USS Pueblo: Evidence from Russian Archives" (Woodrow Wilson International Center for Scholars), 5, accessed September 7, 2019, https://www.wilsoncenter.org/sites/default/files/CWIHP_WP_47.pdf.

7. Pinkston, 14, and Bermudez, 3.

8. Bermudez, 7.

9. A private estimate seen by the author in 2018 suggested three were shipped.

10. Michael Freund, "Fundamentally Freund: When Israel Fought North Korea," *The Jerusalem Post*, October 7, 2014, https://www.jpost.com/Opinion/Fundamentally-Freund-When-Israel-fought-North-Korea-378346.

11. "South Korea," Arab Republic of Egypt Ministry of Foreign Affairs, accessed June 12, 2019, https://www.mfa.gov.eg/English/ForeignPolicy/EgyptandtheWorld/Asia/Pages/republic-of-korea.aspx.

12. "Report of the Panel of Experts Established Pursuant to Resolution 1874 (2009) (S/2019/691)" (United Nations, August 30, 2019), 138, https://undocs.org/pdf?symbol=en/S/2019/691.

13. Pinkston, *The North Korean Ballistic Missile Program*, 16.

14. Prospects for Ballistic Missile Proliferation, National Intelligence Estimate, September 1988.

15. https://www.cia.gov/library/readingroom/document/0001180438.

16. Joshua Pollack, "Ballistic Trajectory," *The Nonproliferation Review* 18, no. 2 (July 1, 2011): 411–29, https://doi.org/10.1080/10736700.2011.583120.

17. Jofi Joseph, "The Proliferation Security Initiative: Can Interdiction Stop Proliferation?," *Arms Control Today*, accessed September 7, 2019, https://www.armscontrol.org/print/1579.

18. Theodore A. Postol, "Lessons of the Gulf War Patriot Experience," *International Security*, Vol. 16, No. 3 (Winter 1991/92), pp. 119–171.

19. Author interview data.

20. Ibid.

21. Steve Fetter, George N. Lewis, and Lisbeth Gronlund, "Casualties and Damage from Scud Attacks in the 1991 Gulf War," Working Paper (Defense and Arms Control Studies Program, Massachusetts Institute of Technology, March 1993), http://drum.lib.umd.edu/handle/1903/4334.

22. Geoff Brumfiel, "Satellite Photos Reveal Extent Of Damage From Iranian Strike On Air Base In Iraq," NPR.org, January 8, 2020, https://www.npr.org/2020/01/08/794517031/satellite-photos-reveal-extent-of-damage-at-al-assad-air-base; Shawn Snow and Meghann Myers, "Nearly 60 Service Members Could Be Eligible for the the Purple Heart Following Iran Ballistic Missile Attack," *Military Times*, February 5, 2020, https://www.militarytimes.com/flashpoints/2020/02/04/nearly-60-service-members-could-be-eligible-for-the-the-purple-heart-following-iran-ballistic-missile-attack/.

23. Author interview data.

24. Iran's success with precision, as seen in the January 2020 strikes, indicates that such technology may soon be within the reach of a country like North Korea, however.

25. Ankit Panda, "Introducing the KN21, North Korea's New Take on Its Oldest Ballistic Missile," *The Diplomat*, 21, accessed September 8, 2019, https://thediplomat.com/2017/09/introducing-the-kn21-north-koreas-new-take-on-its-oldest-ballistic-missile/.

26. Author interview data.

27. Ibid.

28. Ibid.

29. "Supreme Leader Kim Jong Un Guides Strike Drill of Defence Units in Frontline Area and on Eastern Front," *Rodong Sinmun* (blog), May 5, 2019, https://kcnawatch.org/newstream/1557025223–899383687/supreme-leader-kim-jong-un-guides-strike-drill-of-defence-units-in-frontline-area-and-on-eastern-front/.

30. Author interview data. For an early unclassified Australian assessment of the Toksa's 2005 testing, see "Weapons of Mass Destruction: Australia's Role in Fighting Proliferation" (Australian Government, 2005), 92, http://

web.archive.org/web/20060217114222/http://www.dfat.gov.au/publica-
tions/wmd/weapons_of_mass_destruction.pdf. For additional background,
see Paul Kerr, "North Korea Increasing Weapons Capabilities," *Arms Control
Today*, December 2005, https://www.armscontrol.org/act/2005–12/north-
korea-increasing-weapons-capabilities.

31. Quoted in Anthony H. Cordesman and Aaron Lin, *The Changing Military
Balance in the Koreas and Northeast Asia* (Lanham: Rowman & Littlefield,
2015), 185.

32. Author interview data.

33. 오석민, "(2nd LD) N. Korea's 'new' Ballistic Missiles Similar to Russia's
Iskander: Seoul," *Yonhap News Agency*, July 26, 2019, https://en.yna.co.kr/
view/AEN20190726006100325.

34. Scott Neuman, "North Korea Conducts 3rd Missile Test Since Last Week
Amid Stalled Talks With U.S.," NPR.org, August 2, 2019, https://www.
npr.org/2019/08/02/747504332/north-korea-conducts-third-missile-test-
since-last-week-amid-stalled-talks-with-.

35. Author interview data.

36. Aidan Foster-Carter, "Is Kim Jong Un Really Claiming Overall Leadership
On The Korean Peninsula? | 38 North: Informed Analysis of North Korea,"
38 North, April 24, 2019, https://www.38north.org/2019/04/afoster-
carter042419/.

37. Franz-Stefan Gady, "South Korea Test Fires New Ballistic Missile," *The
Diplomat*, accessed May 21, 2019, https://thediplomat.com/2017/04/south-
korea-test-fires-new-ballistic-missile/.

38. "Press Statement by Director-General of DPRK Foreign Ministry," *KCNA
Watch* (blog), August 11, 2019, https://kcnawatch.org/newstream/.

39. "Japanese Radar Stations and MSDF Crews Failed to Track Recent North
Korean Missiles Launches," *The Japan Times Online*, September 23, 2019,
https://www.japantimes.co.jp/news/2019/09/23/national/politics-diplo-
macy/japanese-radar-msdf-failed-to-track-north-korean-missiles/.

40. Jeffrey Lewis, "I Was Very Proud of the 'Hyunmoo Too' as a Moniker.
Sadly, Only Works in Writing.," Tweet, @ArmsControlWonk, September
8, 2018, https://twitter.com/ArmsControlWonk/status/103862353648136
1920.

41. *The Korea Herald*, "Did NK Steal S. Korean Missile Design?," February
21, 2018, http://www.koreaherald.com/view.php?ud=20180221000734.

42. Bermudez, "A History of Ballistic Missile Development in the DPRK," 20.

43. Libya was a rumored customer at one point, but this turned out to be incorrect.

44. Markus Schiller, "The Scope of Foreign Assistance to North Korea's Missile Program," *Science & Global Security* 27:1 (2019): 40–41.

45. Richard Spencer, "N Korea 'Tests New Missile in Iran,'" *The Telegraph*, May 16, 2007, https://www.telegraph.co.uk/news/worldnews/1551868/N-Korea-tests-new-missile-in-Iran.html.

46. Terence Roehrig, *From Deterrence to Engagement: The U.S. Defense Commitment to South Korea* (Lanham: Lexington Books, 2007), 89.

47. Vladimir Tikhonov, "Russia's Nuclear and Missile Complex: The Human Factor in Proliferation," Carnegie Endowment for International Peace, accessed August 2, 2019, https://carnegieendowment.org/2001/03/29/russia-s-nuclear-and-missile-complex-human-factor-in-proliferation-pub-656.

48. Daniel A. Pinkston, *The North Korean Ballistic Missile Program*, 2008, 35, http://www.dtic.mil/dtic/tr/fulltext/u2/a477526.pdf.

49. Pinkston, *The North Korean Ballistic Missile Program*, 35.

50. This statement appears in an October 6, 2009, State Department cable that was released by Wikileaks: "MISSILE TECHNOLOGY CONTROL REGIME (MTCR): NORTH KOREA'S MISSILE PROGRAM."

51. National Air and Space Intelligence Center, Ballistic and Cruise Missile Threat (Wright-Patterson Air Force Base: National Air and Space Intelligence Center), NASIC-1031–0985–17, June 2017, 17.

52. National Air and Space Intelligence Center, Ballistic and Cruise Missile Threat (Wright-Patterson Air Force Base: National Air and Space Intelligence Center), NASIC-1031–0985–13, July 2013, 19.

53. Author interview data.

54. Author interview data.

55. "Kim Jong-Un Orders Full Probe into Musudan Missiles Launches | Yonhap News Agency," Yonhap News Agency, October 28, 2016, https://en.yna.co.kr/view/AEN20161028008400315.

6. FIRE FROM THE SEA

1. H. I. Sutton, "North Korean Submarines," Covert Shores, March 18, 2017, http://www.hisutton.com/North_Korean_Submarines.html.

2. Two years later, a senior North Korean official who defected to the South, known by the alias Ahn Cheol-nam, claimed that the crew responsible had received state honors, including the Hero of the DPRK medal. http://english.yonhapnews.co.kr/northkorea/2012/12/07/31/0401000000AEN20121207008700315F.HTML.

3. Zaloga, 9.

4. Igor Kurdin and Wayne Grasdock, "Loss of a Yankee SSBN," *Undersea Warfare* 7, no. 5 (February 5, 2007), https://web.archive.org/web/20070205125624/http://www.chinfo.navy.mil/navpalib/cno/n87/usw/issue_28/yankee.html.

5. "Kim Jong-Un Tours a Submarine," *CBS News*, June 16, 2014, https://www.cbsnews.com/pictures/kim-jong-un-inspects-submarine/.

6. "Kim Jong Un Inspects KPA Naval Unit 167," *KCNA Watch* (blog), June 16, 2014, https://kcnawatch.org/newstream/.

7. Bill Gertz, "North Korea Building Missile Submarine," *Washington Free Beacon* (blog), August 26, 2014, https://freebeacon.com/national-security/north-korea-building-missile-submarine/.

8. "North Korea: Test Stand for Vertical Launch of Sea-Based Ballistic Missiles Spotted," *38 North*, October 28, 2014, https://www.38north.org/2014/10/jbermudez102814/.

9. "North Korea Appears to Be Developing Missile Submarine: South Korea," *The Straits Times*, September 15, 2014, https://www.straitstimes.com/asia/east-asia/north-korea-appears-to-be-developing-missile-submarine-south-korea.

10. *Nuclear Navy. First Polaris A-Sub Sails On Ocean Patrol, 1960/11/17* (Universal Studios, 1960), http://archive.org/details/1960–11–17_Nuclear_Navy.

11. Author interview data.

12. "Kim Jong Un Watches Strategic Submarine Underwater Ballistic Missile Test-Fire," *KCNA* (blog), May 9, 2015, http://kcna.co.jp/item/2015/201505/news09/20150509–04ee.html.

13. Tony Capaccio and Sam Kim, "North Korea Didn't Launch Submarine Missile, U.S. Officials Say," *Bloomberg*, May 12, 2015, https://www.bloomberg.com/news/articles/2015–05–12/north-korea-didn-t-launch-submarine-missile-u-s-officials-say. Bill Gertz, "U.S. Spy Agencies Closely Watched N. Korea Underwater Missile Test," *Washington Free Beacon*

(blog), May 11, 2015, https://freebeacon.com/national-security/u-s-spy-agencies-closely-watched-n-korea-underwater-missile-test/.

14. Jeffrey Lewis, "DPRK SLBM Test," *ArmsControlWonk*, May 13, 2015, https://www.armscontrolwonk.com/archive/207631/dprk-slbm-test/.

15. Aaron Mehta, "US: N. Korean Nuclear ICBM Achievable," *Defense News*, August 8, 2017, https://www.defense news.com/2015/04/08/us-n-korean-nuclear-icbm-achievable/.

16. Kwang-tae Kim, "(LEAD) N. Korea Apparently Fails to Launch Ballistic Missile from Sub: Official," *Yonhap News Agency*, November 28, 2015, https://en.yna.co.kr/view/AEN20151128001551315.

17. Catherine Dill, "Video Analysis of DPRK SLBM Footage," Arms Control Wonk, January 12, 2016, https://www.armscontrolwonk.com/archive/1200759/video-analysis-of-dprk-slbm-footage/.

18. "Kim Jong Un Guides Strategic Submarine Underwater Ballistic Missile Test-Fire," *Rodong Sinmun* (blog), August 26, 2016, https://kcnawatch.org/newstream/.

19. Ibid.

20. Author interview data.

21. See Colin Zwirko, "North Korean TV Aired Doctored Image in Recent SLBM Test Coverage: Analysis," *NK News—North Korea News* (blog), October 4, 2019, https://www.nknews.org/2019/10/north-korean-tv-aired-doctored-image-in-recent-slbm-test-coverage-analysis/.

22. Author interview data.

23. Ibid.

24. Zachary Cohen and Ryan Browne, "US Detects 'highly Unusual' North Korean Submarine Activity," *CNN*, accessed September 8, 2019, https://www.cnn.com/2017/07/31/politics/north-korea-ejection-test-submarine-activity/index.html.

25. Author interview data.

26. Jamie Crawford and Zachary Cohen, "Satellite Images Suggest North Korea Working to Hide Launch of Missile Submarine," CNN, September 23, 2019, https://www.cnn.com/2019/09/23/politics/north-korea-submarine-images/index.html.

7. TO GUAM AND BEYOND

1. "Kim Jong Un Guides Test-Fire of Surface-to-Surface Medium Long-Range

Ballistic Missile," *KCNA Watch* (blog), February 13, 2017, https://kcnawatch.org/newstream/.

2. Author interview data.

3. Ibid.

4. "Kim Jong Un Supervises Test-Fire of Ballistic Missile," *KCNA Watch* (blog), May 21, 2017, https://kcnawatch.org/newstream/.

5. "Report of the Panel of Experts Established Pursuant to Resolution 1874 (2009) (S/2019/691)," 135.

6. "Rodong Sinmun Praises Kim Jong Un as Brilliant Commander of Songun," *KCNA Watch* (blog), September 18, 2017, https://kcnawatch.org/newstream/.

7. Author interview data.

8. Ibid.

9. Ibid.

10. Matthew Pennington, "Trump Strategy on NKorea: 'Maximum Pressure and Engagement,'" *AP NEWS*, April 14, 2017, https://apnews.com/8662 6d21ea2b45c79457a873a747c452.

11. "Supreme Leader Kim Jong Un Watches Demonstration Fire of Latest Tactical Guided Missiles," *KCNA Watch* (blog), August 7, 2019, https://kcnawatch.org/newstream/.

12. John Schilling, "North Korea's Latest Missile Test: Advancing towards an Intercontinental Ballistic Missile (ICBM) While Avoiding US Military Action," *38 North*, May 14, 2017, https://www.38north.org/2017/05/jschilling051417/.

13. Markus Schiller and Robert H. Schmucker, "A Dog and Pony Show," April 18, 2012, http://lewis.armscontrolwonk.com/files/2012/04/KN-08_Analysis_Schiller_Schmucker.pdf.

14. Author interview.

15. David Schmerler, Jeffrey G. Lewis, and John Schilling, "A New ICBM for North Korea?," *38 North*, accessed September 5, 2019, https://www.38north.org/reports/2015/12/new-icbm-for-nk/.

16. Joshua H. Pollack, "North Korea's ICBM Unveiled," Arms Control Wonk, April 15, 2012, https://www.armscontrolwonk.com/archive/503932/north-koreas-icbm-unveiled/.

8. GOING INTERCONTINENTAL

1. Dagyum Ji, "North Korean State Media Says ICBM Has Range of 'over 6400 Km'," *NK News*, July 24, 2017, https://www.nknews.org/2017/07/north-korean-state-media-says-icbm-has-range-of-over-6400-km/.

2. Kim's desk at missile-viewing events frequently features an empty ashtray. During an August 2019 launch, however, it was shown to be full of cigarette butts.

3. Author interview data.

4. It was an Evolved Enhanced CRYSTAL System, known only as USA-186 (author interview data). In September 2019, U.S. President Donald J. Trump would tweet a very high-res, highly classified image from another of these satellites, showing a space launch accident on an Iranian launch pad.

5. Author interview data.

6. "РФ Передала ООН Данные Минобороны о Проведенном КНДР Ракетном Испытании" *ТАСС*, accessed September 11, 2019, https://tass.ru/politika/4399599.

7. Joshua H. Pollack, "Russia Eyes North Korea," *ArmsControlWonk*, April 7, 2009, https://www.armscontrolwonk.com/archive/502248/russia-eyes-north-korea/.

8. Petr Iliichev, "Letter Dated 8 July 2017 from the Chargé d'affaires a.i. of the Permanent Mission of the Russian Federation to the United Nations Addressed to the Secretary-General," United Nations, July 11, 2017, https://undocs.org/pdf?symbol=en/S/2017/588. "Russia Shared with US Data Indicating North Korea's Missile Was Not Intercontinental," TASS, July 21, 2017, https://tass.com/politics/957331.

9. "Is Russia Sightless or Is It Mimicking Blind: Researcher of Institute for International Studies," *KCNA Watch* (blog), August 10, 2017, https://kcnawatch.org/newstream/.

10. Jeffrey G. Lewis, "That Ain't My Truck: Where North Korea Assembled Its Chinese Transporter-Erector-Launchers," *38 North*, February 3, 2014, https://www.38north.org/2014/02/jlewis020314/.

11. Jeffrey G. Lewis, James Acton, and David Wright, "DPRK RV Video Analysis," ArmsControlWonk, accessed September 12, 2019, https://www.armscontrolwonk.com/archive/1206084/dprk-rv-video-analysis/.

12. Ankit Panda, "US Intelligence: North Korea's ICBM Reentry Vehicles Are

Likely Good Enough to Hit the Continental US," *The Diplomat*, August 12, 2017, https://thediplomat.com/2017/08/us-intelligence-north-koreas-icbm-reentry-vehicles-are-likely-good-enough-to-hit-the-continental-us/.

13. Author interview data.

14. 'North Korea Just Stated That It Is in the Final Stages of Developing a Nuclear Weapon Capable of Reaching Parts of the U.S. It Won't Happen!' / Twitter," Tweet, @*realdonaldtrump* (blog), accessed September 12, 2019, https://twitter.com/realDonaldTrump/status/816057920223846400.

15. Luis Martinez et al., "Tillerson: North Korea Intercontinental Ballistic Missile Test 'Represents a New Escalation' of Threat to US," ABC News, July 4, 2017, https://abcnews.go.com/International/north-korea-tested-1st-intercontinental-ballistic-missile-us/story?id=48429720.

16. "Kim Jong Un Supervises Test-Launch of Inter-Continental Ballistic Rocket Hwasong-14," *KCNA Watch* (blog), July 5, 2017, 14, https://kcnawatch.org/newstream/. Emphasis added.

17. Author interview data.

18. Ibid.

19. Avi Selk, "Flight Crew Saw North Korean Missile 'Blow up and Fall Apart' near Japan," *The Washington Post*, December 4, 2017, https://www.washingtonpost.com/news/worldviews/wp/2017/12/04/flight-crew-saw-north-korean-missile-blow-up-and-fall-apart-near-japan/.

20. Based on an unpublished photograph of the monument, taken from ground-level, seen by the author.

21. Unofficial translation seen by the author.

22. Author interview data.

23. 이해아, "(2nd LD) Dunford Says 'matter of Time' before N. Korea Can Deliver Nuclear Weapon to U.S.," *Yonhap News Agency*, September 27, 2017, https://en.yna.co.kr/view/AEN20170927000252315.

24. Phil Stewart, "U.S. Nuclear Commander Says Assuming North Korea Tested Hydrogen Bomb," *Reuters*, September 15, 2017, https://www.reuters.com/article/us-northkorea-missiles-usa-hydrogen-idUSKCN1BP331.

25. https://kcnawatch.co/newstream/1489800064–168092632/dprk-army-and-people-will-win-final-victory/.

26. Robert D. Walpole, "The Ballistic Missile Threat to the United States," Central Intelligence Agency, February 9, 2000, https://www.cia.gov/news-information/speeches-testimony/2000/nio_speech_020900.html.

27. "North Korea Diplomat Says Take Atmospheric Nuclear Test Threat Literally," *Reuters*, October 25, 2017, https://www.reuters.com/article/us-northkorea-nuclear-warning-idUSKBN1CU2EI.

28. Author interview data. "Report of the Panel of Experts Established Pursuant to Resolution 1874 (2009) (S/2019/691)," 135.

29. Author interview data.

30. Zachary Cohen and Barbara Starr, "Satellite Images of North Korea Reveal New Work at Military Site Linked to Production of ICBMs," CNN, December 21, 2019, https://www.cnn.com/2019/12/21/politics/north-korea-satellite-images-building-expansion/index.html.

31. https://fas.org/irp/threat/missile/nie99msl.htm.

32. Tenet also underlined the possibility that the North Korean Taepodong-1 and associated technology could be proliferated, including to Iran. Years later, it emerged that Iran had facilitated development of the March 8 Revolution engine that powered North Korea's first true test-flown ICBM design, the Hwasong-14.

33. Author interview data.

34. "Space Is Common Wealth: KCNA White Paper," *KCNA Watch* (blog), November 29, 2011, https://kcnawatch.org/newstream/.

35. "Report of the Panel of Experts Established Pursuant to Resolution 1874 (2009)" (United Nations, June 11, 2013), 16–17. See also Schiller, "The Scope of Foreign Assistance to North Korea's Missile Program," 42.

36. David Brunnstrom, "North Korea Satellite Not Transmitting, but Rocket Payload a...," *Reuters*, February 11, 2016, https://uk.reuters.com/article/uk-northkorea-satelitte-missiledefense-idUKKCN0VJ2PF.

37. Will Ripley and Tim Schwarz, "North Korean Official: Satellite Launch Imminent," *CNN*, accessed September 4, 2019, https://www.cnn.com/2015/09/23/asia/north-korea-space-center-ripley-schwarz/index.html.

38. Damien Gayle and Justin McCurry, "North Korea Rocket Launch: UN Security Council Condemns Latest Violation," *The Guardian*, February 7, 2016, https://www.theguardian.com/world/2016/feb/07/north-korea-launches-long-range-rocket-it-claims-is-carrying-a-satellite.

39. Ankit Panda, "Why North Korea Is Likely Planning a Satellite Launch in 2018," *The Diplomat*, January 12, 2018, https://thediplomat.com/2018/01/why-north-korea-is-likely-planning-a-satellite-launch-in-2018/.

40. Vladimir Khrustalev, "North Korean Plans for Two New Satellite Types

Revealed," *NK News* (blog), December 8, 2017, https://www.nknews.org/2017/12/north-korean-plans-for-two-new-satellite-types-revealed/.

41. John Schilling, "Satellites, Warheads and Rockets: Is North Korea's Space Program Really about Missile Development?," *38 North*, February 5, 2016, https://www.38north.org/2016/02/schilling092815/.

42. https://kcnawatch.co/newstream/1530458135–792391479/kim-jong-un-guides-ballistic-rockets-reentry-environmental-simulation/.

43. http://www.dtic.mil/dtic/tr/fulltext/u2/a056390.pdf.

44. In December 2019, North Korea's Academy of National Defense Science announced that two tests had been conducted at the larger Sohae test stand—the one that was supposed to have been disabled after the September 2018 Pyongyang summit. One of these tests may have involved stress-testing for a new re-entry vehicle design, though Pyongyang released no images or information on the nature of the experiment. All it said was that the test was "crucial ... for further bolstering the reliable strategic nuclear deterrent." "Spokesman for Academy of Defence Science of DPRK Issues Statement," KCNA Watch, December 15, 2019, https://kcnawatch.org/newstream/.

45. Dave Schmerler, "Revealed: North Korea's under-Development Space Environment Test Center," *NK PRO* (blog), June 25, 2019, https://www.nknews.org/pro/revealed-north-koreas-new-space-environment-test-center/.

46. Author interview data.

47. Ibid.

48. These probabilities did not take into consideration the damage-limiting role of U.S. missile defense, or the possibility of U.S. fighters destroying the missiles in North Korea before they could be used.

49. "Report of the Fifth Plenary Meeting of the 7th Central Committee of the WPK (Kim Jong Un's 2020 New Year Address)," NCNK, January 2, 2020, https://www.ncnk.org/resources/publications/kju_2020_new_years_plenum_report.pdf/file_view.

9. FEAR, COMMAND, CONTROL

1. Bruce G. Blair, *Strategic Command and Control: Redefining the Nuclear Threat*, first edition (Washington, D.C: Brookings Inst Pr, 1985), 281.

2. Scott D. Sagan, "Armed and Dangerous," *Foreign Affairs*, January 29, 2019,

https://www.foreignaffairs.com/articles/north-korea/2018–10–15/armed-and-dangerous.

3. "Law on Consolidating Position of Nuclear Weapons State Adopted," *KCNA Watch* (blog), April 1, 2013, https://kcnawatch.org/newstream/. 유청모, "N. Korea Calls Itself 'Nuclear-Armed State' in Revised Constitution."

4. Trump, "North Korean Leader Kim Jong Un Just Stated That the 'Nuclear Button Is on His Desk at All Times.' Will Someone from His Depleted and Food Starved Regime Please Inform Him That I Too Have a Nuclear Button, but It Is a Much Bigger & More Powerful One than His, and My Button Works!"

5. William Burr, "The 3 A.M. Phone Call: False Missile Attack Warning Incidents, 1979–1980," *National Security Archive*, March 1, 2012, https://nsarchive2.gwu.edu/nukevault/ebb371/.

6. Jeffrey G. Lewis and Bruno Tertrais, "OP #45: The Finger on the Button," James Martin Center for Nonproliferation Studies, February 18, 2019, https://www.nonproliferation.org/op-45-the-finger-on-the-button/.

7. "Declassified Documents Concerning Russian President Boris Yeltsin, Clinton Digital Library," accessed July 14, 2019, https://clinton.presidentiallibraries.us/items/show/57568. "Memo: Clinton and Yeltsin on the Nuclear 'Football,'" Arms Control Association, November 2018, https://www.armscontrol.org/act/2018–11/features/memo-clinton-yeltsin-nuclear-%E2%80%98football%E2%80%99.

8. Author interview data, 2017.

9. Nate Thayer, "The Odd Tale of a Lone Israeli Spy and North Korea," *NK News* (blog), June 20, 2013, https://www.nknews.org/2013/06/the-odd-tale-of-a-lone-israeli-spy-and-north-korea/.

10. "Hyundai Group Suggests Patience and Generosity Towards North Korea; Notes from Kim Jong Il Meetings," Wikileaks, February 26, 2009, https://wikileaks.org/plusd/cables/09SEOUL282_a.html.

11. Peter D. Feaver, "Command and Control in Emerging Nuclear Nations," *International Security* 17:3 (1992): 160–87, https://doi.org/10.2307/2539133.

12. In a 2018 work of speculative fiction on a nuclear war between the United States and North Korea, a confused North Korean air defense crew shoots down a civilian South Korean airliner, sparking a crisis. See Lewis, *The*

2020 Commission Report on the North Korean Nuclear Attacks Against the United States.

13. Terence Roehrig, "The Abilities—and Limits—of North Korean Early Warning," *Bulletin of the Atomic Scientists* (blog), November 27, 2017, https://thebulletin.org/2017/11/the-abilities-and-limits-of-north-korean-early-warning/.

14. Paul Bracken, *The Command and Control of Nuclear Forces* (New Haven: Yale University Press, 1983), 68–71.

15. John W. Lewis and Litai Xue, *China Builds the Bomb*, first edition (Stanford: Stanford University Press, 1988), 202–3. Quoted in Scott D. Sagan, "The Perils of Proliferation: Organization Theory, Deterrence Theory, and the Spread of Nuclear Weapons," *International Security* 18:4 (1994): 102, https://doi.org/10.2307/2539178.

16. For a deeper discussion of these issues, see Narang, *Nuclear Strategy in the Modern Era.*

17. Peter Hennessy, *The Secret State: Whitehall and the Cold War*, Revised edition (London: Penguin Global, 2004).

18. Lewis and Tertrais, "OP #45: The Finger on the Button," 31.

19. William Burr, "U.S. Had Plans for 'Full Nuclear Response' In Event President Killed or Disappeared during an Attack on the United States," National Security Archive, December 12, 2012, https://nsarchive2.gwu.edu/nukevault/ebb406/.

20. Karen DeYoung, Ellen Nakashima, and Emily Rauhala, "Trump Signed Presidential Directive Ordering Actions to Pressure North Korea," *The Washington Post*, September 30, 2017, https://www.washingtonpost.com/world/national-security/trump-signed-presidential-directive-ordering-actions-to-pressure-north-korea/2017/09/30/97c6722a-a620–11e7-b14f-f41773cd5a14_story.html.

21. DeYoung, Nakashima, and Rauhala, "Trump Signed Presidential Directive Ordering Actions to Pressure North Korea."

22. Author interview.

23. William J. Broad and David E. Sanger, "U.S. Strategy to Hobble North Korea Was Hidden in Plain Sight," *The New York Times*, March 4, 2017, https://www.nytimes.com/2017/03/04/world/asia/left-of-launch-missile-defense.html.

24. David E. Sanger and William J. Broad, "Downing North Korean Missiles Is Hard. So the U.S. Is Experimenting.," *The New York Times*, November

16, 2017, https://www.nytimes.com/2017/11/16/us/politics/north-korea-missile-defense-cyber-drones.html.

25. Spencer Ackerman, "Revealed: Pentagon Push to Hack Nuke Missiles Before They Launch," May 22, 2018, *The Daily Beast*, https://www.the-dailybeast.com/revealed-pentagon-push-to-hack-nuke-missiles-before-they-launch.

26. Author source interview.

27. Tom McCarthy, "Dozens of US Nuclear Missile Officers Caught up in Drug and Cheating Scandals," *The Guardian*, January 15, 2014, https://www.theguardian.com/world/2014/jan/15/nuclear-missile-officers-suspended-drug-cheating-scandals.

28. Christopher Clary and Ankit Panda, "Safer at Sea? Pakistan's Sea-Based Deterrent and Nuclear Weapons Security," *The Washington Quarterly* 40:3 (July 3, 2017): 153, https://doi.org/10.1080/0163660X.2017.1370344.

29. Author interview data. In the early 2000s U.S. intelligence assessed that a nearby site had a role in the testing of conventional explosives for use in nuclear weapons.

30. Author interview data.

31. For the science of PALs, see Steven M. Bellovin, "Permissive Action Links," accessed July 14, 2019, https://www.cs.columbia.edu/-smb/nsam-160/pal.html.

32. Michael Krepon, "Safe Nuclear Weapons," *ArmsControlWonk*, April 29, 2015, https://www.armscontrolwonk.com/archive/404598/safe-nuclear-weapons/.

33. Joseph Trevithick, "The Time When A Burning B-52 Nearly Caused A Nuclear Catastrophe 'Worse than Chernobyl,'" *The Drive*, September 20, 2019, https://www.thedrive.com/the-war-zone/29945/the-time-when-a-burning-b-52-nearly-caused-a-nuclear-catastrophe-worse-than-chernobyl.

34. Sagan, "The Perils of Proliferation."

10. THE ARSONIST AND THE FIREFIGHTER

1. Tony Munroe and Jack Kim, "North Korea's Kim Says Close to Test Launch of ICBM," *Reuters*, January 1, 2017, https://www.reuters.com/article/us-northkorea-kim-idUSKBN14L0RN.

2. Philip Ewing, "That 'Armada' Heading to North Korea? Actually, It Sailed South," *NPR.org*, accessed September 16, 2019, https://www.npr.org/

sections/thetwo-way/2017/04/18/524560773/that-armada-heading-to-north-korea-actually-it-sailed-south.

3. Kevin Liptak, Sunlen Serfaty, and Ted Barrett, "Senators: Little Learned during Rare All-Hands North Korea Briefing," *CNN*, accessed September 16, 2019, https://www.cnn.com/2017/04/25/politics/trump-senators-north-korea-briefing/index.html.

4. Ankit Panda, "A Presidential Misunderstanding of Deterrence," *The Atlantic*, September 20, 2017, https://www.theatlantic.com/international/archive/2017/09/trump-kim-north-korea-nuclear-united-nations/540447/.

5. 'This Week' Transcript 8-13-17: Lt. Gen. H. R. McMaster, Anthony Scaramucci," ABC News, August 13, 2017, https://abcnews.go.com/Politics/week-transcript-13-17-lt-gen-mcmaster-anthony/story?id=49177024.

6. For a fuller cataloguing of the 2017 crisis' most dangerous moments, see Jackson, *On the Brink*, 199.

7. Author source interview.

8. Hyung-jin Kim, "North Korean Leader Kim Called Trump a What? A 'Dotard,'" *Associated Press*, September 22, 2017, https://apnews.com/c2d919f8a5864d838e638d88ac5e8569.

9. Carol Morello, "North Korea Threatens to Shoot down U.S. Warplanes," *The Washington Post*, September 25, 2017, https://www.washingtonpost.com/world/national-security/north-korea-asserts-its-right-to-shoot-down-us-bombers/2017/09/25/74da66c4-a204-11e7-8cfe-d5b912fabc99_story.html.

10. "Rodman Gives Trump's 'The Art of the Deal' as Gift for North Korea's Kim: AP," *Reuters*, June 15, 2017, https://www.reuters.com/article/us-usa-northkorea-rodman-idUSKBN1961EK.

11. Gerry Mullany, "North Korea Praises 'Fire and Fury' Book on Trump Administration," *The New York Times*, January 11, 2018, https://www.nytimes.com/2018/01/11/world/asia/north-korea-trump-book-michael-wolff.html.

12. Gerald F. Seib, "Amid Signs of a Thaw in North Korea, Tensions Bubble Up," *The Wall Street Journal*, January 9, 2018, https://www.wsj.com/articles/amid-signs-of-a-thaw-in-north-korea-tensions-bubble-up-1515427541.

13. Andrew Jeong, "Kim Jong Un Says He Has a Nuclear Launch Button on

His Office Desk," *The Wall Street Journal*, January 3, 2018, https://www.wsj.com/articles/kim-jong-un-says-he-has-a-nuclear-launch-button-on-his-office-desk-1514770845.

14. Fifield, *The Great Successor*, 241.

15. Benjamin Haas & David Smith, "North Korea Open to Relinquishing Nuclear Weapons, Says Seoul," *The Guardian*, March 6, 2018, https://www.theguardian.com/world/2018/mar/06/north-korea-says-kim-jong-un-keen-for-vigorous-efforts-to-calm-military-tensions.

16. "Remarks by Republic of Korea National Security Advisor Chung Eui-Yong," The White House, March 8, 2018, https://www.whitehouse.gov/briefings-statements/remarks-republic-korea-national-security-advisor-chung-eui-yong/.

17. "DPRK Report on the Third Plenary Meeting of the Seventh Central Committee."

18. "Stipulations for Peace: Excerpts from the Inter-Korean Military Agreement," *Stars and Stripes*, accessed September 17, 2019, https://www.stripes.com/news/pacific/stipulations-for-peace-excerpts-from-the-inter-korean-military-agreement-1.548844.

19. *Turning Nuclear Swords Into Plowshares in North Korea: Introduction and Panel 1*, accessed September 17, 2019, https://www.youtube.com/watch?v=O7EFBL8pT48&feature=youtu.be&t=819.

20. As stated by Gen. Vincent Brooks (Retd.), former U.S. Forces Korea commander, on April 3, 2019.

21. Grace Oh, "S. Korea Says N.K. Firing Drills Violate Peace Agreement," Yonhap News Agency, November 25, 2019, https://en.yna.co.kr/view/AEN20191125003700325.

22. Christina Wilkie, "Trump Cancels Pompeo Trip to North Korea, Cites Lack of 'sufficient Progress' on Denuclearization," *CNBC*, August 24, 2018, https://www.cnbc.com/2018/08/24/trump-cancels-pompeo-trip-to-north-korea-cites-lack-of-sufficient-progress-on-denuclearization.html.

23. "Pyongyang Joint Declaration of September 2018," *NCNK*, September 19, 2018, https://www.ncnk.org/node/1633.

24. Author interview data.

25. Ibid.

26. Will Ripley and Tim Schwarz, "North Korea Blows up Tunnels at Punggye-Ri Nuclear Test Site," *CNN*, accessed September 17, 2019,

https://www.cnn.com/2018/05/24/asia/north-korea-nuclear-test-site-intl/index.html.

27. "DPRK Report on the Third Plenary Meeting of the Seventh Central Committee."

28. "Trump-Kim Summit: How Did It All Fall Apart?," *BBC News*, May 25, 2018, https://www.bbc.com/news/world-asia-44247860.

29. "Trump Should Insist on Libya-Style Denuclearization for North Korea: Bolton," *Reuters*, March 23, 2018, https://www.reuters.com/article/us-usa-trump-bolton-northkorea-idUSKBN1GZ37A.

30. "Full Text: North Korea Calls John Bolton Repugnant and Threatens to Bail on Summit with Trump," *Quartz*, accessed September 17, 2019, https://qz.com/1279247/full-text-north-korea-calls-john-bolton-repugnant-and-threatens-to-bail-on-summit-with-trump/.

31. Choe Sang-Hun, "North Korea, Calling Pence Remarks 'Ignorant and Stupid,' Issues New Warning on Summit," *The New York Times*, May 23, 2018, sec. World, https://www.nytimes.com/2018/05/23/world/asia/north-korea-trump-pence-summit.html.

32. Tracey Shelton, "Gaddafi Sodomized: Video Shows Abuse Frame by Frame (GRAPHIC)," *Public Radio International*, accessed September 17, 2019, https://www.pri.org/stories/2011-10-24/gaddafi-sodomized-video-shows-abuse-frame-frame-graphic.

33. Choe Sang-Hun, "North Korea, Calling Pence Remarks 'Ignorant and Stupid,' Issues New Warning on Summit," *The New York Times*, May 23, 2018, https://www.nytimes.com/2018/05/23/world/asia/north-korea-trump-pence-summit.html.

34. "Joint Statement of President Donald J. Trump of the United States of America and Chairman Kim Jong Un of the Democratic People's Republic of Korea at the Singapore Summit," The White House, June 12, 2018, https://www.whitehouse.gov/briefings-statements/joint-statement-president-donald-j-trump-united-states-america-chairman-kim-jong-un-democratic-peoples-republic-korea-singapore-summit/.

35. Robert B. Abrams, "Statement of General Robert B. Abrams, Commander, United Nations Command; Commander United States-Republic of Korea Combined Forces Command; and Commander, United States Forces Korea Before the Senate Armed Services Committee," Senate Armed Services Committee, February 12, 2019, https://www.armed-services.senate.gov/imo/media/doc/Abrams_02-12-19.pdf.

36. "North Korea to work towards denuclearization in exchange for security guarantees," *NK News*, June 12, 2018, https://www.nknews.org/2018/06/north-korea-to-work-towards-denuclearization-in-exchange-for-security-guarantees/.

37. "North Korea Begins Dismantling Key Facilities at the Sohae Satellite Launching Station," *38 North*, July 23, 2018, https://www.38north.org/2018/07/sohae072318/.

38. Ankit Panda, "US Intelligence: North Korean Engine Dismantlement at Sohae Reversible 'Within Months,'" *The Diplomat*, July 25, 2018, https://thediplomat.com/2018/07/us-intelligence-north-korean-engine-dismantlement-at-sohae-reversible-within-months/.

39. Sheena Chestnut, "Illicit Activity and Proliferation: North Korean Smuggling Networks," *International Security* 32:1 (June 26, 2007): 99, https://doi.org/10.1162/isec.2007.32.1.80.

40. Warren P. Strobel, "CIA Korea Expert Who Spurred Talks Sees Hope in Summit," *The Wall Street Journal*, February 23, 2019, https://www.wsj.com/articles/cia-korea-expert-who-spurred-talks-sees-hope-in-summit-11550884856.

41. Shashank Bengali, "In Vietnam, Trump and Kim Jong Un Find Symbolism, History—and a Shared Goal of Keeping the Press at Arm's Length," *Los Angeles Times*, February 27, 2019, https://www.latimes.com/world/la-fg-north-korea-donald-trump-vietnam-20190226-story.html.

42. Julie Hirschfeld Davis, "Obama Hosts a Top Official From Vietnam at Oval Office," *The New York Times*, July 7, 2015, https://www.nytimes.com/2015/07/08/world/asia/obama-hosts-a-top-official-from-vietnam-at-oval-office.html.

43. "North Korean Leader Heads to Vietnam Ahead of Trump Meeting, Follows Grandfather's Footsteps," *The Global Times*, February 23, 2019, http://www.globaltimes.cn/content/1139842.shtml.

44. John Hudson, "In a First for North Korea's Secretive Leader, Kim Jong Un Takes a Question from a Foreign Journalist," *The Washington Post*, accessed September 21, 2019, https%3A%2F%2Fwww.washingtonpost.com%2Fworld%2Fnational-security%2Fin-a-first-for-north-koreas-secretive-leader-kim-jong-un-takes-a-question-from-a-foreign-journalist%2F2019%2F02%2F28%2F5c4cbcd9-c4434d43-a2a1-537e1e73ab57_story.html.

45. Lesley Wroughton and David Brunnstrom, "Exclusive: With a Piece of Paper, Trump Called on Kim to Hand over Nuclear Weapons," *Reuters*, March 30, 2019, https://www.reuters.com/article/us-northkorea-usa-document-exclusive-idUSKCN1RA2NR.

46. "Remarks by President Trump in Press Conference | Hanoi, Vietnam," The White House, February 28, 2019, https://www.whitehouse.gov/briefings-statements/remarks-president-trump-press-conference-hanoi-vietnam/.

47. Ellen Nakashima and Joby Warrick, "North Korea Working to Conceal Key Aspects of Its Nuclear Program, U.S. Officials Say," *The Washington Post*, accessed February 16, 2019, https://www.washingtonpost.com/world/national-security/north-korea-working-to-conceal-key-aspects-of-its-nuclear-program-us-officials-say/2018/06/30/deba64fa-7c82–11e8–93cc-6d3beccdd7a3_story.html.

48. Author interview data.

49. Ibid.

50. "DPRK-U.S. Ties Can Never Become Victim of Political Scramble in U.S.," *Ryugyong* (blog), accessed February 16, 2019, https://kcnawatch.co/newstream/1536120030–245359690/dprk-u-s-ties-can-never-become-victim-of-political-scramble-in-u-s/. The editorial originally appeared in *Rodong Sinmun* on August 20, 2018. See http://www.rodong.rep.kp/en/index.php?strPageID=SF01_02_01&newsID=2018–08–20–0010.

51. Author interview data, from Hanoi during the summit.

52. Ibid.

53. Victor D. Cha, "What Do They Really Want?: Obama's North Korea Conundrum," *The Washington Quarterly* 32:4 (October 1, 2009): 119–38, https://doi.org/10.1080/01636600903224837.

54. "Report of the Fifth Plenary Meeting of the 7th Central Committee of the WPK (Kim Jong Un's 2020 New Year Address)".

55. Philip Rucker and Josh Dawsey, "'We Fell in Love': Trump and Kim Shower Praise, Stroke Egos on Path to Nuclear Negotiations," *The Washington Post*, accessed September 22, 2019, https%3A%2F%2Fwww.washingtonpost.com%2Fpolitics%2Fwe-fell-in-love-trump-and-kim-shower-praise-stroke-egos-on-path-to-nuclear-negotiations%2F2019%2F02%2F24%2F46875188–3777–11e9–854a-7a14d7fec96a_story.html.

56. "Report of the Fifth Plenary Meeting of the 7th Central Committee of the WPK (Kim Jong Un's 2020 New Year Address)".

57. "DPRK Will Always Emerge Victorious with Its Strong Military Muscle for Self-Defense: Rodong Sinmun," *KCNA Watch* (blog), August 31, 2019, https://kcnawatch.org/newstream/.

58. Lei Liu, "'Dog-Beating Stick': General Zhang Aiping's Contribution to the Modernisation of China's Nuclear Force and Strategy since 1977," *Cold War History* 18:4 (May 15, 2018): 403, accessed January 9, 2019, https://www.tandfonline.com/doi/abs/10.1080/14682745.2018.1434507?utm_campaign=buffer&utm_medium=social&utm_content=buffer53473&utm_source=twitter.com&journalCode=fcwh20.

59. "Report on 4th Plenary Meeting of 7th Central Committee of WPK," *KCNA Watch* (blog), April 11, 2019, https://kcnawatch.org/newstream/.

60. "Report on 4th Plenary Meeting of 7th Central Committee of WPK."

61. "Practical Measures for Solving Food Problem," *KCNA Watch* (blog), April 25, 2019, https://kcnawatch.org/newstream/.

62. Jeong-ho Lee, "China, Russia, North Korea Call for Adjusted Sanctions against Pyongyang," *South China Morning Post*, October 10, 2018, https://www.scmp.com/news/china/diplomacy/article/2167931/china-russia-north-korea-call-adjusted-sanctions-ahead.

63. Michelle Nichols, "China, Russia Propose Lifting Some U.N. Sanctions on North Korea, U.S. Says Not the Time," Reuters, December 17, 2019, https://www.reuters.com/article/us-northkorea-usa-un-idUSK-BN1YK20W.

11. A DANGEROUS COEXISTENCE

1. Vann H. Van Diepen and Daniel R. DePetris, "Putting North Korea's New Short-Range Missiles Into Perspective," *38 North*, September 5, 2019, https://www.38north.org/2019/09/vvandiependdepetris090519/.

2. Elizabeth Shim, "Kim Jong Un has purged, executed more than 300 people, spy agency says," *UPI*, December 28, 2016, https://www.upi.com/Top-News/World-News/2016/12/28/Kim-Jong-Un-has-purged-executed-more-than-300-people-spy-agency-says/7071482971899/.

3. Jane Perlez and Choe Sang-Hun, "With No Mention of Korea, China Warns of 'Chaos,'" *The New York Times*, April 8, 2018, https://www.nytimes.com/2013/04/08/world/asia/from-china-a-call-to-avoid-chaos-for-selfish-gain.html.

4. Joshua H. Pollack, "The Most That Can Really Be Said? North Korea Has

Denuclearized Kim Il Sung Square. (End)," Tweet, *@Joshua_Pollack* (blog), September 9, 2018, https://twitter.com/Joshua_Pollack/status/1038853 334474678278.

5. Donald J. Trump, "Just Landed—a Long Trip, but Everybody Can Now Feel Much Safer than the Day I Took Office. There Is No Longer a Nuclear Threat from North Korea. Meeting with Kim Jong Un Was an Interesting and Very Positive Experience. North Korea Has Great Potential for the Future!," Tweet, *@realdonaldtrump* (blog), June 13, 2018, https://twitter.com/realdonaldtrump/status/1006837823469735936?lang=en.

6. "'This Week' Transcript 8/13/17: Lt. Gen. H. R. McMaster, Anthony Scaramucci."

7. Michael R. Gordon, Helene Cooper, and Michael D. Shear, "Dozens of U.S. Missiles Hit Air Base in Syria," *The New York Times*, April 6, 2017, https://www.nytimes.com/2017/04/06/world/middleeast/us-said-to-weigh-military-responses-to-syrian-chemical-attack.html.

8. "U.S. Missile Attack on Syria Unpardonable: DPRK FM Spokesman," *KCNA Watch* (blog), April 8, 2017, https://kcnawatch.org/newstream/.

9. Jackson, *On the Brink*, 199.

10. See, for example, U. S. Government, U. S. Military, and Department of Defense, *Hitting a Bullet with a Bullet: A History of Ballistic Missile Defense (BMD)—Nike, Sprint and Spartan, Strategic Defense Initiative (SDI) Star Wars, Patriot versus Scud Gulf War, THAAD, Lasers* (Progressive Management, 2016).

11. Jason Sherman, "GAO: True Cost of GMD Program $67 Billion and Counting, 63 Percent Higher than MDA Estimate," InsideDefense.com, May 31, 2018, https://insidedefense.com/daily-news/gao-true-cost-gmd-program-67-billion-and-counting-63-percent-higher-mda-estimate.

12. Ankit Panda and Vipin Narang, "Deadly Overconfidence: Trump Thinks Missile Defenses Work Against North Korea, and That Should Scare You," *War on the Rocks*, October 16, 2017, https://warontherocks.com/2017/10/deadly-overconfidence-trump-thinks-missile-defenses-work-against-north-korea-and-that-should-scare-you/.

13. Trump during a Fox News interview on October 11, 2017, on "Hannity," https://video.foxnews.com/v/5606494547001/?playlist_id=93090 9813001#sp=show-clips.

14. Panda and Narang, "Deadly Overconfidence;" System effectiveness for n

interceptors against i targets with k single-shot kill probability (SSPK) per interceptor is calculated using the expression $(1-(1-k)n)i$. Assuming four interceptors, a single incoming ICBM, and an SSPK of about 57 percent, the odds of a successful intercept scenario thus rise to 97 percent. This calculation, however, ignores the possibility that each successive interceptor's chance of successful kill might not be independent of the previous one, due to correlated factors such as design shortcomings, leading to a lower overall success rate.

15. Michael J. Zagurek Jr., "A Hypothetical Nuclear Attack on Seoul and Tokyo: The Human Cost of War on the Korean Peninsula | 38 North: Informed Analysis of North Korea," *38 North*, October 4, 2017, https://www.38north.org/2017/10/mzagurek100417/.

16. Erik Ortiz and Arata Yamamoto, "Sen. Graham: Trump Says War with North Korea an Option," *NBC News*, August 1, 2017, https://www.nbc-news.com/news/north-korea/sen-lindsey-graham-trump-says-war-north-korea-option-n788396.

17. Author interview data.

18. Ibid.

19. Author interview data. For comparison, the U.S. Defense Intelligence Agency estimates that Russia's Yamantau facility (identified in 2019 as the most hardened military target in the world) would require a 66 megaton surface blast or 3.7 megatons with 9 meters of surface penetration.

20. Alida R. Haworth, Scott D. Sagan, and Benjamin A. Valentino, "What Do Americans Really Think about Conflict with Nuclear North Korea? The Answer Is Both Reassuring and Disturbing," *Bulletin of the Atomic Scientists* 75:4 (July 4, 2019): 179–86, https://doi.org/10.1080/00963402.2019.1 629576.

21. Haworth, Sagan, and Valentino.

22. Author interview data.

23. Joshua Stanton, "The 'Experts' Were Wrong. The Sanctions Are Working.," *OneFreeKorea* (blog), April 23, 2019, https://freekorea.us/2019/04/23/the-experts-were-wrong-the-sanctions-are-working.

24. Leo Byrne, "Security Council Adopts Measures Capping N. Korean Oil, Banning Migrant Labor," *NK News*, December 22, 2017, https://www.nknews.org/2017/12/security-council-adopts-measures-capping-n-korean-oil-banning-migrant-labor/.

25. Cameron Trainer, "How North Korea Skirts Sanctions at Sea," *The Diplomat*, September 2019, https://magazine.thediplomat.com/#/issues/-LnBlVlS_1DsiVyAVtMQ/read.

26. For a suggested alternative sanctions regime on North Korea, see Adam Mount and Andrea Berger, "International Study Group on North Korea Policy," *Federation of American Scientists*, n.d., 108.

27. Thomas C. Schelling and Morton H. Halperin, *Strategy and Arms Control* (Twentieth Century Fund, 1961), 1.

28. Michelle Ye Hee Lee, "More than Ever, South Koreans Want Their Own Nuclear Weapons," *The Washington Post*, accessed September 22, 2019, https%3A%2F%2Fwww.washingtonpost.com%2Fnews%2Fworldviews%2Fwp%2F2017%2F09%2F13%2Fmost-south-koreans-dont-think-the-north-will-start-a-war-but-they-still-want-their-own-nuclear-weapons%2F.

29. Yong Ho Ri, "Statement by H.E. Mr. Ri Yong Ho, Minister for Foreign Affairs of the Democratic People's Republic of Korea at the General Debate of the 72nd Session of the United Nations General Assembly," United Nations, September 23, 2017, https://gadebate.un.org/sites/default/files/gastatements/72/kp_en.pdf.

30. Author interview data. Also publicly stated by Gen. Vincent Brooks (Retd.), former commander of U.S. Forces Korea, on April 3, 2019.

31. William J. Perry, "How to Contain North Korea," *Politico*, January 11, 2016, https://www.politico.eu/article/how-to-contain-north-korea-nucelar-weapons/.

32. Ellen Nakashima and Philip Rucker, "U.S. Declares North Korea Carried out Massive WannaCry Cyberattack," *The Washington Post*, December 19, 2017, https://www.washingtonpost.com/world/national-security/us-set-to-declare-north-korea-carried-out-massive-wannacry-cyber-attack/2017/12/18/509deb1c-e446-11e7-a65d-1ac0fd7f097e_story.html.

33. Colin Zwirko, "North Korea Appoints Vice Foreign Minister as New Ambassador to Russia," NK News, February 6, 2020, https://www.nknews.org/2020/02/north-korea-appoints-vice-foreign-minister-as-new-ambassador-to-russia/; Oliver Hotham, "North Korea Names Ex-Ambassador as New Ruling Party Foreign Policy Chief," NK News, January 22, 2020, https://www.nknews.org/2020/01/north-korea-names-ex-ambassador-as-new-ruling-party-foreign-policy-chief/.

34. "North Korea Unlikely to Give up Nuclear Weapons: U.S. Spy Chief Coats," *Reuters*, January 29, 2019, https://www.reuters.com/article/us-usa-north-korea-nuclear-idUSKCN1PN1Y7.

APPENDIX

1. As confirmed to the author by U.S. intelligence sources over multiple interviews.

INDEX

INDEX

INDEX

INDEX

INDEX

INDEX

INDEX

Mupyong-ni Arms Factory, 199

Musharraf, Pervez, 106

Musudan-ri, North Korea, 154, 217

Mutual Defense Treaty (1953), 40

Mutually Assured Destruction (MAD), 75

Nagasaki atomic bombing (1945), 35, 36, 113, 156

Nakamura, David, 275

Nampo, North Korea, 174

Narang, Vipin, 78, 79, 234

National Aerospace Development Administration (NADA), 216, 217

National Air and Space Intelligence Center, US, 159, 189, 200, 214

National Defense Commission, DPRK, 18, 288

National Geographic, 37

National Intelligence Council, US, 213

National Intelligence Estimate, US, 139, 213

National Photographic Interpretation Center, US, 139

National Security Agency, 246

Nazi Germany (1933–45), 36, 136

negative controls, 244–8

neorealism, 27

nerve agents, 15–16

Netherlands, 105

New York, United States

denuclearization agreement (1993), 46, 47, 267

ICBM threat, 85, 287

United Nations in, 63

New York Times, 44, 46, 74, 114, 241

New Yorker, 22–3

NHK, 3

Nie Rong-zhen, 233

912 Project Office, 172

Nixon, Richard Milhous, 3, 40, 42, 269, 272

No First Use, 78

Nobel Peace Prize, 272

Nodong missiles, 106, 139, 154–6, 157, 160, 223

Nonproliferation Review, The (Pollack), 290

Non-Proliferation Treaty (NPT), 4, 173, 305–6

collaboration and, 246–7

Israel and, 22

South Korea and, 42, 43

United States and 4

China and, 4

Russia and, 4

France and, 4

United Kingdom and, 4

North Korea and, *see* Non-Proliferation Treaty and North Korea

Soviet Union and, 7, 28, 40, 42

Non-Proliferation Treaty and North Korea, 45–6, 48, 58, 75, 173, 303, 305–6

INDEX

INDEX

INDEX

INDEX

INDEX